D0275529

GETTING THINGS
DONE

GETTING THINGS
DONE

A RADICAL NEW APPROACH TO MANAGING TIME
AND ACHIEVING MORE AT WORK

ROGER BLACK

Michael Joseph
London

First published in Great Britain by
Michael Joseph Ltd,
27, Wrights Lane, London W8 5TZ
1987
Second impression, April 1988

© Duncan Petersen Publishing Ltd 1987
© Roger Black 1987

Conceived, edited and designed by
Duncan Petersen Publishing Ltd,
5, Botts Mews, London W2 5AG

All rights reserved. No part of this publication may
be reproduced, stored in a retrieval system or
transmitted in any form or by any means,
electronic, mechanical, photocopying, recording or
otherwise, without the prior permission of the
copyright owners.

British Library Cataloguing in Publication Data
Black, Roger
Getting things done
1. Success
1. Title
158'.1   B5637.S8
ISBN 0-7181-2842-7

Filmset and originated in Great Britain by
Modern Reprographics Ltd, Hull

Printed and bound in Great Britain by
The Bath Press,
Lower Bristol Road, Bath

Getting *Things Done* is divided into one hundred short sections, listed below, each a step towards better management of time and achieving more.

The book is also divided into five main sections:

> **PLANNING**
> **DIRECTION AND GOALS**
>
> **YOUR TIME**
>
> **KNOWING, MOTIVATING AND**
> **IMPROVING YOURSELF**
>
> **DEALING WITH OTHERS**
>
> **RESULTS**

Although they follow each other sequentially, their order does not imply relative importance. In fact, the five sections have a special relationship:

Time is central to the issue, but unless the other areas are looked after, even an eternity is not enough to get the results you want.

CONTENTS

PLANNING
DIRECTION AND GOALS

Section
Number

Getting Things Done

Using this book

This questionnaire is designed to give you some instant *personal* clues to how you could perform better and waste less time. If you answer 'yes' to any question, or if you are unsure of your answer, look up the section indicated by the number below. You will find that those sections will act as a useful personal focus.

Don't, however, let this prevent you from working through the whole book sequentially: every section is a self-contained step towards better performance, and many assume an understanding of what has come before.

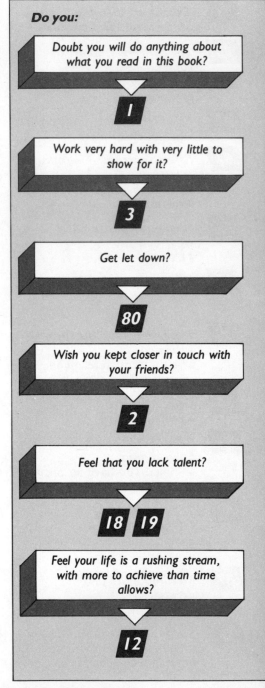

Do you:

Doubt you will do anything about what you read in this book?

1

Work very hard with very little to show for it?

3

Get let down?

80

Wish you kept closer in touch with your friends?

2

Feel that you lack talent?

18 **19**

Feel your life is a rushing stream, with more to achieve than time allows?

12

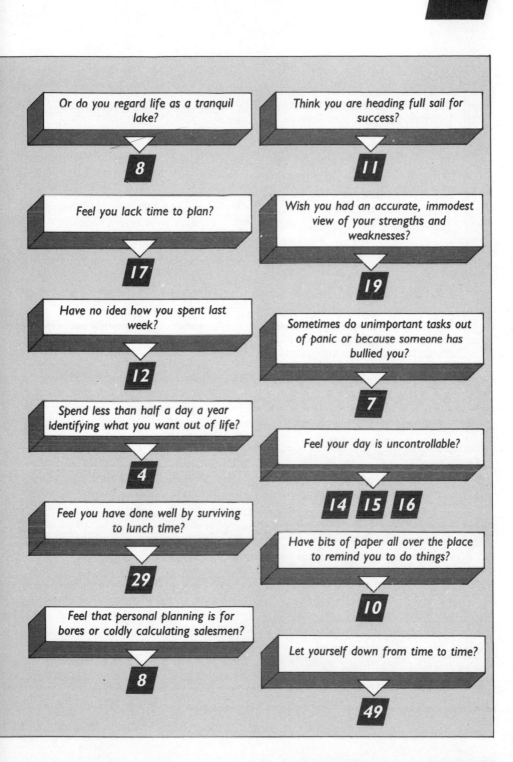

Or do you regard life as a tranquil lake?

8

Feel you lack time to plan?

17

Have no idea how you spent last week?

12

Spend less than half a day a year identifying what you want out of life?

4

Feel you have done well by surviving to lunch time?

29

Feel that personal planning is for bores or coldly calculating salesmen?

8

Think you are heading full sail for success?

11

Wish you had an accurate, immodest view of your strengths and weaknesses?

19

Sometimes do unimportant tasks out of panic or because someone has bullied you?

7

Feel your day is uncontrollable?

14 **15** **16**

Have bits of paper all over the place to remind you to do things?

10

Let yourself down from time to time?

49

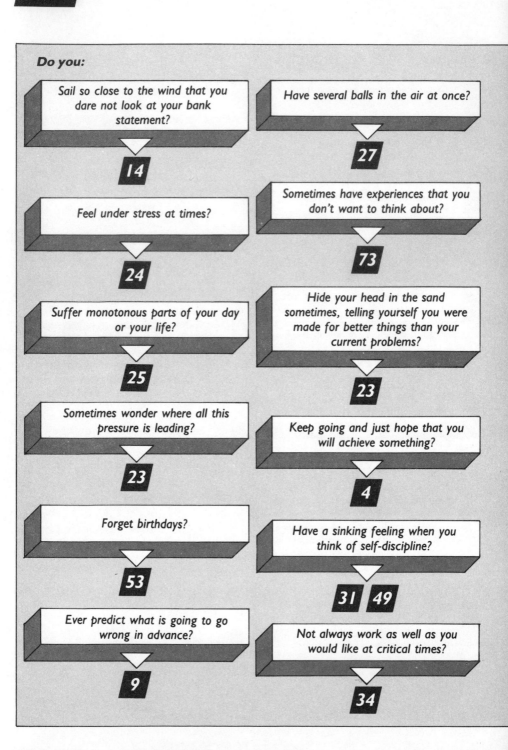

Do you:

Sail so close to the wind that you dare not look at your bank statement?

14

Feel under stress at times?

24

Suffer monotonous parts of your day or your life?

25

Sometimes wonder where all this pressure is leading?

23

Forget birthdays?

53

Ever predict what is going to go wrong in advance?

9

Have several balls in the air at once?

27

Sometimes have experiences that you don't want to think about?

73

Hide your head in the sand sometimes, telling yourself you were made for better things than your current problems?

23

Keep going and just hope that you will achieve something?

4

Have a sinking feeling when you think of self-discipline?

31 **49**

Not always work as well as you would like at critical times?

34

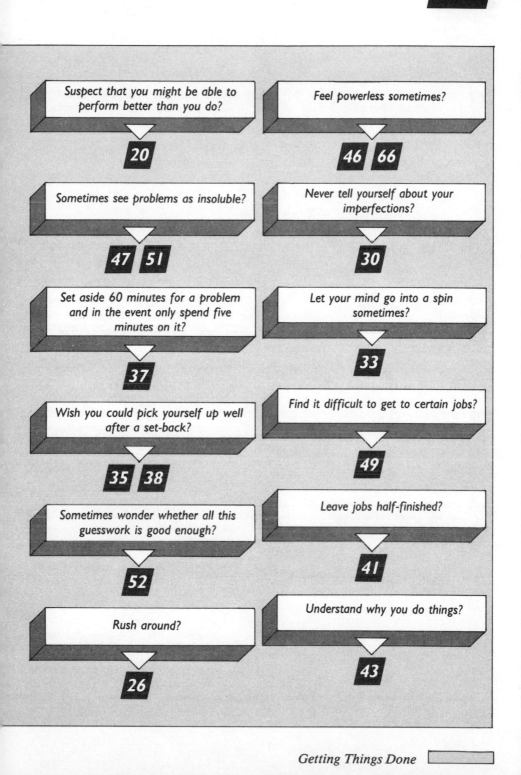

Suspect that you might be able to perform better than you do?

20

Feel powerless sometimes?

46 **66**

Sometimes see problems as insoluble?

47 **51**

Never tell yourself about your imperfections?

30

Set aside 60 minutes for a problem and in the event only spend five minutes on it?

37

Let your mind go into a spin sometimes?

33

Wish you could pick yourself up well after a set-back?

35 **38**

Find it difficult to get to certain jobs?

49

Sometimes wonder whether all this guesswork is good enough?

52

Leave jobs half-finished?

41

Rush around?

26

Understand why you do things?

43

Do you:

Write off 'positive thinking' as cranky?

47

Get too involved in projects and generate too much information?

51

Wish you could calm down when you need to?

33 34

Find it difficult to prepare thoroughly?

51

Put things off?

49

Doubt you will cope with your next major shock adequately?

94

Day dream?

46

Never take risks with your life?

64

Find New Years' resolutions difficult to implement?

31

Talk more than do?

3

Get over-critical of your ideas?

54

Hare around doing and don't stop to think?

3

Getting Things Done

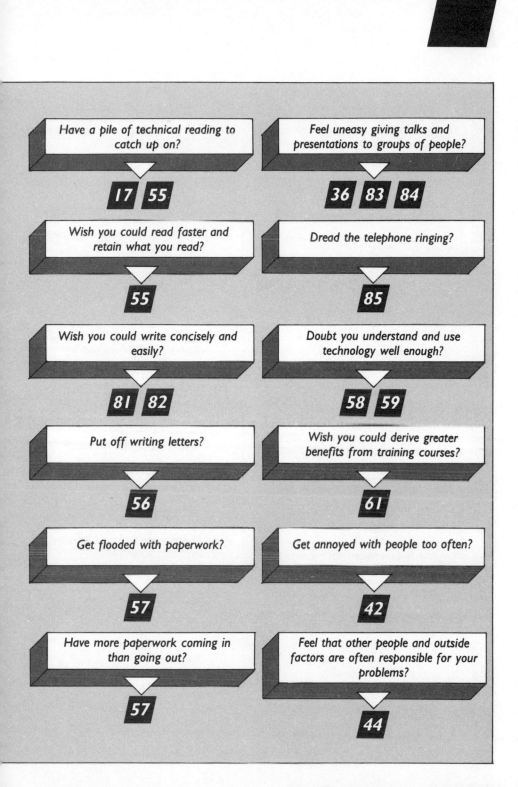

Have a pile of technical reading to catch up on?

17 **55**

Feel uneasy giving talks and presentations to groups of people?

36 **83** **84**

Wish you could read faster and retain what you read?

55

Dread the telephone ringing?

85

Wish you could write concisely and easily?

81 **82**

Doubt you understand and use technology well enough?

58 **59**

Put off writing letters?

56

Wish you could derive greater benefits from training courses?

61

Get flooded with paperwork?

57

Get annoyed with people too often?

42

Have more paperwork coming in than going out?

57

Feel that other people and outside factors are often responsible for your problems?

44

Do you:

Have difficulty knowing whether to be firmer or softer?
65

Feel that some people are difficult to understand?
78 **79**

Wish you were more persuasive?
69

Fail to excite some people with your ideas?
75

Think that there is a limit to manipulating others?
69

Fail to get agreement after all your efforts at persuasion?
76 **77**

Occasionally feel your relations with some people amount to banging your head against a wall?
91

Get accused of not listening?
80

Find that some people make you feel tense?
47

Assume other people know what you want?
86

Feel you cannot control conversations?
73

Find it difficult to deal with aggressive or sulky people?
67

Wish you could inspire other people?

40

Feel unable to influence meetings?

90

Have difficulty in getting people to do things for you?

66 68

Wish you could influence your boss and your boss's boss?

91

Wish you could be just as approachable, but with fewer interruptions?

87

Spend more time arguing within your organization than dealing with outsiders?

92

Wish you could feel better about telling people off?

88

Doubt you blow your own trumpet enough?

60

Wish you could give bad news more easily?

88

Suspect you are insensitive to other people's pressures?

93

Attend boring meetings?

89

Getting the best from this book

Which of these is you?

■ *'I'm in a mess; this book looks useful; I'll read it when I've got myself sorted out.'*

■ *'I'll start in the middle, with the interesting bits.'*

■ *'There's nothing new in this book. I'm doing most of these things already. Surely there must be something new?'*

■ *'These books are excellent in theory, but you can never put them into practice.'*

■ *'It'll take ages to cover each step thoroughly.'*

■ *'I bet it won't work.'*

■ *'I want to get on and do something, not read about doing something.'*

■ *'It'll inhibit my relationships with people.'*

■ *'I can't control my life, other people do.'*

■ *'This book looks fantastic. It'll solve all my problems.'*

■ *'It's not productive to think of my weaknesses.'*

■ *'I'll read the first couple of pages in the bookshop and the rest on holiday.'*

■ *'I'm not going to enjoy it.'*

I f any of the statements in column one apply to you – and at least one or two apply to everybody – you can get something from this book. Reading it, like any other task, will be subject to your natural weaknesses, barriers and distractions, and it is designed with those in mind.

Start it now, when you have finished this section.

Don't leave it until you are in less of a muddle. The book is designed to help you out of muddles. If you feel deeply cynical about whether the book can help you, go straight to 2 and try implementing that. You should in general, however, *work through in sequence, from the beginning.*

Although each step can stand alone, the logical sequence of getting things done has to be:

> **1** Know where you are going

> **2** Get yourself organized and working well.

> **3** Cope with outside distractions.

Getting Things Done follows that logic, and so should you. Putting 3 ahead of 1 is potentially disastrous; it gives you a perpetual excuse for staying in stalemate.

■ **Gain something from each step,** however humble. Even if you think 'I'm already doing that', check again whether you are. If you are, ensure it is logged in your mind as a definite strength.

■ **Believe you can make it work.** All the suggestions are practical; they have all worked for other people.

■ **Don't be prejudiced.** Beware of writing off ideas because 'That doesn't sound like me'.

■ **Set yourself a deadline** for completing the book. Don't get bogged down re-trying suggestions if they don't work first time. A couple of months would be a sensible time scale for going through the whole book. You can always go back over topics again, so finish the book first.

■ **Use your imagination.** Seeing things as black or white can be a barrier to taking action. If you see something as black (i.e. negatively) try and look at it temporarily in a different, brighter colour, even if you don't believe you can change your mind about it in the long run. This gives at least a chance of fair trial.

■ **Be patient.** Many of us spend too much time hopping around and not enough stopping and thinking. Slow down, think about the ideas and then try them out.

■ **Be positive.** Remind yourself that these ideas are designed to enhance relationships; to give you more time with other people, *and* more time to work alone, protected from distractions.

■ **Be self-critical.** Blaming other people and circumstances for your own difficulties means three things:

– You are fooling yourself
– You are obstructing your personal development
– You will not gain from this book.
In fact, you cannot gain from a book like this until you accept some of the blame – and credit – for yourself.

■ **Be realistic.** Don't expect the book to be a cure-all; simply expect it to improve your performance.

■ **Use the cross-referencing.** Almost every section ties in with another section; success has to be built on. If you think you are benefiting from the book, all the more reason to reinforce this by looking up related issues.

■ **Finish it.** Two things could happen while reading the book:
– You imagine you have practically finished it, and put it down.
    Another interest captures your imagination.

The final section is particularly important: it contains a checklist which will enable you to see how you may, or may not, have benefitted from reading the book.

2 *The magic hour*

This is perhaps one of the most effective basic tricks of time management, convenient and easy to apply to *private* life, but also relevant at work. It is included at this early stage because it gives *immediate* results: a morale-booster to those who lack confidence in their ability to improve personal performance, or faith in books about time management.

> *"I just don't get the time"*?

But practically everyone has the same amount of time to achieve these essentially personal tasks. If you are honest, you must acknowledge that some people you know achieve more in these areas than you do. It follows that "I just don't have the time" is self-deception. So what do you do with your 'free' time? More important things?

> *"Of course I remembered it was your birthday . . . it's just that I had much more important things on . . . I mean not more important things, but things that would get me into trouble with more important people than you. I was really enjoying myself and I didn't remember until it was too late; I'm sorry."*

People fail to achieve these types of task because:
- They seem relatively unimportant.
- The consequences of not achieving them are not particularly unpleasant.
- Other things are more pleasant to achieve.
- They forget.

 Action

Try allocating these activities to a 'magic hour' at least once a week.

Imagine you have one extra hour every week: your 169th hour. It occurs whenever you want it to, and you can do whatever you want with it. You don't have to see anyone that you don't want to see, or write letters to them, or do anything that you're currently feeling guilty about.

■ Write down five things that would make you happy in that hour (don't give yourself any restrictions or nagging guilt feelings about other jobs to be done).

■ Write down five things that would give pleasure to someone else in that hour.

■ Finally, write down five important things that you have been putting off, that you could at least start in the hour.

Then consider:
If you could have last week all over again, where could you fit in the magic hour? Resolve to fit it into this week at that same point.

If you find that simply the process of deciding to do this makes you feel good, you probably are not making enough decisions of this nature.

Make the magic hour a weekly habit.

In reality, how much time do you get to:

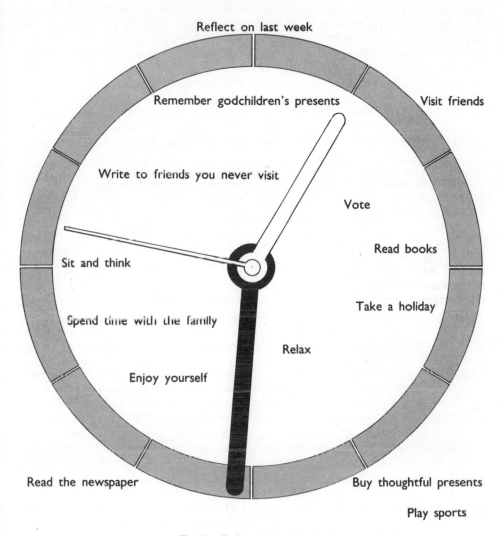

Reflect on last week

Remember godchildren's presents

Visit friends

Write to friends you never visit

Vote

Read books

Sit and think

Take a holiday

Spend time with the family

Relax

Enjoy yourself

Read the newspaper

Buy thoughtful presents

Play sports

Think of the week ahead

Sit and do nothing

Listen to music

Be a good neighbour (don't be cynical)

3 *Thought and action: achieving a balance means achieving more*

Y ou worked hard last week: but what did you achieve? You may wince at expressions like 'There's no room on the scoreboard for "I tried"'; but achievement relates directly to earning power, to mental well-being, and what is usually meant by job satisfaction.

Imagine two days next week. On each one you have the same list of routine tasks to achieve. On day one, you complete the list. On day two, nothing gets done: plenty of effort and running around, talking to people in a lively way, but nil results.

How do you feel at the end of each of those two days? Bright and energetic after day one? Frustrated, flat and tired after day two? It does not matter *what* you are trying to achieve; only that you achieved.

Below is a list of achievements, all essentially run-of-the-mill: most people manage most of them as a matter of routine; or at any rate without drama:

- Meeting sales targets
- Learning to drive
- Booking a holiday
- Getting the bank balance into credit
- Buying a birthday present
- Teaching children to swim
- Hanging a picture
- Keeping in touch with friends

- Starting to do social work
- Finishing a book
- Completing the next step in a language course
- Joining a political party
- Passing an examination
- Writing a letter
- Mending the car
- Painting a picture

Consider them carefully, however, and it should be evident that whatever their relative value, all give real satisfaction – but only if achieved.

By achieving - completing – tasks like these, you remind yourself of your abilities, or at any rate of your capacity for self-discipline. When things are not completed, you are vulnerable to nagging doubts about your ability to control time and events. Moreover, these doubts are the type which build up; indeed, they can snowball. This is why such self-evident clichés as 'It's results that count' carry a certain weight of truth.

The universal barrier

This book covers most of the reasons why people don't achieve; but this section concentrates on the most all-embracing: the fact that human beings tend to spend either too much time thinking about work and not doing it, or the other way round: too much time running around doing, without stopping to plan.

Peter Drucker, one of the most widely respected writers on management, describes the common denominator for all consistently successful people, whether artists or engineers, as their perfect balance between thought and action. They possess not too much, or too little, of either.

There is a simple verbal trick that can help you achieve this balance most of the time – now read on to .2.

2 **The importance of 'why' and 'therefore'**

The trick lies in the use of these two words. First, however, you need to make a basic judgement about your personal style. Do you spend too much time thinking, or do you spend too much time doing?

The first type spends hours in detailed planning, re-planning and analysis, leaving little time in which to actually achieve. Being in meetings with people like this is like negotiating a maze: every three-quarters of an hour you realize, in despair, you are passing the same point.

The latter type spends days working without let-up, only to feel that little has been achieved. They consider planning and reviewing a dangerous waste of time, the occupation of people in boring jobs.

■ If you spend too much time planning, keep adding the word THEREFORE to every waking thought:

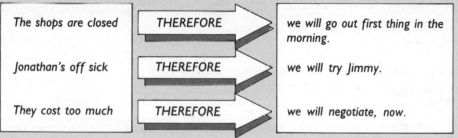

The shops are closed	THEREFORE	we will go out first thing in the morning.
Jonathan's off sick	THEREFORE	we will try Jimmy.
They cost too much	THEREFORE	we will negotiate, now.

■ If, on the other hand, you spend too much time doing, keep asking yourself why you are making all this effort:

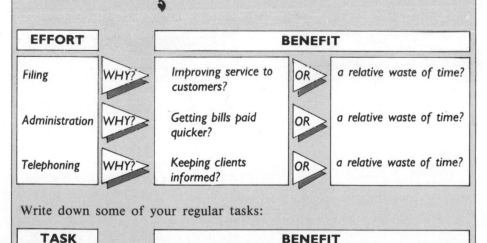

EFFORT		BENEFIT		
Filing	WHY?	Improving service to customers?	OR	a relative waste of time?
Administration	WHY?	Getting bills paid quicker?	OR	a relative waste of time?
Telephoning	WHY?	Keeping clients informed?	OR	a relative waste of time?

Write down some of your regular tasks:

TASK	BENEFIT

4

What would you like to do with your life?

S pend some time mulling over the following questions. Write your answers down.

■ *What do you regret not having done so far in your life?*

■ *What do you wish for?*

■ *What do friends tell you that you ought to try?*

■ *If you had more free time, to what would you devote it?*

■ *Which activities give you greatest pleasure?*

■ *At the end of your last holiday, what sort of hopes for the future did you have?*

> **"** *Most people don't have a clear long-term objective. Very few people actively work towards an objective. Most successful individuals and organizations do have an objective and a plan.* **"**
> – Michael Edwardes

1 ▶ Why do people fail to set objectives?

Probably because they underestimate their talents. They imagine the sequence of:

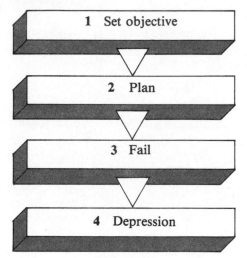

So they avoid thinking about it. Yet if you look back over your answers to the questions above you will find nearly all of them achievable. It is likely that achieving those aims requires not a major change in lifestyle, but a relatively minor change in your habits; spending time on one area rather than another.

Working out objectives

Right now, prepare a set of long-term objectives for yourself. Use the list below to generate your ideas. Allow yourself time to consider each heading. At this stage write everything down, don't exclude an objective because achieving it may seem impossible.

Income

Work
– Ambition/status
– Type of work
– Kind of organization

People
– Family
– Friends
– Neighbours
– You don't yet know
– Helping others

Mind
– Knowledge
– Stretching
– Spiritual/religious

Body
– Fitness
– Sport
(watch/participate)

Politics

Material things
– Home – size, style, location
– Car
– Other possessions

Travel
– New places
– Re-visiting
– Day trips
– Holidays

You
– Style and attitude
– Time to yourself
– Relaxation
– Habits
– Creativity
– Health

Interests
– Hobbies
– The arts
– Natural world
– Making things
– New skills

 Grading objectives

■ Mark against each item a D for desirable and an E for essential. This gives you a single statement of priority.

■ Try and give each item better definition by applying to it a time scale or potential costing, or a measure of quantity or quality to be achieved.

■ Plan to review these objectives each month.

■ Re-design your objectives each year.

Imagine having achieved your list. How would you feel?

Towards more realistic goals

In **4** you thought about what you want to do with your life generally and made a wide-ranging list of objectives. Having that list is useful, but translating it, or any single item on it, into reality is another matter.

Many of the sections in this book, but particularly **3** and **32**, should refine your insight into why there can be such a gulf between thought and action. Here, by contrast, we confront the gulf head-on. You have, for the first time, thought out a set of concrete personal goals. You may well feel quite excited by their potential. Suppose, in fact, that you crave the chance to translate one of them into reality.

Suppose, too, that you also have that leaden feeling, born of previous experience, that your thoughts, however well-defined, practically never translate into reality because:
– You lack will power.
– They lose their sparkle when subjected to reality; they are impractical, impossible to implement.

Also suppose that under the heading 'Work' in 4 you put down 'Start part-time business'.

What next?

 Antique discovery

Sally-Anne Duke and Carola Sutton both had thriving careers, but wanted to give them up to start a part-time business. They were married, and expected to have children; but wanted an interest that would take them outside the home and family as well as provide an independent income.

While still in their full-time jobs they:

I *Decided to start a service for people who needed to buy antique furniture for pleasure or investment, but who lacked the knowledge or time to undertake the considerable work involved.*

The idea at this stage was no more than a hunch, fuelled by their mutual interest in and love of antiques. They had to prove to themselves before committing money that the market existed; but they had no professional experience of the antiques world, or in market research.

Their only assets at this stage were, therefore, that they liked their goal, and that it fitted their perception of how they would like to be in a few years' time.

2 *Attended a course of evening classes in the decorative arts. During this period they also:*
– *Made a partnership agreement.*
– *Defined the objectives of the service to be offered, named the company Antique Discovery, investigated grants for small businesses, and found out the costs of accounting, book-keeping and other overheads.*

3 *Listed a set of objectives for firm action and assigned a date to each.*

4 *Decided to commit just £500 each against overhead costs to give the business a trail run of six months.*

5 *Systematically researched all sources of antique furniture from scratch and familiarized themselves with the operation and commercial terms of every aspect of the market from country auctions to major London salerooms.*

At this stage, they considered themselves ready to go.

A year later, the business was successfully established.

---

2 **Analysis**

Key points about the story:

■ **Motivation:** both women needed to continue work for persuasive reasons of finance and self-respect.

■ **Self-image:** both saw themselves, looking into the future, not just as mothers but as career women.

■ **They liked antiques.** The goal of working in the antiques world was attractive, likeable.

■ Almost everything about the later stages of achieving their goal was *realistic and practical,* particularly the six-month trial period. However, at the beginning, they had no guarantee that it was realistic and practical; *yet they were still sufficiently motivated to carry on.*

■ They proceeded in *clearly-defined steps.* Once the first one or two steps were taken, the project gained a momentum of its own and they were able to take some steps simultaneously.

Could the business have been set up without some of these factors? Probably not, *but* two of the ingredients, motivation and self-image, do seem to be at least as important as the rest. If a goal looks like satisfying self-interest and self-image – how one sees oneself now or in the future – this is usually enough to make you take the first step towards it *even* if at the outset you cannot tell whether it is realistic, likely to succeed.

Add to these first two ingredients the element of attraction, and you gain significant extra impetus. Add to this a healthy determination to make a goal realistic, and the practical expedient of

breaking it down into steps that appear manageable and not too daunting, and you have what amounts to a formula for success.

3 **The time factor**

One other key factor remains – time. Most people ignore it.

You will probably never achieve resolutions which do not pass the motivation and self-image tests. Human beings, in other words, tend to achieve what they want to achieve. However, the knowledge of what you want to achieve can lie buried in the sub-conscious.

One of the best ways of finding out what your sub-conscious has to 'say' is to address it – nag it – *over a period of time.* The subconscious has a way of working in delayed action; what starts as an idea can grow into conviction. If you do have a conscious personal goal, repeatedly asking 'Can I see myself doing this?' or picturing yourself performing the role often has the effect of turning an idea into reality or into an equally clear conviction that it will never work because it 'isn't you'.

The process benefits from time because time is a test of all things, especially ideas or personal goals born of the moment.

Do you really want to change?

"Change is not achieved without inconvenience, even from worse to better."
– Richard Hooker, 16th Century

Y ou have a choice to make. Do you wish to make things happen? To improve your performance? To bring about change in yourself and other people? Or are you inclined to stay as you are? Everything in the world changes, but your particular choice is whether to accept the changes as they come, or to attempt to force the pace.

 The gap between ambition and reality

In **4** you worked out what you would like to achieve. Imagine how it would be if you never achieved any of these goals; if nothing changed; that you will spend your time next year exactly as you did this year.

Is there a gap between what you would like to achieve and what you are likely to achieve? Will you have plenty of spare time in which to achieve your chosen goals? Have you proved in the past that you can change established habits?

For most of us the answers are, of course, 'yes', 'no' and 'no'. Many discover this simple truth when it is too late – when we have already failed.

Taking an honest look at the gap between your ambitions and the likely outcome is a useful way of addressing the fundamental question of whether you really want change. If for example you are so depressed by the gap that you spend time wondering how to reduce it, then it is of course likely that you really do want change.

 Closing the gap

If you think you really do want change, you need to take further time dispassionately considering the five main ingredients of change. The first four you have to have in some measure, the last are essential. All involve 'inconvenience'.

■ **Ability:** suppose you think you lack certain skills to achieve your goal; for example, you would like to work in Germany, but don't know the language; or start using a microcomputer, but don't know how to type.

The trouble with limitations is that the more you honestly acknowledge them, the more you believe in them; they become, in computer language, 'logged' – part of you.

The most effective antidote to this type of negative thought is shame. Remind yourself of other people who have developed skills they did not know they possessed. The world is full of mothers joining their daughters on nurses' training programmes; 40-year-olds doing university degree courses; grandmothers learning to paint in oils. If they can, so can you.

■ **Resources:** you probably have little spare time, less spare cash. At work you probably have no spare people to help you achieve more. But people do achieve without resources: they build their own houses because they have no cash, and they work their passage around the world.

Einstein, who failed mathematics at school, had developed his Special Theory by the age of 26; all the work was done in his spare time while working at the Swiss Patent Office. It was not for another four years that he enjoyed the luxury of being based full-time at a university.

■ **Opportunity: see 95.** Chance can play a large part, and good fortune cannot be supplied to order. So, you have to manufacture it. At the very least, you can be in the right places at the right time, speaking to key people. Terence Conran, frustrated by complete lack of outlets for his furniture and household designs, created his own 'luck' by setting up a new shop which eventually turned into the Habitat empire.

■ **Discipline:** too many people don't know the correct meaning of the word. Its primary sense is learning or instruction, and it has secondary meanings of training, or following a course. Discipline is *not necessarily* self-inflicted punishment. Try regarding it as a conscious commitment to learning, training or following a predetermined course; as a means to a desirable end.

■ **Desire:** it is easy to be temporarily motivated by someone else's enthusiasm, but second-hand enthusiasm soon fades. Unless you have personal commitment (see **5**) you will almost certainly fail.

▶ But do you really want change?

It is worth returning to this question once more. Why not stay as you are? Living life as it comes can have an element of excitement. There is a certain integrity in trusting that things will remain the same: that you will live in the same house, go the same way to work every day and have the same colleagues. Change involves learning to cope with new people and new circumstances. Staying the same is likely to mean that other people will not change their opinion of you. Change can draw adverse comment from other people. Those who change religion, or actively seek promotion, all experience pressure from their fellows not to upset the equilibrium of the team.

You may well have your current situation under control, knowing just how to influence the people around you and how to get things done – as far as they go. The security this gives will certainly be undermined by taking a new course. Could you live with this threat?

If you weigh the factors for and against change in this way and as a result suspect deep down that you don't want to change, the gap between ambition and reality will look different to how it was described in .1. Rather than depressing, it will appear natural and inevitable. After all, most people harbour some ambitions they know they cannot achieve, and find them a continuing source of mildly ironic amusement.

It requires, after all, energy and commitment to sustain the *status quo*; within that framework, there is opportunity for improving yourself, getting things done, and a more fulfilling existence.

7 *The urgent versus the important*

T he kind of planning suggested in **4, 5** and **6** for establishing clear, viable personal goals is a powerful tool in managing your time. But even the best-laid time-management schemes and life plans can come to grief if you don't have the habit of discriminating between the urgent and the important.

Some of the problems that can occur are neatly illustrated by the experiences of a publishing editor attempting to mastermind a massive encyclopaedia project, section by section, to a series of tough deadlines.

Publishing, perhaps more than most businesses, revolves around deadlines, and this editor set up his diary to ensure that no deadline was missed.

Every deadline date was entered; all the work was broken down into components, and each was carefully assigned to a period in which from experience the editor knew it could be completed.

At first it went well; he was able to commission authors to write the entries well in advance. The authors' briefs were so clear and thorough that nearly every entry could be sent straight on to the typesetter virtually unaltered.

But as the project advanced, things began to change. As more and more people inside and outside the company became involved, more and more 'urgent' questions came the editor's way:

"Would you mind if I deliver next week, not this week?" Or "Could I over-write by 250 words? It's such an important topic." To compensate, the editor soon found himself writing increasingly short and hurried briefs. He was still using his diary religiously, but every day his carefully worked out list of tasks to be achieved was thrown by unforeseeable problems that seemed to demand urgent attention.

Before long, he was commissioning authors so late that they were barely able to complete the work on time. Then, as a key deadline loomed, an author fell ill and

was late with his copy, while another, failing to understand the hurredly written brief, delivered a piece which was totally unusable. Unable to retrieve the situation, the editor missed the deadline, costing the company thousands.

What went wrong?
The editor felt that he was the victim of circumstances, and that he had done his best. But was he?

Urgent or important?

The editor failed to understand that:

■ Surprisingly few tasks are both urgent and important.

■ Urgent tasks assume importance simply because they *seem* to demand immediate action. A colleague comes into your office and says he must have certain figures by the end of the morning; if he is good at selling himself, you tend to oblige, and put more important but less urgent tasks on the back burner.

■ Since most people confront 'urgent' problems nearly all the time – a telephone call, someone walking into the office with a query – long-term goals are consistently put aside for the sake of the 'urgent'.

Ask yourself honestly, how many important resolutions you set over the last year fell by the wayside simply because you did not have the time? Were you going, for instance, to:

– Revamp the filing system?
– Set new budget controls?
– Plan strategy months in advance?
– Take Spanish lessons?
– Write more often to friends?
– Keep fit?

Far too many important tasks only get done when they become urgent as well.

If you suffer from this problem acutely, you can find yourself living in a permanent state of crisis, juggling one deadline against another, scraping through just in time – *even though you plan your schedule meticulously.*

---

2 **Recognizing priorities**

The solution is to develop a sixth sense for assessing whether tasks are important or urgent; you need to be capable of judging their status instantly, so that outside requests can be rejected or undertaken on the spot.

Some time-management writers suggest rating priority with scores out of ten. This is fine in theory, and can work for some people, but is probably unnecessarily complex. A cruder approach tends to make you much more decisive. Just ask yourself whether it is urgent or important. For example:

■ **Urgent, but not important:** a colleague rushes in to your office say-ing "God, we haven't tested the fire alarm for 18 months; we're break-ing the law." You are just about to start planning next year's sales strategy. ACTION "George, I know it is urgent, but if we could test the day after tomorrow I'd keep quiet about it between now and then."

■ **Urgent and important:** you are dialling the printer to make a critical change to a report when your secretary rushes into the office say-ing your husband has been taken to hospital after an accident.
ACTION Tell your secretary to telephone the printer, while you go to the hospital; resolve to check she has made the change properly by calling the printer from the hospital.

8 *Plan your life* and *remain normal*

M any people's private definition of 'planner' runs roughly like this: 'Person (usually boring) who wastes time describing work whilst others are working.' Similarly with the verb to plan: (i) to produce a complicated list of times and tasks irrelevant to the real world; (ii) to waste time.

Planning is often felt to be: inflexible; dangerously time-wasting; dull.

Inflexible?
It depends how you plan. A plan does not have to be anything more than a guide to making better decisions. When a crisis comes along, you usually adapt to circumstances anyway, regardless of the requirements of a master plan. Many people fear the in-flexibility of planning when all along they are more than capable of adapting plans as circumstances dictate.

Dangerously time-wasting?
But obviously, it *can* be dangerous not to plan.

A threat to spontaneous relationships?
Only if planned time accounts for every minute of your life.

Dull?
Sometimes: doing is, for most of us, much more exciting. But you can easily counteract this type of negative feeling by reminding yourself, as you plan, that planning leads to the pleasurable experience of doing.

 Planning to achieve objectives

If you have read **4** and **5**, you already know where you are going. By following the steps below with each of your objectives in mind, you can discover the sequence of steps that will take you there. Win each of these battles and you have won the war.

■ Take one of your objectives and write down all the stages to achieving it. Don't worry about logical order at this stage, but don't forget the very first steps of getting organized, and the very last ones of tidying things up. Next,

■ *Don't try and order them yet.*
■ Against each step, jot down the small component tasks required to achieve it, and further divide these if necessary.

You should now have a list, long or short, of all the necessary steps to reduce the project into manageable pieces.
■ Still don't try and order them.
■ Make connections between the inter-dependent steps.
■ Asterisk the critical steps: those which will hold everything up until they are completed.

■ *Now you can order them.*
■ Put against each job the time it will take, including interruptions.
■ Put the first step in your diary – and do it.

 Your response to the exercise

If you found it boring or difficult, your brain probably prefers to make creative jumps; but it probably also needs to be disciplined to gather more facts before jumping ahead.

On the other hand, if you loved the whole process, you are probably too fond of detail, which could eventually overwhelm the object in view.

9 *Planning to avoid crises*

A few people at the top of the tree live in a perpetual state of crisis – and would not want it any other way. They relish the sense of power given by keeping cool in an emergency; they thrive on and may even be addicted to the buzz of their own adrenalin. But they are the exception.

It is axiomatic that most successful people have a knack for avoiding crises. They may be busy. They may have as much pressure on their time as anyone; yet they are rarely caught off-guard. The true art of crisis management is managing to avoid crises.

Crises undeniably add spice to life, and many people are indeed highly adept at riding them out. But as Jean Kerr so aptly put it in her book *Please Don't Eat the Daisies*: 'If you can keep your head when all about you are losing theirs, it's just possible you haven't grasped the situation.'

If you continually find yourself confronting crises, either at work or at home, consider:

■ Crises are stressful.

■ Crises undermine good time management habits and prevent you achieving important goals.

■ If you are continually beset by crises – however well-managed – you will not inspire confidence in your colleagues.

■ Eventually you will be hit by a crisis out of which even you cannot wriggle.

1 ▶ Why crises occur

Mostly because of basic failure to anticipate:
– You failed to act on warnings.
– You failed to act until the matter was urgent.
– You underestimated what time each part of the job would take.
– You failed to allow time in your schedule for possible mishaps and breakdowns.
– You did not lay enough contingency plans.
– You did not check up on people to whom you delegated.

2 ▶ Anticipating crises

Setting a deadline is, of course, the key to anticipating crises: indeed it means you have anticipated a crisis point in a piece of work. It is therefore worth going to a great deal of care over the way in which deadlines are set.

Most people tend to allow work to build up towards one crucial date. Seven or eight times out of ten, perhaps, this works – at the expense of a few frayed nerves. But a 70 or 80 per cent success rate is not good enough. So instead of setting one main deadline, set a series of interim targets to ensure that jobs are broken down into compents and that the work flows, rather than goes in as last-minute rush.

■ **Be realistic about schedules.** Depending on the type of work to be completed, you should build in different amounts of slack time. *Not* adjusting the amount of slack time to suit the project is a sign that you are not giving each schedule the individual attention it deserves.

It would be wrong to give any concrete guidelines here about slack time: ▶

9

▶ if you don't do this particular piece of thinking for yourself, you take the first step towards crisis.

■ **Listen for the routine (but not always obvious) warnings.** Assume all your work tasks divide into three categories:

> 1 for highest priority
> – jobs you must do now, and do well, or face the consequences;

> 2 for routine importance
> – things you must do this week or a crisis will occur;

> 3 for tasks you can postpone indefinitely.

Generally speaking, anyone capable of holding down a job does 1s and 2s but procrastinates 3s in the knowledge that out of every 100 3s, 99 never develop into a crisis. But what of the 3s that do turn into 1s? See the box.

3 ▶ A nose for a crisis

All the advice given in this section far depends on specific action or specific awareness. But there is another dimension to anticipating crisis: using intuition. If you run complex projects or manage large numbers of people, you probably cannot get away without it.

It is not enough to be merely alert to what could go wrong. You have to let the mind range over every area of your control "sniffing" for trouble. Successful operators have a sixth sense for:

■ **The 'deafening silence':** hearing nothing from a particular source may be a sure sign of impending crisis. Most people to whom you delegate work want to let you know they are getting on with it and do so by making little noises. If you don't hear any such noises, act quickly.

■ **Protesting too much:** by contrast, some people to whom you delegate will betray lack of confidence in their ability to complete by making too many noises: they want cover for their non-action. Only your intuitive ear can detect when such noises top the safety level.

■ **The crisis-prone:** some people, and some projects are, for no apparent reason, crisis-prone. You can improve your nose for these trouble-makers by regular reviews:
– Do crises almost always revolve around one particular type of project, task or person? Or is it the same part of the system, or piece of equipment that plays up?

4 ▶ Contingencies

'Of course', you say; of course I have contingency plans. But are they sufficiently concrete? Will they need thinking out or refining after the crisis has occurred?

The only way of ensuring contingencies are concrete is by being pedantic:

■ Break the project down into steps. Write a list of everything that could go wrong at each stage.

■ Go through the list with a colleague. Two brains are better than one, and everyone connected should share in a healthy fear of what might go wrong.

■ Speculate only on the likely: don't make contingency plans for snow in the Sahara.

■ Think outside the project as well as within its orbit. In particular, speculate on what might happen at home. Children ill? Building work? Anything which might prevent you from working late through a critical pre-deadline period?

■ Work out an escape route for each crisis on the list.

■ Keep the list in an accessible place.

Anatomy of a crisis

1 Thursday. *A memo arrives on your desk from the sales director asking for the manufacturing price of a product not due out for 18 months. You rate it 3.*

2 The following Wednesday, *another memo from the sales director: friendly enough, but reminding you he wants the price. No deadline mentioned: you still rate it 3.*

3 Friday. *The sales director's secretary (an interfering woman) says to you by the coffee machine: "Did you get my memo?" "Yes," you say, "I got the two memos you typed for the sales director." Not wishing to demean yourself by asking why this trivial matter has suddenly become so urgent, you change the subject and re-rate the task as a 2.*

4 The following Monday. *An angry telephone call from the managing director – for it was he who asked the sales director for the price in the first place in order to assess the worth of some secret new development with a similar specification. "If you can't get me the price by tomorrow, we'll have to have a serious talk about your future with this company."*

CRISIS Whole day on telephone to manufacturer, who cannot possibly get the price within 12 hours.

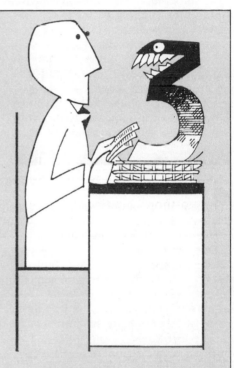

The warning signs

■ It was a memo: requests in writing usually mean business.

■ The memo was followed up. Never be fooled by the friendly tone of follow-ups: people like to think they delegate in a friendly manner.

■ Being nagged on a second front: if someone bothers for you to be nagged on a second front, act.

10 *Your diary*

Do you think you know how to keep a diary? I often conduct informal polls at my courses on diary-keeping habits. Two interesting facts almost always emerge. More than half think that keeping an efficient diary means simply ensuring that all appointments are meticulously entered; and at least a third think that it would be time-saving to hand the running of the diary over entirely to a secretary.

A diary ought to be a tool not only for recording appointments, but for planning *every* function you fulfil at work or at home, including talking to people, letter-writing, reading, going to the bank or nipping out to buy your son's birthday present. And a really useful diary, for the reasons given below, is far too personal – far too interesting – a document to hand over to someone else. By all means involve a secretary in planning your schedule and recording appointments - as long as the diary never leaves you.

This may sound as if a well-kept diary is, as some advertisements claim, the key to effective time management; indeed that all you need to be well-organized is a 'system' (meaning a range of expensive printed inserts to fit a loose-leaf binder).

In fact, a well-maintained diary, given the nature of life and time, is anything but systematic or neat: it is full of tentative plans, plans re-planned, crossings-out, scribbled ideas and items suddenly remembered.

The only diary 'system' worth having is simplicity and flexibility; even then, it will be no more than a tool of time management. More important by far is a realistic attitude to planning – see **14** and **15** .

1 ▶ What a diary should be:

■ A book offering enough space to list one day's appointments AND, *on the same page*, sufficient room for extensive notes on the far more complex business of when and how to perform the rest of the day's work: letter-writing, telephoning, thinking and planning.

■ A notebook for every area of your life, whether home- or work-related. It should be capable of carrying your notes of meetings (later transferred to files); lists of all sorts; goals; thoughts and ideas; records of self-appraisal; as well as all the practical paraphernalia of expenses, anniversary dates and essential telephone numbers.

One of the advantages of loose-leaf systems is that they allow blank pages for notes to be interleaved with diary pages. Some people have practical objections to loose-leaf diaries – for example, the discomfort of writing when the ring-binder is in the way; and a tendency for the holes in the pages to wear larger than their proper size. If you share these objections, you will choose a conventionally-bound desk diary with pages measuring at least 140 mm (width) X 210 mm (depth).

■ A means of planning complex, long-term projects over at least a whole year.

■ Interesting: record ideas and plans in a diary, and it becomes a book you will want to keep dipping into.

2 ▶ What a diary can do for you:

■ Increase self-confidence and control because all the key points of your life are in one place.

10

■ Enable you to summon ideas without resorting to memory.

■ Reduce the stress of doubting you have remembered appointments.

■ Ensure that you perform adequately, even on bad days.

■ Remind you that time has an economic *and* a spiritual value.

Below, and on the next two pages, examples of inserts available for one of the more sophisticated loose-leaf diary systems. An interesting variation on both the traditionally-bound and the loose-leaf diary is the mid-year diary. This can cover as long as 15 months. The usual 31st December year-end is in some respects an unnatural one for the executive – for many, the new year begins at the end of the summer holiday season. Also, it can be surprisingly useful to carry a diary that enables one to look forward, and back, further than the usual maximum of 12 months.

Actual page size 210 × 300 mm

▶

November 1987

One whole week to view

MONDAY **2**	TUESDAY **3**	WEDNESDAY **4**
These are examples of appointments pages; the system allows blank pages to be interleaved with them to allow individually tailored day plans as described in section 15.		*Space for early morning appointments*

9.00

Space for each of four working hours before one o'clock

10.00

11.00

12.00

1.00

Space for each of four working hours after lunch

2.00

3.00

4.00

5.00

Space for after-work appointments

November 1987

THURSDAY

5

This system is also available in the brief-case sized format of 210 × 150 mm.

9.00

10.00

11.00

12.00

1.00

2.00

3.00

4.00

5.00

FRIDAY

6

SATURDAY

7

SUNDAY

8

Aspects of time, fast and slow

ime is measured in hours and minutes, but not all hours and minutes are the same length. The number of expressions in daily use which describe time's ability to pass quickly, slowly, or stand still, testifies well to how capricious it can be. The phenomenon is immutable; those who ignore it invariably come off worst; the only option is to understand it better. This section is about a basic understanding; the next considers in greater detail time's extraordinary ability to slip away.

 How accurately do you measure time?

QUESTION ONE Write down the day, month and year when you think the events below took place. If you can, write down the day too. This is not a test of your general knowledge, but of your consciousness of the speed of time passing.

a Concorde's inaugural commercial flight to New York.

b The first man on the moon.

c J.F. Kennedy's assassination.

d The occupation of the U.S. Embassy in Tehran and seizure of the hostages.

(The answers are at the bottom of the next page.)

QUESTION TWO Without looking at your watch, estimate what time it is now. TARGET: accuracy to the nearest five minutes.

QUESTION THREE Estimate the passing of one minute by looking away from your watch and turning back when you think that 60 seconds have elapsed. Don't try to count the seconds, do it by guesswork. TARGET: less than ten per cent error.

These questions, among many others, are sometimes posed by personnel departments and head hunters seeking high achievers. A large proportion of these consistently under-estimate elapsed time, *or* are extremely accurate; they are most likely to give dates considerably more recent than the actual date, or to be within six months of it.

Don't draw any definite conclusions about yourself as a result of these tests; they are no more than measures of an individual's potential in the context of a large number of other questions. However, they should provide food for thought, especially in relation to what follows.

2 **Reasons for over- and under-estimating the speed of time**

■ The ability to estimate time operates in the same area of the brain as verbal skill and logic (see 32). The more time you spend 'in' the other side of the brain thinking creatively, or using creative or intuitive skills, the less aware you are of time passing. For instance, if you are immersed in a book or an emotional conversation, you are likely to be surprised by how much time has passed when you finish.

■ "Tomorrow" is the universal safety valve of procrastinators to avoid the reality of time pressure. Time suffers progressive devaluation, like an inflating currency, when there is always plenty more "tomorrow", and with this devaluation goes a decreasing ability to estimate its speed of passing.

■ As Einstein suggested, time 'flies' when you are enjoying yourself: so the brain must judge the speed of time passing by measuring the gaps between moments of enjoyment. For instance, you hate writing reports. Today you must spend all your time on a departmental report. If your last enjoyable moment was breakfast at home and the next pleasure will be the evening meal, then time will drag all day.

■ Time sometimes stands still. At the Helsinki arms talks in 1986, the official clock was stopped to enable agreement to be reached before the agreed deadline. This is not, of course, the true meaning of time 'standing still'. Time stands still of its own accord at moments of ecstasy or terror such as falling in love or falling off a bridge.

 Effects of estimating time inaccurately

■ **Stress:** it may well be that people who under-estimate time passing are achievers, but they can cause others with whom they work a good deal of trouble. They will commit themselves to too many jobs because they genuinely estimate they will fit their schedule. The gradual realization that they will not fit the schedule stresses both the person attempting the impossible, and those waiting for the unfulfilled promises.

Such people are constantly aware of time: continually trying to fill the 'unforgiving minute' with 120 second's worth of work – and failing.

■ **Under-achievement:** those who over-estimate time required for tasks often suffer from stress too. They usually negotiate reasonable deadlines, but their tendency to stay in the right hand side of the brain causes stress and irritation to achievers who depend on these slow coaches to produce work.

Moreover, those who over-estimate often fail to realize many of their talents by protecting themselves too well from time pressures that draw out latent ability.

4 ▶ **Action**

■ Practise estimating time passing.

■ If you persistently over-estimate what you can achieve in a given space of time, take the commonsense precaution of building slack into every deadline, however confident you feel. If you feel you will finish by Thursday, tell your boss it will be Friday.

■ If you consistently over-estimate how long jobs last, take more risks with time and push yourself harder, even though this is against your instincts; justify this apparent folly by reflecting that stretching yourself develops potential.

Answers to questions in **11.1:**
a 22.10.77   b 21.7.69
c 22.11.63   d 4.11.79

12 *Gauging where time goes*

As your bank manager ever had to tell you that you have less money than you thought? And have you then ever spent one of those long Sunday afternoons working out in depressing detail exactly where it has all gone? As a result of what you discovered, did things improve? (At least until the next period of neglect?)

The chances are that you answered "Yes" to all these questions, in which case you know, at any rate in moments of honesty, that time is like money: a finite resource, easy to spend without knowing exactly on what. Your bank manager writes to you when you are overdrawn on cash; you have to do the chasing-up yourself if you are overdrawn on time. It is important to match the way in which you do this to your own particular style.

▶ Basic time check

First, whoever you are, and regardless of whether you think you are overdrawn on time or not, run this basic check once yearly. Answer with brutal honesty:

a What is your span of concentration?
b Where are you giving time away, and where are people taking it from you?
c What distractions are you allowing?
d How much time is spent on the important, how much on the unimportant, how much on crises and how much on planned events?
e How often do you avoid, or fail to achieve really important tasks or projects?

If you find the answers to these questions are:
a Less than . . .
b Don't really know
c Don't really know
d Don't really know
e Once too many
then you need a more searching method of assessing where your time goes: a detailed time log.

Time log

This, for most people, is a difficult procedure. (If you find it easy, that in itself can be an indication of underlying problems: see ▪ 4).

There are two main methods of keeping a detailed time log: which you choose depends upon the number of interruptions you normally experience in a day.

If you have constant interruptions:
▪ Decide on a time unit say 15 minutes .
▪ During one whole day, jot down at 15-minute intervals whatever task you are currently working on: be honest,

and resist the temptation to put down what you have just done, or are about to do because it sounds better than drinking coffee.

■ At the end of the day, list all the tasks you *had* to do, and award each one a point for every time you logged yourself doing it. Compare the totals.

■ The longer you keep the log, the more accurate a picture you will develop of where your time goes.

The log could look something like this:

10.00	*phone out*
10.15	*chatting with Ken*
10.30	*writing letter*
10.45	*writing letter*
11.00	*phone in*
11.15	*car*

If you have a day that is not constantly bombarded by other people's interruptions:

■ Write down the starting and finishing time for each task.

■ Ensure that interruptions and distractions are all logged.

■ Ensure that unproductive and unpleasant uses of time are logged as well.

■ Add up time spent that day on each job and compare totals.

It is worth repeating the exercise once each month.

The value of time logs

If you mistrust the exercise, remind yourself that it will at least give you a partial picture of where time goes, and that this is less misleading than none at all. Try to use the log to pinpoint threats, potential or actual, to getting things done; distinguish between threats which are your fault, and those which are genuinly beyond your control.

The very act of logging time makes you more than usually aware of time; and it can improve your use of time without further effort.

Further benefits to be gained from a time log lie in your consideration of the following questions:

■ Is the spread of time appropriate on each of the topics you listed?

■ Are you assertive enough – or too rigid in your use of time?

■ How many events are planned beforehand? How realistic are these plans?

■ How much of your time do you control?

■ Could you control more?

4 ► Dangers of time logs

■ If you are naturally logical, you may waste time on too much detail-gathering or analysis.

■ If you are a creative type, you may think the process is anathema to the creative process, or you may log dishonestly, or you may reject the inevitable conclusions.

If you are either of these types, confine the time log period to just two hours, but repeat every other day until you have done the exercise four times. Then, before rejecting the exercise as unproductive, analyse the jottings. They should reveal whether you spend any time at all on:

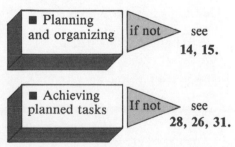

Analysing a time log

In 12 you kept a detailed log of your time usage and considered the results in general terms. Now you are in a position to analyse it in detail and, if necessary, re-direct your efforts.

▶ Lessons from time logs

Have some jobs taken longer than you thought they would? Why?
- Did someone let you down?
- Did you under-estimate?
- Don't you like these types of jobs?
- Did you get distracted?
- Do you detect a pattern of low concentration with these jobs?
- Were some tasks difficult to get into?
- Were some too tempting to resist?

How long did telephone calls take?
- Incoming?
- Outgoing?
- Were some people particularly long-winded?
- Did people telephone back when they said they would? How long were meetings?
- Which ones could have been shorter?

How long do letters take you to write?
- In total, after checking and signing?

How long do regular reports take you?
- Could you delegate part of this job?

How much time did you spend liaising (or were you chatting)?
- How productive was it?

How much time was spent travelling?
- Was this an average week?

How often did people interrupt you with queries?
- And you interrupt them?
- How often were you thrown off course by someone's interruption?
- Was it really important?

How much time was spent pottering?
- Was this important in gathering your thoughts or giving your brain a rest?
- Or were you avoiding the next job?

What were the main surprises in terms of length of time taken on tasks?

What was the longest time spent on one job without interruption?

What times of day did you concentrate for the longest periods?

Have you used your time exactly as you wanted?

Did you consciously give yourself enough breaks (rather than let them be dictated by others)?

If this was someone else's time log, what constructive advice would you give them?

Proactive or reactive?

Now look at the headings below. They should represent the main elements of your job (with managing as the optional extra). Write down the percentage of your total working time that *you would like to, or feel you should*, spend on each of the categories.

CATEGORY	% TIME
Thinking *(reading, reflecting, developing ideas).*	
Planning *(daily, yearly, budgetting, forecasting, planning for meetings, organizing rotas).*	
Doing *(technical work, answering queries, dealing with customers, users).*	
Managing *(motivating, appraising, communicating, answering queries, coaching).*	
Administering *(writing letters, filling in forms, dealing with the mail).*	
Reviewing *(on a daily, weekly, monthly, yearly basis).*	
	TOTAL: 100%

Now, on a blank sheet of paper, put six columns: **T,P,D,M,A,R.** Lay this against each sheet of your time log and use it to add up the total amount of time that you did spend on each of the categories. How do the two compare? Mark which categories need to have more time spent on them.

Having made this comparison, look at one more factor. Part of your job and your personality will mean that you are reacting to things and to people: reacting to customer, client or user problems; reacting to your own staff queries; reacting to your boss; reacting to colleagues. The rest of your time is spent being proactive, making things happen. For instance, making the time to think about new ways of doing things or motivating your boss. Everyone's job will have a different ratio of reactive to proactive.

Consider whether you would like your life to be a little more or less reactive. It is very likely that if you said earlier that you would like to spend more time on thinking, planning or reviewing that you want to be more proactive. It is an interesting point that some people often feel that reading and sitting thinking are luxuries. Are you the sort who automatically pushes papers away when someone comes in? In which case, you probably need to be more proactive.

To carve out the time for thinking, reading or planning requires you to be proactive, to be strong and assertive over youself and others. Though being reactive demands many interpersonal skills, if it often easier to be reactive than to make time the to reflect. The balance between being proactive and reactive is the balance in your relationships. If you are totally reactive it is always you who says "yes", who soaks up the pressure. The more proactive you can become the more you can shape those relationships to give more time for reflective activities.

14 *How much time can you control?*

As Charles Dickens' Mr Micawber pointed out:

" *Annual income twenty pounds, annual expenditure nineteen pounds, nineteen shillings and sixpence – result happiness. Annual income twenty pounds, annual expenditure twenty pounds, ought and sixpence – result misery.* "

How many people are free to spend all of their income just as they please?

Most of us have commitments in the shape of mortgages and household budgets. If after these have been paid there is nothing left for yourself, you are quick to realize something is wrong. It ought to be the same with time.

Credit balances of money, or time, don't have to be big, but they do have to exist.

Being heavily in debt can wretchedly inhibit your freedom to act; in the same way, having no control over your time can be deeply de-motivating. Think back to the last time you had more things to do than time available. How did you feel? Would you like to find a way of avoiding that feeling coming up again?

▶ A typical week's time balance sheet

Opening credit   **168 hours**
(You will never improve upon that figure)

Items	Debit	Balance
Sleeping	51 hrs	117 hrs
Travelling to and from work	6 hrs	111 hrs
Other travelling	18 hrs	93 hrs
Meetings	15 hrs	78 hrs
Monthly budgets	3 hrs	75 hrs
Speaking to customers on the telephone	12 hrs	63 hrs
Interruptions	10 hrs	53 hrs
Writing letters	6 hrs	47 hrs
Staff appraisal and coaching	10 hrs	37 hrs
Eating	25 hrs	12 hrs
Showering, dressing	3 hrs	9 hrs
Watching TV	9 hrs	0 hrs
Keeping fit	3 hrs	– 3 hrs **O/D**
Weekend jobs	6 hrs	– 9 hrs **O/D**
Time spent with family/friends	12 hrs	– 21 hrs **O/D**
Reading	5 hrs	– 26 hrs **O/D**

Unlike money, time cannot be borrowed to tide you over a bad patch.

 Uncontrollable time

For the average executive, 50 to 90 per cent of time is taken up by:
- Heads round the door
- Telephone interruptions
- Requests from boss/staff
- Formal meetings
- Informal chats over coffee
- Mail, budgets, travelling
- Speaking to customers and suppliers

What remains can in theory be used for:
- Planning ahead
- Spending unpressured time with staff
- Relaxing, reflecting
- Learning and teaching new skills
- Delegating
- Meeting key people whom you don't normally meet
- Being creative

There is no point in trying to get more done – or in reading more sections in this book – unless you can first be really tough with yourself over the basic issue of how much time is left after the basic regular debits. It is not much fun reflecting on last week, last month, last year and honestly admitting how much time was left for uninterrupted work, creative thinking and planning. But it has to be done.

Three additional factors will influence how much controllable time you have:

■ Your Job
The more contact you have with people, the less time you will have to control. And what you do have will come in endless little bits much less useful than a whole clear day.

■ The Boss
The autocrat and the worrier will interrupt his subordinate's day much more than the trusting delegator.

■ You
The friendlier you are, the more time you will give away to others.

With these 'wild cards' in mind, look back over the time log made in **12** and mark off the parts of each day when your time was controlled by or committed to other people and things. What you are left with is the amount of each day that you had at your disposal: your controllable time.

Now ask yourself if your controllable time is sufficient for the jobs you regularly set out to achieve each day. If you keep carrying jobs over from day to day, is it because you do not have enough controllable time to spend on them?

3 **Common misconceptions about controllable time**

■ *Having a small amount of disposable time is a bad thing.*
Wrong. Many jobs exist for the purpose of providing feed-back to customers or in-house personnel, and some personalities are attracted by, and suited to, these 'reactive' jobs. This is not to say, however, that you will not benefit by being a little less reactive than you are: social interaction is like a drug to many people: the more they get, the more they depend on it for their sense of well-being.

■ *Disposable time is equivalent to doing nothing.*
Probably wrong. It is time you might spend on a Magic Hour – see **2**; or you could use it for reading and reflecting.

Controlling your day

By 'controlling time', I mean control – no more, no less. This section is about damage limitation: stopping things getting out of hand.

1 ▶ Immediate action

Below are some pieces of advice, some of which most people use occasionally, but rarely all together on a regular basis. Combined, they make a potent time control scheme.

■ **What must you do tomorrow?** What would you like to do? Make a list of all those things. *Mark off the most important.* Rate them according to their value to you . . . . . . not according to how much you like them.

The value is decided by you.

■ **How long will these jobs take?** The one certain thing about tomorrow is that it will only contain 24 hours. No more, and no less. It is also pretty likely that what you have to do plus all your interruptions will add up to more than 24 hours.

■ **Now picture tomorrow.** First, how much time is already committed? Make sure that all your appointments are in your diary. Block off the total time this will take. Be realistic. Don't hope that tomorrow, for the first time in history, your regular monthly meeting will take half the time. There is no alternative to blocking this off as it is definitely going to happen. Now you can see how much time you will have tomorrow B.I. (Before Interruptions).

■ **How much time is likely to be taken up by the unknown interruptions?** See **14**. This is likely to be the most time that you will get to yourself tomorrow.

■ **Commit yourself to times for the important jobs.** You probably change your meetings with other people less easily than the plans you make for yourself, so treat yourself with more respect. Commit yourself to a meeting with yourself to do one of the jobs on your list. Pencil it into the diary. This gives you the flexibility to move the appointment around when tomorrow's crises DO occur.

You will now be making more decisions about the way you spend your time. Every time you get an interruption, you must ask yourself which is more important: the current task, or the interruption?

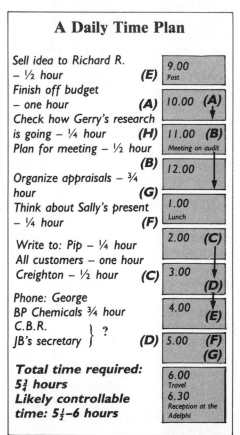

A Daily Time Plan

Sell idea to Richard R. – ½ hour **(E)**	9.00 Post
Finish off budget – one hour **(A)**	10.00 **(A)**
Check how Gerry's research is going – ¼ hour **(H)**	11.00 **(B)** Meeting on audit
Plan for meeting – ½ hour **(B)**	12.00
Organize appraisals – ¾ hour **(G)**	
Think about Sally's present – ¼ hour **(F)**	1.00 Lunch
Write to: Pip – ¼ hour All customers – one hour Creighton – ½ hour **(C)**	2.00 **(C)** 3.00 **(D)**
Phone: George BP Chemicals ¾ hour C.B.R. } ? JB's secretary } **(D)**	4.00 **(E)** 5.00 **(F)** **(G)**
Total time required: 5¾ hours Likely controllable time: 5½–6 hours	6.00 Travel 6.30 Reception at the Adelphi

It is not your fault that you cannot control the day. You are overloaded with work by other people who are insensitive to existing pressures on your time. Or is it your fault?

Just as you are waking up, a little thought reminds you of today's jobs . . .

THEREFORE

late getting up . . .

THEREFORE

not enough time at home in the morning

THEREFORE

don't have time to talk to anyone else

THEREFORE

are told you don't have time for anyone

THEREFORE

go out of the door in a bad frame of mind . . .

THEREFORE

forget something . . .

THEREFORE

have to sneak back to get it . . .

THEREFORE

later than usual . . .

THEREFORE

plans for first half of morning spoiled, so decide to cut losses by having cup of coffee . . .

THEREFORE

meet a colleague . . .

THEREFORE

spend some time discussing the day . . .

THEREFORE

only have time to look at the post, not to do anything with it . . .

THEREFORE

add to your pile of outstanding paperwork (most of which will go in the bin when you do get to look at it) . . .

THEREFORE

feel under even more pressure . . .

THEREFORE

make a list of all outstanding jobs . . .

THEREFORE

feel uncomfortable . . .

THEREFORE

start the job you like most (instead of the one which needs doing first) . . .

THEREFORE

fail to concentrate, because you know there is something much more important you should be doing . . .

16 *Reviewing a daily plan*

You have read and tried **15**. You have therefore planned today. The most important jobs were given priority, times were estimated and the tasks were allocated to particular times in the day.

Now it is the end of the day. The daily log looks a mess, covered in crossings out, arrows and additions. So what next?

1 How to approach a daily plan

■ **Expect it to look a mess.** Daily life is usually a bit of a mess. If you have used the plan throughout the day, every interruption will have been a decision point. To deal with the interruption or the planned job, that was the question. And if you changed course from the planned job, then you had to re-slot the task. Hence the scribblings.

In fact, they represent the working day's planning and re-planning. It is messier, but more effective, to budget both money and time on paper rather than in your head: on paper you have a more complete picture than your memory can ever reproduce; you can study it without being distracted by the thought that your memory is inadequate.

■ **Don't spend too long reviewing.** About a quarter of an hour at the end of each day should be sufficient to untangle today and plan tomorrow.

■ **Give praise where it is due.** Tick off the planned jobs that you achieved. This starts you off in a positive frame of mind. Usually you only carry around in your head the jobs that you have not done, which means you forget the progress you have made in other areas. Keeping a day plan is therefore more self-motivating than other

'methods' because it recognizes success as well as unfinished tasks.

■ **What about the jobs that did not get done?** Plan when you will do them – tomorrow or next week. Review your priorities in the light of today.

■ **What if only a small percentage of the tasks were achieved?** This happens regularly; don't stop planning – the pressure will not go away if you do that. Instead, analyse and act. Ask yourself:
– Have you under-estimated your controllable time?
– Should you be more assertive with people to protect your plan from interruptions?
– Should you be persuading your boss to re-arrange your deadlines, or to take someone else on to help you?
– Which of today's tasks could have been delegated?
– Could you introduce a system to cope better with the work?
– If none of these is applicable, when will you be having your nervous breakdown trying to achieve the impossible?

■ **Don't fall into the 'My life's too complicated to plan' trap.** The more complicated your life is, the more important it is to know what all your commitments are at any one time.

2 Learning from a daily plan

■ **There is no more need for time logs (12 and 13).** They are useful, but they are also an extra job, and in any case a day plan becomes a time log if you review it each evening.

■ **Were there some jobs that you avoided,** even though you had committed them to specific times? Why was this? See **31** and **49**.

■ **Did some jobs take longer than estimated?** Did you forget the invisible extras, such as travelling to a meeting during rush-hour, gathering thoughts before writing a letter, or checking the final proof of a report? Day plans, like time logs, should account for *all* the components of a task.

■ **Did you stay too long on one job?** See **3** and **8**, and guard against unnecessary perfectionism.

■ **Were you too selfish with your time?** A common misconception about day planning is that it requires you to shut yourself away from everybody and concentrate only on objectives. In doing so you can hinder colleagues and therefore the overall working of your organization.

This is, in fact, a truly problematic issue. When starting to implement day plans, one tends, in one's determination to make the system work, to be over-protective of one's time; and it is almost impossible to judge subjectively where to draw the line.

The solution is to take your cue from colleagues. Noticing a change in your behaviour, they will probably pass comment. Don't take the first remark as a major criticism and over-react, apologize and revert to your old habits. However, if colleagues continue to comment adversely on your unavailability, then you can be more or less sure that you have gone too far. Still don't scrap the daily plan; just dilute it.

■ **Have you also found:**
– The time of day in which you work best?

– That you are beginning to group particular types of task, like telephoning or dictating or visiting the warehouse?
– That you are planning and thinking ahead more, and thus saving yourself time?
– That you feel more confident, knowing as you do that at worst you have a list of what has not been done today, rather than a vague fear that something essential has not been done?

3▶ **Questions for the future**

■ How can you extend your control of time?

■ How many more jobs can you delegate?

■ How can you plan, think and review more while doing less?

Remember that in the absence of day plans, you

■ don't know exactly what is going on in your life.

■ cannot learn from your mistakes easily.

■ will not even feel better as a result of getting a few things done.

17 *Bonus time*

Are there days when getting up, having breakfast and travelling to and from work are almost unbearably frustrating? You want – you urgently need – to be at your desk, but mundane considerations of dressing, make-up, shaving and public transport hold you back.

Have you, like everyone else, concluded that this 'peripheral' time, as some time-management theorists call it, should be put to better use? Before reaching your place of work have you tried not only to read the papers, but to go through a contract, decide on replies to the letters you brought home yesterday, rehearse for the morning's first meeting and perhaps have a couple of good ideas too?

And when you opened your briefcase on the train, did the sight of the contract, with its dense print and dozens of potential snags, suddenly make you feel that working on it before you reached your desk might be self-defeating? Did you conclude that doing the job properly would need consultation with colleagues, two or three telephone calls, and a generally calmer atmosphere than that of the 7.32?

And when you arrived at the office (having spent the rest of the journey reading the sports pages) did you find that the whole contract needed a quick read-through before you could start on the contentious clauses, *which might well have been done on the train*?

1 Peripheral time can be bonus time

– But only if you match the work to the nature and *quality* of the time.

Most tasks can be divided into components: and of course, it is the components needing low-grade concentration which are suited to peripheral time which, by definition, offers too many distractions for serious work.

Once you start actively identifying the low-grade components of work, and completing them during travelling time to and from the office, you achieve not necessarily a quicker work rate, but something equally valuable: an awareness of which are the key components of a task; and extra time in which to focus on them in a calm and purposeful way once you reach your proper working environment.

Arriving at your desk knowing you can go straight to the core of a task is therapeutic: it gets you down to work quicker; it makes you feel effective, competitive, in control. Bonus time is best not for achieving whole tasks, but for easing pressure on office time.

2 Bonus time within bonus time

Having read the above don't, however, decide you are going to fill each and every moment of your peripheral time: you will just create more pressure.

Peripheral time may be potentially useful; it is also essential as relaxation. If you are capitalizing on it to keep on top of work during a particularly busy period, you should be especially determined to use it for relaxation. Reward yourself generously for reading right through the contract: spend the second half of the journey reading something entertaining.

This way you make commuting time a varied experience, not just a slog.

Travelling to and from work is the most obvious form of peripheral or bonus time in most people's working lives, but not the best. There are plenty of other opportunities, some obvious, some not so self-evident. The knack is not so much in identifying when you can 'pirate' extra hours or minutes, but in realistically assessing the quality of the time available, and thus what type of task to assign to it.

- ☐ Top-quality bonus time, worthy of creative thought, long-term planning, brain-storming sessions, formulating key documents and operations.

- ○ Average-quality bonus time, useful for catching up on important routine tasks, *including writing the diary* and planning long-term schedules.

- ◇ Low-grade bonus time: allocate simplest tasks.

* The suggestions made under TYPES OF TASKS SUITED are *selective* examples, not an exhaustive list.

OPPORTUNITY	COMMMENTS	TYPES OF TASKS SUITED*
☐ Days in wake of public holidays	Following winter or summer holidays, the office tends to be in limbo, poorly attended, staff and business slow to pick up. 　A day or two spent working at home may well be feasible, and more productive than at the office.	Long term planning: batteries recharged, you can view prospects with a fresh and constructive state of mind; developing business plans; conception of new projects and systems.
☐ Business trips, conferences	Almost always involve hours of slack time without the distraction of regular office demands.	Long- and short-term planning; matters and ideas arising from conference discussions.
☐ Holidays	Yes, holidays. It is a fallacy that holidays should be a total break from work to be properly therapeutic. To anyone taking their job seriously, two weeks enforced idleness is bad for the nerves. Allocate a period every day short enough for the family/fellow	Related reading: selected key articles in professional journals, culled by yourself or your secretary before leaving; strictly rationed telephone calls (say one a week) to colleagues at the office to keep you in the picture, and staff on their toes.

▶

holidaymakers not to notice.
Don't advertise your activity: disappear without making a fuss. Half an hour
every day over two weeks
makes one whole day.

○
Sunday mornings

Make the work period short
enough for the family/part-
ner not to complain. Three-
quarters of an hour over 50
weekends amounts to more
than a whole week's work.

Rough drafts of difficult letters; long office memos;
Next week's diary/schedule.

○
Waiting at
doctor/dentist

The medical professions'
waiting rooms are usually a
peaceful environment;
reading matter provided
tends to be out of date;
capitalize on this otherwise
wasted time.

Reading short reports,
selected articles in professional journals/trade press;
the rest of the day's
schedule.

○
Taking less sleep

Some time management
theorists are very keen indeed on telling people to rise
early. True, there are untold
hours to be gained by cur-
tailing sleep, and there are
people who take more sleep
than they need. BUT it is
unrealistic, and possibly bad
for the health over the long-
term, to suddenly expect
yourself to start rising say as
much as an hour earlier
every day. Most consistent
early risers have built up the
habit over a long period.

Without doubt, the early
morning is prime bonus time
if you are feeling fresh and
if the home or the office is
peaceful. Try getting
straight ahead with the day's
work, taking an hour or
more in *lieu* later in the day
for talking to staff and colleagues.

○
Breakfast
meetings; early
evening meetings

Breakfast meetings are fine,
as long as you are not carried away by the idea. They
should be a time in which to

Run-of-the mill work and
business-social encounters;
exploratory sessions for new
projects within the organiza-

clear routine meetings and conferences which would otherwise clutter up the rest of the day.

On the same principal, there are many encounters which can be shunted right to the end of the day; and you can take the heat out of them by having a drink at the same time. This is the time to set up meetings which you want to get through quickly, but which the other side may wish to prolong: having to get home is one excuse you can give without offending.

tion, or with other organizations; putting ideas into people's heads; staff problems.

○ Walking

Everyone has a trigger, if only they knew it, that sets in train the process of thought. For some it is black coffee, for others it is listening to jazz, or reading Jane Austen. For a significant number, it is just walking: the most natural form of exercise available. It can be excellent for setting the the mind working – once you gain your stride, and the legs start taking care of themselves, the mind starts moving in sympathy. Try to walk at least half a mile a day, with a set problem to ponder *en route*; if it works for you, try weekend walks, or walking holidays.

Pondering problems, untying knots; having ideas; self-appraisal.

○ Last ten minutes before getting out of bed.

Provided you have actually woken up, a buffer period between sleep and waking activity can provide a truly useful period for clear-

Rehearsing the key commitments of the day; identifying crunch points, people and paperwork which need extra careful handling.

▶

17

minded reflection. BUT beware of letting this become a time for anxiously recalling tasks you had forgotten.

○
Seeking stimulating company

University teachers often comment on how good exam results run in groups of friends: the brightest minds not only thrive on each other's company, but attract average ones as a useful audience. The results of the group as a whole benefit because of the atmosphere of exchange; because simply expressing ideas tends to clarify them.

In business, or indeed any walk of life, this translates to marking out people you admire and, if possible, taking the trouble to talk to them, or at any rate finding out about their methods.

You won't get anything tangible done, but you will at the very least increase your awareness, gain some perspectives. Just getting an interesting view on a situation that does not directly concern you can turn out to be a trigger for a new idea, or a solution to a problem.

◇
Listening to tapes while dressing or driving

Dressing and driving make very low-grade peripheral time – unless someone does the work for you.

J.F. Kennedy listened to Shakespeare while shaving; so could you.

Serious, or light reading/music you would not otherwise experience.

◇
Lunch hour

Over-rated and misused: no one ever caught up with themselves by working through lunch, and painfully few 'business' lunches earn their cost.

Lunch-hour, except for exceptionally important occasions or meetings, should be lunch-hour or not at all.

Many use lunches 'on the firm' for raising staff morale, but this rarely works well unless there is a group: when a junior is face-to-face with a senior, conversation is practically never spontaneous; it is exhausting for both sides to have to perform right through a meal.

So EITHER take a modest lunch break and don't get ulcers trying to work at the same time; OR work through the day without a formal lunch break, pausing for a snack or a sandwich.

◇
Taking work home in the evening

The lowest of low-grade peripheral time: as bad as breaking the Sabbath. Much better stay late at the office and make it up to your spouse/partner by offering to take him or her out for a meal afterwards.

Your personal resources

People can be asset-stripped as well as companies. A job that uses all your energies but only half your talents takes a greedy toll on your vitality and can eventually reduce your worth in the labour market. Too many people passively accept this process because they have a woolly, half-baked idea of their personal and mental assets. The simple cure is to list them: it may seem an unnaturally formal exercise, but it does enable you to mentally register your own worth; once done, you need only review, rather than re-write, the inventory.

Stage one
Before reading any more of the book, use the checklist below to audit your personal assets.

Stage two
Look at the list you have created and ask yourself:
- Have you been optimistic or pessimistic?
- Where are the surprises? If none, you have not dug deep enough.
- Which of these assets have yet to be exploited fully?
- Are you looking after your resources well?

Finally
If you met someone with an identical profile, what would your positive advice be to them? Does the same apply to you?

 Resource checklist

List, in as much detail as possible, your current position, using the headings in the next column.

■**Material assets**
- Earnings: Now
             Potential
- Cash balance: Cash
                Debts
- Bank Manager: Attitude of
- Borrowing facilities: Bank
                         and other
- Savings
- Insurances/assurances
- Home What facilities?
- Other possessions

■ **Other people**
- Immediate family
- Relatives
- Friends and neighbours
- Boss/colleagues/staff
- Contacts: Current
            Potential
- Enemies

■**You**
- What makes you happy/unhappy?
- Interests Current
           Past
- Knowledge: Academic
             General
             Opportunities to learn
- Skills (work): Used
                 Unused
- Skills (leisure): Useful
                    Indulgent
                    Unindulged
- Common sense
- Past successes/failures: Recent
                           Ancient
- Are they likely to reccur?
- Personality: (strengths as well as
               weaknesses)
               The last compliment
               paid to you
               Spare time
               Level of motivation
               Future prospects

19 *Know your natural strengths and weaknesses*

> **"A swan! Me a swan!"**
> **And they said 'Yeh, take a look in the lake and you'll see.'**
> **And he looked . . . and he saw . . . and he said "Weeeeee . . . I AM a swan"**

M ost people under-estimate and under-utilize their talents. This section could save you a trip to the lake.

Imagine someone asks you to invest some money in their business.
"What's it going to do?" you ask.
"Do you know, I'm not really very clear about that. I haven't really had the time to think about it. I've been setting it all up. I'll come back to you on that one."
"What are its special talents and strengths, then?"
"Now that's an interesting question. I'm not too sure. Nothing out of the ordinary, I don't suppose."
"Right. What are the threats to its success?"
"Oh, quite a lot."
"But what are they?"
"Well, that'd be temping fate, wouldn't it. Let's wait and see."

But could that company be you? As individuals, we also need not just a sense of direction (4 and 5), but clarity in our perception of our true strengths and weaknesses.

▶ Realistically auditing strengths

■ Write down as much as you can think of that you have achieved in your life, of which you are proud. (If you are feeling depressed and fed up, then make this a list of your least disastrous disasters.)
■ Now list some of your failures.
■ Go slowly through your successes. Against each one plot the strengths that contributed to your success. Include relevant aspects of your:
- Personality
- Knowledge
- Skills
- Motivation and drive
- Ability to communicate

With your failures, list the weaknesses that contributed to the outcome. Use the same prompts.

Add to your two lists compliments and criticisms that you have received in the past – even if you don't fully agree with them. If they have been repeated, they almost certainly contain some truth.

Finally, show the list to someone you respect and ask them to add any others to either side.

You now have a list of your major established strengths and weaknesses: ones with a record of success or failure.

Look at the list of strengths once a fortnight. Determine to use them.

■ Always check, when planning to achieve something, that you are capitalizing on these strengths. If what you want needs other strengths, reconsider the goal.

■ When depressed, remind yourself of your strengths.

■ Following the above two procedures reduces the impact of your weaknesses.

20 *Personal standards*

> **" I have a very rigid set of personal and moral standards. And if you don't like them I've got others. "**
> – Anonymous mid 20th-century salesman

The salesman who can be all things to all people is an easy target. But could you write down your own personal standards? Apart from obvious moral standards, what others do you have?

Do you have any governing your day-to-day performance?

Organizations like Sony, IBM and Avis publicize their standards of production or service as part of their marketing strategy. Hotel chains and tour operators invite guests to fill in a questionnaire at the end of their stay to demonstrate their concern with setting and maintaining high standards of hospitality. Having set standards, these organizations train and manage their staff to ensure the standards are met. Setting standards does not mean that the organizations become perfect, but it does increase their chances of success.

You have the same opportunity as these organizations to set and maintain standards around the qualities that you care about: for example, keeping your promises to phone back; meeting deadlines; your treatment of and attitude to other people. You are more likely to meet goals if you have the back-up of realistic standards; they maintain and improve existing levels of performance.

Like many useful habits, standards get a bad name from those who practice them to extremes. The ex-army officer with an obsession for shiny shoes and meticulous time-keeping tends to achieve his standards at the expense of relaxation, creativity and risk-taking. You don't have to make that mistake. Standards *can* be liberating and *can* encourage creativity.

 Standards for you alone

Use the list below to generate standards especially relevant to yourself. Use the examples to spark off additional areas that you value or feel are important.

Time
- Spent with family each week
- Spent thinking, planning and reviewing
- Time-keeping for appointments
- Meeting deadlines
- Leaving home early once a week
- Starting meetings on time
- Having a daily quiet time

Communications
- Replying to letters within 24 hours
- Improving spelling and handwriting
- Telephoning back when you say you will
- Setting aside half an hour for each member of staff once a week

Quality of work
- Nil complaints
- Receiving praise

Work rate
- Minimum daily/monthly targets

Your desk
- Tidying your desk each night
- Clearing away before moving on to the next job
- Filing systematically and regularly

Diet and fitness
- Maintaining an ideal weight
- Jogging or equivalent aerobic exercise twice a week
- Walking part of the way to work
- One day a week off alcohol
- Having a lavish meal just once a month
- Minimum of seven hours sleep a night

Treatment of others
- Courtesy; stopping at pedestrian crossings

- Voluntary work
- Not criticizing people behind their backs
- Smiling regularly

Finance
- Borrowing limits
- Budgetting each month
- Giving yourself a 24-hour cooling-off period when tempted to make an impulse purchase
- Savings, per month

Legal
- Not speeding
- Not drinking and driving

Relaxation
- A weekly hour to yourself
- Monthly visits to the theatre or cinema
- Reading a book a month

 Realistic standards

■ **Make them measurable.** 'Motivate staff' is too vague. Try instead 'Fortnightly meetings with each member of staff'.

■ **Set them at their *current* level,** however high or low; don't set them as you would like them to be. You can always try to improve on them later. Unrealistically high standards which you continually fail to meet can be a source of anxiety. If you are embarrassed by how basic a standard is, for example, 'smile once a month', then you have already identified one to work on and improve.

■ **Realize that you will fail sometimes.** Realistic standards help maintain an average performance rate. Intermittent failure is a built-in feature.

■ **Pick out, say, half a dozen standards which really are important** to you, or ones which are the most difficult for you to keep. These are going to become second nature to you. Don't throw the others away. Make a private written record of all your standards, and review them from time to time. Looking back on them in 20 years will be interesting. *If other people start noticing an upturn in your performance, you will know that you are setting and maintaining realistic standards.*

21 *Controls*

S uccessful manufacturing businesses have to use production control techniques to ensure that they meet their targets. But could you, should you, have a set of controls? If you already have standards – see **20** – do you need controls too?

Comparing plans with performance is, like a set of accounts, a 'snapshot' of an individual's or an organizations's performance at a given moment, no more, no less. Just one such snapshot can be misleading, if not unfair; but a set of them, taken at carefully and fairly selected opportunities, can tell an interesting story.

1 ▶ Controls, a definition

Controls should be identified critical points or stages in a project which are in some way measurable, and which will give an indication of whether the overall target is going to be met to the required standard. Monthly financial reviews, which compare a budget with actual expenditure, are a typical example.

2 ▶ Personal controls

Richard Hadlee, the world-class New Zealand all-rounder, describes in his book Double Century *how he set out to achieve the 'impossible' target of a thousand runs and a hundred wickets in the same season. The English county cricket championship consists of 24 matches, half played at home and half played away. Hadlee set himself bowling and batting targets for each match. The targets he set were slightly easier for home matches than for away matches, and also took into account, as far as possible at the beginning of the season, the skills of the opposing sides.*

With this set of controls he could check after every match whether his hopes were going to be realized. He succeeded in his goal. Obviously this was not just because of the controls, but they did keep his mind on the target.

When setting up personal controls, use the following system:

> Identify an objective or project which really matters to you.

> Work out the route which will take you there (see **8** and **27**).

> Pick out several critical points, probable watersheds, in the project. These could appear in terms of expenditure, or time-scales, or quality and quantity achieved, but, most important, they should be useful indicators of success or failure. You might choose a monthly accounting point, or you might just choose a Friday morning for a spot check on yourself.

> Decide what you will do if your controls show shortfall or failure.

> Review the results together, not in isolation.

22 *The power of routines*

> **"** *If the human being is condemned and restricted to perform the same functions over and over again, he will not even be a good ant, not to mention a good human.* **"**
>
> – Norbert Wiener, American mathematician.

Do you resent, or try to avoid:

– **Calculating monthly expenses?**

– **Updating files?**

– **Chasing up bad debts?**

Trivial tasks like these can seem to get in the way of the real business of living, but if neglected they build up into a major source of anxiety and self-doubt. This section looks at routine as a means of fitting them into your life more comfortably; as a way of making sure that they don't compete with more exciting activities. It should be read in conjunction with section **49** – Procrastination.

 Into the habit

Routines, humble as they are as a time management tool, are a natural part of life. Much of the work of modern behavioural psychology is on just this theme. It confirms what everyone suspected all along: that we are creatures of habit.

Whole lives can be built around habit: after all, one rises at the same time most week days; washes, dresses and makes tea in the same order.

The distinction between habit and routine is worth making; habits you fall into; routines should be created.

The philosopher Alfred North Whitehead forcefully expressed the positive aspect of routine in his book Adventure in Ideas (1933): 'Routine is the god of every social system; it is the seventh heaven of business, essential component in the success of every factory, the ideal of every statesman. The social machine should run like clockwork.' But because routines can be performed without thinking, they can all be exploited to ensure workers do the job expected of them without complaining.

 Action

■ **Don't let routines multiply.** Tie a new routine into an existing one. In any case, it is easier to establish routines around fixed reference points. If you determine, for example, to update your address book on the twentieth day of each month you are courting failure. But if you do it at the same time as writing weekly letters or paying bills, you have a much better chance of success.

■ **Avoid making routines once-monthly.** Most people's lives are organized on a daily/weekly basis; try, for example, chasing debtors once a week for a morning, rather than once-monthly for two days.

■ **Associate routines with a reward,** however minor. When you sit down to go through the invoices, have a cup of coffee and a chocolate biscuit. Tie in unpleasant routines with pleasant ones; save the pleasant ones until last.

23 *Do you live to work, or work to live*

Ponder the question above, and write down your answer: only committing it to paper will give it the necessary definition.

Most people answer this question as if work should be put in its 'proper' place: they give 'working to live' as the 'right' answer.

They admit that all too often they do 'live to work' meaning that work is allowed to dominate their existence; but that it would be much healthier, more pragmatic to adopt the attitude of 'working to live', looking at work as a means of earning a living rather than as a vocation.

Ironically, this is the opposite of what the writer Dorothy L. Sayers had in mind when she first put the question. She was firmly convinced that people really should live to work, and argued that work, like it or not, is the focus of life. While not everyone would agree with her, it is certainly worth examining your own attitudes to work in the context of her view.

1 ▶ Why do you do the work you do?

■ If your answer is that you do it simply to earn a living, ask yourself, have you ever:
- Stayed behind after work to complete an important letter which could have waited until tomorrow?
- Rearranged a holiday to avoid coinciding with a particularly important week at work?
- Taken work home in the evening?
- Talked about work at home, other than to complain?
- Been interested in promotion?
- Been disappointed with the standard of your work?

The chances are you answered "yes" to all of these questions. So why did you do all these?

■ On the other hand, you may already be 'living to work' in the worst possible sense – spending so much time working that there is room for little else in your life.

Do you think you might be addicted to work – a 'workaholic'?

Do you, for example:
- Find yourself working well into the evening most nights?
- Find yourself unable to take holidays because of pressure of work?
- Think about work all weekend?
- Forget names easily?
- Take little interest in the world around you?
- Find youself bored by small talk at home?
- Find yourself unable to speak to friends about anything but work-related topics?

If the answer to more than a few of these questions is "yes", ask yourself honestly: would the bills not get paid, or would anyone think the worse of you, if you did not let work dominate your life so much?

2 Taking control

The problem with both of the two extremes described above – failure to acknowledge that work is important to you, and becoming addicted to work – is that you lack control. You have allowed work to dictate to you, rather than approaching it on your own terms.

■ If work is important to you – as it is for most people – define for yourself just what it is that you value in it.

You may find it simplest to approach the question obliquely:
– Make a list of everything you don't like about your current job. Include even the little things, such as the way there are never any pencils in the stationery cupboard.
– Make a list of everything you like about your current job. Again include the little things, like your chats with Stephen in the lift every morning.
– Now ask yourself what *you* want from work, as opposed to what it *happens* to provide. The like/dislike lists make an excellent basis for defining this crucial element.

Could your present job give you what you want? If so, on what terms?

■ Now examine your life outside work, and establish your priorities here using the suggestions in section 4.
– How much time do you spend working?
– How much would you like to spend, now you have considered your job in the light of the three lists?

The value of going through this course of self-examination is to pin-

point whether you can approach work on your *own terms*. Unless you do this, work will never have a legitimate perspective in your life.

3 For workaholics

■ Are you unable to get on top of your job because you are using your time badly?
■ Are you happy to be buried in work for reasons unrelated to interest in your job?
– Lack of confidence? You take on extra work to give yourself a sense of importance.
– An uncomfortable home, socially, emotionally, or just physically?

There are numerous other possibilities, not least that society places a high value on dedication to work, or that you need to distract yourself from the emptiness of the rest of your existence. Ultimately there is but one answer to every 'reason' for being a workaholic: working 'round the clock' means that you are allowing your life to become dominated by activity rather than achievement. Resolve, as suggested in 4, to make your life turn around specific achievements, both at work, and outside it; you will probably feel considerably less inclined to continue as a workaholic.

24 *Are you stretched, or overworked?*

Just how demanding can your schedule be? There is a critical difference between being stretched and being over-worked.

The image of the over-worked executive is now commonplace – and the effects of overwork are familiar too. All too many people have seen in friends and relations the damage that the stress of overwork can do – ulcers, coronary heart disease . . . and broken marriages.

Despite this, few people sit down and think how it may apply to them – one reason, of course, why the problem is so familiar.

1 ▶ Overwork is bad; but how bad?

■ **Physiological effects:** sustained over-work causes stress, and stress has been clearly shown to increase the chances of coronary heart diease, ulcers and a variety of other health problems. A recent study of a group of young coronary patients showed 70 per cent worked more than 60 hours a week and 25 per cent had two jobs. Another showed that *people working more than 48 hours a week were twice as likely to die from coronary heart disease* as people working under 40 hours.

Additionally, over-work is clearly linked with cigarette smoking. Another survey showed that people who had more telephone calls, more office meetings and more visits during the day smoked more cigarettes as well.

■ **Psychological effects** are less familiar, harder to quantify, but just as real. People who work too hard are prone to go on drinking binges, to absenteeism, to low self-confidence, lack of inventiveness, and (ironically) to poor motivation to work.

On the face of it, low self-confidence seems an odd bedfellow for over-work – but on reflection, the connection should be clear. How much is cause and how much effect varies from individual to individual. Essentially people work too hard because they lack self-confidence – they take on excessive work in order to boost their self-image.

Others lack self-confidence because they work too hard – a nagging voice keeps telling them that if they had more ability, they could get through their work quickly.

■ **Reduced efficiency:** cramming in too much leaves *no margin for error*. You end up missing deadlines simply because the job took marginally longer than anticipated, or because you had no time to spare to cope with the unexpected.

Overwork also puts you the wrong side of *the law of diminishing returns*: as you become more and more tired, your work-rate diminishes; you can actually find yourself achieving less than someone working less hard.

If you are over-tired or have to hurry a job too much, you inevitably make more mistakes. Finally, over-work puts you in a state of constant crisis. Because you have little time to spare, even minor unexpected difficulties are elevated into crises.

2 ▶ Recognizing overwork

Although it is not always easy to recognize stress, objectively judging whether you have too much work to do is easy. The principle is roughly the same as for How much time can you control? **(14)**, only the calculation needs to be made over a longer span.

■ Make a list of all the work-related

24

tasks that you *must* do over the next month. Work out roughly how long each should take – be realistic, conducting a few experiments if necessary. Add up the time needed to complete all these tasks.

■ Repeat the process for essential non-work tasks – paying the gas bill, unblocking the sink, writing to your mother, and so on. Try to remember just how many of these crop up 'unexpectedly' each month.

■ Work out how many hours you would like (and can reasonably expect) to devote to family, social and leisure activities.

■ Calculate how many hours you will need for important, though not essential, tasks at work. These might include up-dating the text of a mailing shot, or changing the oil in the car.

■ Calculate how long you might expect to give to any special projects.

Add all these totals together, add a dozen hours for the unexpected, another dozen for simply doing nothing and a further ten (only half an hour a day) for planning your work schedule and keeping your diary.

There are 720 hours in a 30-day month, and you need to allow at least eleven hours a day for sleeping, eating, dressing and washing. Does your monthly total fit into the remaining 320 hours? If not, you are taking on too much.

Some people regard the process outlined above as a long-winded way of proving the obvious: and that is precisely its value. Overwork creeps up on you insidiously; it is a knot which takes time to unravel.

You will never tackle the problem radically unless you force yourself to reflect *at leisure* on the various components of your overload. Pedantically writing down tasks and times is the only way of doing this: merely 'thinking it over' in an idle moment is much too vague.

When you review the hours you need in a month:

735
734
733
732
731
730
729
728
727
726
725
724
723
722
721
720
719
718
717
716
715
714
713
712
711
710
709
708
707
706
705
704
703
702
701

■ Draw the obvious conclusion if time needed is substantially, i.e. 12 hours or more, over time available.

■ Don't kid yourself into thinking all is well if time needed is just inside the 720-hour limit, or just exceeds it: everything takes longer than you expect. A viable minimum time needed figure is around 708 hours. At this level you are sensibly stretched.

■ If your time needed figure is below 708 hours, you are not stretching yourself, and you are, or soon will be, bored.

25 *Variety* is *the spice of life*

" *Consistency is the last resort of the unimaginative* **"**
– Oscar Wilde

A job with little or no variety kills the imagination. Everyone needs variety: monotonous work is not only unsatisfying and unrewarding; it is stressful. People in dull, repetitive jobs are just as prone to stress-related illness as those in demanding jobs.

While it is true that people can 'switch off' and coast through repetitive work, *they cannot always switch off the stress created by maintaining this split between thought and action.*

1 Are you *seriously* bored?

Not as easy a question to answer as it seems: you need to be fair on your job. Variety in work does not necessarily mean performing a wide range of tasks. The same tasks, done at different paces, at different times, in different environments, with different people can be genuinely absorbing. It may be up to you to try and introduce this type of variation.

Probably the most reliable indication of true boredom is difficulty concentrating.

Today did you:

■ Find your mind constantly wandering?

■ Get up to make a cup of tea or coffee more than once during the morning?

■ Go to the lavatory more than two or three times?

■ Spend considerable time keeping your desk tidy?

■ Make only partially necessary telephone calls?

■ Try to keep each of your tasks (for example answering queries, writing letters, showing people around) as short as possible, even when you were not pressed for time?

Feeling guilty if you answered 'yes' to any of these questions is probably misplaced. These types of activity are natural defensive reactions to relieve the stress of boredom. The problem that needs tackling is not your taste for tea or your fascination for the telephone, but lack of variety in your work.

2 Getting into a rut

The first sign of boredom may well be tiredness. Once you have slumped into the state of lethargy that a boring job induces, it is doubly difficult to summon up the energy to change it. You get used to working at a fraction of your real potential: the prospect of variety can begin to seem frightening. You are in a rut.

And often you transfer your boredom, and the stress it induces, to your family and social life.

All work, no play . . .

One of the classic ways to become bored with work, without necessarily realizing it, is to overwork – see **24**. *The more your work starts eating into your home and social life, the less varied your life as a whole becomes; you run the risk of being boring company.*

 Solutions

■ Acknowledge the problem.

■ Consider a new job. Don't wait for the job of your dreams, nor one that lifts you a step up the career ladder; consider a move sideways. Even if the new job is no more varied than your current job, the environment and people will be completely new. Landing a new job improves self-confidence, in any case. Also, changing jobs almost always improves career prospects, broadens your experience and increases your range of contacts.

In the past, employers put a high premium on staying power; nowadays, they can be just as impressed by someone who recognizes when to make a move, and has the will to act accordingly.

■ If you think you are overworked, see **24**.

■ Look for ways of introducing variety into your work. Think about the way you perform each task. For example, do you save up your letters to answer in a blitz at the end of each week? Could you instead answer them as and when they come in?

Could you visit some of your regular contacts in their offices, rather than always meet in yours?

---

5 ▶ **The stress of boredom**

Boredom is rarely thought of as a major cause of stress, yet it can be. Just how stressful boredom can be was revealed by a study of the Institute of Social Research at the University of Michigan in the mid 1970s.

Each of the workers in the study was asked to assess his/her own boredom rating, and not surprisingly, assembly-line workers rated their jobs very boring indeed, while family doctors rated their jobs very low in boredom. More surprising, however, was the discovery that the pressure on the doctor was actually more healthy than the tedium of the assembly-line worker.

The findings were summarized as follows:

"Assembly-line workers have boring jobs, but ones that do not involve long hours, unwanted overtime, much concentration or responsibility. They report the most dissatisfaction with their job and show the greatest stress-related disorders. By contrast, family physicians who work the most hours per week, with heavy demands on their free time, concentration, and personal responsibility are most satisfied with their jobs. They also have fewest somatic complaints or other stress effects of any occupation studied."

26 *How to cope with too much work*

More and more people suffer from overwork – and not just at the office. Genuine work overload is like trying to pour a whole bucketful of water into a small wineglass: the absurdity of it ensures you actually achieve less than a 'glassful', however hard you try. Far too often, overload is accepted as part of modern working life:

> ❝If you find it too hot in the kitchen, sit it out next door.❞
>
> ❝I work for myself, I can't turn work down; I may have none next week.❞

Accepting long-term overload is accepting long-term stress.

Reasons for overload

course, work overload can be caused by economic pressure on a company or an organization; if finances do not allow adequate overall staffing, work overload will be common among most or all of the employees.

Our concern here is the overloaded *individual*. The problem occurs when someone

> *either*
>
> Has too much to do
>
> *or*
>
> Does too much

If you have *too* much to do it is probably because you say "yes" too often: to your boss, your customers or your staff, not to mention the nagging little voice in your head constantly prompting you to do more and to do it more perfectly. If you *do* too much, you are not stopping and analysing enough. You are addicted to achievement. Like other addictions, it can land you in a mess.

Action

■ **Understand your pressures.** If overload is a *regular* occurence, then your planning is unrealistic – see **8** and **12-16**. Every day that unfinished work is carried over you must ask yourself who is unrealistic; you or your boss?

■ **Don't get worked up.** Look back at last year and think of the times you were under pressure. List what put you under pressure. With hindsight, were those issues really so important? Practically no job is more important than your health.

■ **Don't blame everything on your own laziness.** Most of us are lazy in some way or other. Successful people often claim to be lazy (they are constantly trying to find quicker ways of doing things). But the reason why some of your jobs are undone is almost certainly not simply your laziness. If you were active for every minute of the day, you would still have too much to do.

■ **Walk away from the problem.** One famous American bank based in London has made 'walking away' a set policy for its staff. When anyone finds things getting too much, they are encouraged to leave the building and walk around the block. No doubt stretching the legs and a breath of fresh air stimulates the mind: but the main benefit is reminding executives that they are more important than their problems.

■ **Estimate time for tasks.** By estimating how long each job is going to take before each day or each week, and by knowing roughly how much of the day you control – see **15** – you can discover beforehand, rather than afterwards, whether you are embarking on mission impossible.

■ **Agree priorities.** Don't let superiors say to you: "They are all priorities, I want them all done." You must agree beforehand that if you only have time for one job, which one it will be. You should not have to cope with the stress of too much work as well as making decisions which should be the responsibility of someone further up the line.

■ Above all **remind yourself regularly that there is only so much time.** Your objectives *can* be changed, your boss *can* soak up more pressure, your customers or clients *can* accept different time scales. The only element that *will not* change is time.

 Personalities, complications

> *"It's all very well, but you don't know my boss, I can't go and tell him that I've got too much work to do. He'd be furious."*

What would you say if you overheard somebody who worked for you making that statement? Would you not rather they came and discussed their overload with you before it became a mess?

But when you do go to your boss, make sure you suggest *alternative* ways of coping with the problem. Ensure that you appear constructive; don't just moan.

> *"I agree with all that, but I haven't got the time to sort it all out."*

When you last made the time to sort out your workload, did you find that it was actually an easier job than you thought it would be? Addictive 'doers' often dislike and therefore avoid all jobs that are not immediately productive. Get into the habit of stopping and sorting out occasionally. Spend a little bit less than a hundred per cent of your time doing.

> *"Well, I can't. It's no good me saying I can do any of these things, because I never know what's going to happen next. In my job I've got constant interruptions."*

Just a few executives really do have to deal with constant interruptions; the minute one person leaves the room, or goes off the telephone, another is waiting. But this is truly a rare occurence. If it really is the case, accept it, and also the consequences: no time for creative work; no time for reports or budgetting, or anything else, including this book.

It is more likely that you are not being assertive enough, not shaping the relationships around you. It is not enough merely to deal with interruptions. You need to spend more time pondering potential problems rather than solving existing ones.

> *"My organization always expects more than I've got the time to do."*

Maybe you have to find another job; perhaps they would be better off with somebody who can achieve miracles. *But* it would be better for you, and the organization, if you had one more try at persuasion. See **77**.

27 *Handling complex projects*

In their book *The Peter Principle* Laurence J. Peter and Raymond Hull made the classic management observation that everyone rises to the level of their incompetence – that is, they are promoted to a level where their deficiencies begin to show up and no further. In few areas of business is the Peter Principle more aptly demonstrated than in the handling of complex projects.

Many people new to management fall into the trap of relying on the 'active' skills that have earned them promotion – selling, accounting and so on. They allow the project to manage them, instead of managing the project, concentrating on the minutiae of day-to-day running, rather than directing the overall flow.

To get on top of major projects you need to develop new skills that emphasize efficient deployment of time and resources. *Effective handling of complex projects requires a strategic, not a tactical, perspective.*

Strategy for handling complex projects has two main thrusts, planning and control. There is overlap between the two, but it is helpful to think of them separately.

1 ▶ Planning

■ The most fundamental task in planning an elaborate project, just as in planning your career (**4**), or the day's work (**15** and **16**), is to establish goals. This sounds obvious enough, but it is all too easy to plunge straight into detailed planning without having a clear idea of what you want to achieve.

Don't be content with having the goals in the back of your mind. Write them down; they may be less clear cut than you imagine. A project to establish a new branch office in a provincial town, for example, might have three goals:

---

1 Open a new office in Newport

2 Boost sales in the Newport region

3 Increase company profits

If you forget the second two the office you end up with may be more trouble than it is worth.

■ With the goals clearly in mind, you can commence detailed planning by making a list of all the tasks that need to be completed to achieve these goals.

The new office project, for instance, might entail:
■ Locating an office.
■ Assessing what changes need to be made to the office layout.
■ Finding a manager to run the new office.
■ Conducting market research to

establish whether the local market is strong enough.

- Arranging finance.
- Preparing a budget.
- Advertising for and hiring new personnel.
- Checking local bylaws.
- Ensuring the communications are adequate: telephone, FAX, telex and so on.
- Checking the competition.
- Working with the new manager to ease him/her into the job.

■ On some projects it does not matter what order the tasks are completed, but on most, poor sequencing means the whole project is vulnerable to being held up waiting for the completion of a trivial, but essential process.

Working out the sequence can be an immensely complex process, and many planners have developed systems such as critical oath analysis and 'PERT' to assist them (see box). But with projects of average complexity, a simple, but effective strategy is to start at the end and work backwards, visualizing the sequence as a simple branching network.

Starting with the end project, draw in branching lines to all the tasks that need to be completed immediately prior to achieving the end result. Take it back another stage, drawing branching lines to tasks that need to be completed immediately prior to the penultimate tasks, and so on.

This system provides an effective working plan; critical path analysis and other techniques are designed to improve the efficiency of this basic plan.

■ With the sequence of tasks established, you need to work out exactly what resources are needed for each – personnel, materials, finances, and so on. Remember to allow some margin for error (illness, short supply and so on).

■ Finally, you need to establish a time frame for the completion of each stage. See 9 for ideas on realistic scheduling.

2 ▶ **Control**

To maintain control, you need to delegate effectively – see **68, 86** and **87**. To stay in control, you must monitor progress carefully at every stage. Effective control means inspecting, not expecting – see **9** and **87**.

With complex projects, the wall chart comes into its own. Put it in a prominent position; ensure it lists all the tasks along with the name of the person responsible for each, and the date for completion. Leave a blank space to be filled in when the task is complete. Everyone involved should be able to tell at a glance which tasks are still to be done, and who is working on them.

Finally, don't forget that controls, **21**, come into their own with complex projects.

Critical path analysis

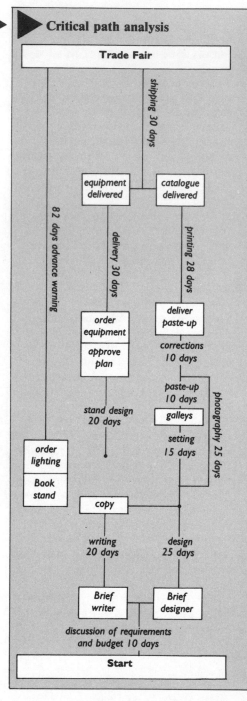

Critical path analysis shows the shortest possible way of completing a complex project, and exactly what the effect of speeding up a particular task will be on overall project time. This is important because almost any task can be speeded up given the will, but it is a waste of time and effort if it has no effect on the overall length of the project.

Draw a chart showing activities (tasks to be done) as arrows and events (stages in the progress of the project) as circles. If the project is to start up a new sales drive, briefing the staff would be an activity, the completion of that task would be an event. Starting from a baseline, the activities and events are drawn in the sequences they need to be performed. The length of each arrow should be approximately equal to the estimated time needed for the completion of the activity – in calendar days rather than working days.

The critical path is the longest path through the network. It is the 'critical' path because to shorten the overall project time, you must shorten the time spent on activities that lie along this path. Taking up the slack time in activities lying on other parts will have no effect on the overall project time, unless you also shorten the critical path.

Critical path analysis can be very sophisticated if computerized, but even if done with only pen and paper it can be invaluable, highlighting problems with time and cost that might otherwise be overlooked. Moreover it clearly reveals the total time for the project, and indicates which tasks can proceed simultaneously.

28 *Achieving makes you feel better*

A middle-aged man I know was so bored and disillusioned with his job that he began, on his own admission, to start making a mess of it. His lifetime's obsession happened to be parachuting. For weeks he had been deriding himself for having such an outlandish dream when he could not even get it together to be a competetent member of a third-rate pension fund team.

He decided to leave his job, and, with nothing to lose, took a week's unscheduled holiday – devoting it, as "a sort of sick joke against myself" to the longed-for parachuting course. He loathed the preliminary training, and the other people on the course; but went through with it mainly to avoid losing face. On the last day, he made the solo jump.

Waiting to jump out of the aeroplane he reached his lowest point: to restlessness and dissatisfaction he had now added terror.

Heaving himself out into the slipstream required what he described as an enormous act of self-subjugation. Every instinct he possessed had to be 'shut down': he had to forget about his dissatisfaction, boredom, indeed he had to "forget about himself" in order not to "flunk out" completely.

When his parachute opened, he found himself "in a different world". He was suspended "half-way between both sets of troubles": the pre-jump terror of the areoplane, and the boredom of his nine-to-five existence below.

It was a euphoric experience, but it also changed him. The troubles now seemed trivial. I asked him why they seemd so trivial, given that he knew he was floating back towards them. His reply: "Momentarily evading them was

enough, but as a matter of fact, the sense of achievement has stayed with me for good.

Feeling in charge

Going parachuting is an extreme way of reminding yourself that achievement makes you feel better – but the story does illustrate well the central reason why a single achievement can be so effective at breaking the stalemate of boredom and disatisfaction. We all need to be reminded that we *can* be in charge.

Day-to-day existence, especially at the lower and middle levels of an organization, can seem as if you are utterly at the beck-and-call of superiors and colleagues; as if it would not matter *anyway* if you suddenly took the law into your own hands.

For most people, most of the time, the one-off winner, like parachute jumping or climbing the Matterhorn, are impractical. But small, routine achievements like wiring a plug, mending the broken cup or sorting out a file can be a substitute for the grand gesture if you see them as part of an overall strategy for satisfaction. If you are at the mercy of an over-bearing superior, plan your day around that. Adopt a jackdaw-like attitude towards time: constantly on the look-out for the odd spare moments, to fill with little achievements of your own. The sum of them can convert a flat day into a moderately useful day, can make you feel is if you are still in charge, against the odds.

29 *Looking after body and mind*

> **" My body needs attention and my mind's in a mess. "**
> – Paul McCartney, 1986

Visitors from outer space would surely be puzzled by the way in which humans treat their brains and bodies. Having used them to master the environment and dominate the animal world, we nonetheless attempt to damage these marvellous tools irreparably by drinking too much alcohol, eating too much food and failing to exercise body and mind.

The Ancient Greeks believed fitness had a high moral purpose; perhaps something of this consciousness is returning in the second half of the 20th century. Certainly, modern understanding of brain and body provides numerous examples of how the two are inseparably linked. Psychosomatic illnesses can show the same symptoms as their actual counterparts; impotence and respiratory disorders are among common complaints that are generally recognized as having both physical or mental causes.

The first step towards looking after body and mind must be to recognize their closeness. If you doubt the significance of this, consider the placebo effect: an innocuous pill with no physical healing properties is given to a patient complaining of, say, stomach pains. The imagined healing powers are sufficient to cure the pain. Mind overcomes matter.

Just as your mind can influence body, so body can affect mind. If you take regular exercise, both mind and body will feel fresher, more alert and more resilient all the time. You will be quite happy with the prospect of the next bout of mental, or physical, exercise. On the other hand, a period of physical lethargy makes the mind slower, more desirous of maintaining the status quo.

If you want to get things done, don't be one of those people who treats a new car with more respect than body or brain. By the same analogy, don't be the type of person who never takes a car out in the rain for fear of rust.

What follows is a prescription for 'balanced' care of mind and body. It has been thought out with 'average' people in mind: there is nothing in it that requires exceptional dedication or will-power. It will give results if you alter your life just a little for the better in each of the categories described.

1 ▶ Body

■ **Regular exercise** need not and should not involve exhaustion, a red face and a thumping heart. It should be enough to raise your pulse and a little perspiration. Various programmes have been developed over the years to help with fitness, the most effective being those that use the pulse rate as an indicator of the amount of exercise to take.

A fully fit person of 20 should work to a maximum pulse rate of 200 per minute. To gauge the maximum desirable pulse rate during exercise, add to your age in years a handicap of 40 if you are unfit and subtract from 200. So, if you are now 40, add another 40 for unfitness and subtract the total from 200. Your ideal exercise programme should take your pulse rate to no more than 120 per minute. There are many programmes that enable you to get fit with only 40 minutes' exercise in a week, usually in two bouts of 20 minutes. Moreover the exercises can be done in your own home without any special equipment. Swimming is considered the best all-round exercise, but at almost any exercise is better than none at all.

■ **Food and drink:** A 5ft 10in man should weigh approximately 12st 12lbs, while a 5ft 6in woman should weigh 10st. How close are you to these weights? Do you remember feeling better the closer you have been to them? Sudden shock diets are one way of reducing weight, but many people find that weight lost quickly is often put back on quickly.

The most effective long-term method of weight loss and healthier living is to pay attention to diet. Reduce quantity and increase the quality of food.

How easy would you find it to have a week on alcohol and a week off? Why not try it? You may well discover that it is a little more difficult than you thought. If you succeed, you will discover a freshness of mind that does not need outside stimulus. There are other ways of relaxing at the end of the day than having a double whisky.

2 ▶ Mind

Give your mind the same sort of regular exercise that you give your body. For instance:

■ **Memory:** use the techniques outlined in **53** to learn by heart some information that could be particularly useful to you, perhaps a set of facts or figures that you regularly have to look up in a reference book.

■ **Crosswords and brain-teasers:** crosswords particularly are excellent exercise for both sides of the brain. To be really successful, you need a blend of logic, free-ranging creativity, plus memory skills to recall the regular ploys of crossword compilers.

■ **Creativity and silliness:** if you find yourself telling people that you are not really creative, or if someone says you are losing your sense of humour, pause for serious reflection. The more inhibited, and the less silly you become, the more you limit your potential. The majority of successful people in all walks of life emphasize enjoyment of life as an actual element of their success. Find ways of re-introducing frivolity. Go to a purely social event. Allow yourself to see the funny side of things. Make yourself laugh, often.

30 *Self-appraisal*

" I often marvel that while each man loves himself more than anyone else, he sets less value on his own estimate than on the opinions of others. "
– Marcus Aurelius, Meditations, 2nd Century

Most people in organizations accept the potential value of formal performance appraisals with their boss or some third party conducting the session. Some progressive organizations are now beginning to encourage *self*-appraisal, whereby individuals go through regular self-analysis to devise their own development plans. This has the advantage that people tend to be more committed to plans devised by themselves; but it has its pitfalls too. It is important not to fall into the same traps that your boss does when he appraises you.

1 ▸ How not to conduct your first self-appraisal

Don't keep cancelling this meeting with yourself; and don't allow interruptions. Don't only talk about the bad things. Don't stumble into the subject:

'Right, well let's look at how you've been doing. It really has been pretty awful, hasn't it? I mean, look at your in-tray – it's piled up. You've got files on the floor, you've got papers all over the desk. You've got reports two weeks behind schedule. You've still got masses of queries that are outstanding, PLUS all the things you've promised yourself, which other people don't even know about. I'm not surprised you hold your head in your hands. What have you done well? OK, you've run a few meetings, implemented a few

systems, got a fairly happy team. But what's that compared with . . . '

This kind of litany has a way of getting longer and longer, while the positive points become shorter and shorter; with you feeling more and more miserable and less and less motivated.

2 ▸ Positive self-appraisal

You cannot properly appraise your performance when you are not clear what you have been trying to achieve. Look *forwards*. There is nothing you can change about the past; it has just one use: to provide information which will help you make positive changes in the future. Have regular informal self-appraisals, say every three months, when you are feeling optimistic.

Unfortunately, people tend to appraise themselves informally at odd and inappropriate times: coming back from bungled meetings, or sitting in front of the television after a wasted day – in other words, while brooding. Remove, or escape temporarily from outside pressures like the telephone; ensure peace and quiet. Discipline yourself to jot down tasks you performed well and not so well. Keep these notes somewhere, ideally in your diary – see **10**. They will help you make a well-balanced appraisal of both the positive and the negative points.

■ Look at your weaknesses *comprehensively*. What are you going to do to try and limit their effects?

■ End up with an action plan.

■ The next time you catch yourself grumbling that it has been ages since you had an appraisal with your boss, ask yourself when you last had a constructive self-appraisal.

Self-appraisal blueprint

Most or all of these questions need to be worked through systematically in a self-appraisal session:

The Past
■ What were you trying to achieve?
■ What have you achieved?
■ How realistic have you been about your workload?
■ Have you been stressed, stretched or bored?
■ How have you made the best use of your talents?
■ Which of your weaknesses have you tried to eliminate?
■ Which of your strengths have you tried to enhance?
■ How have you controlled:
■ Money and resources?
■ People?
■ Time?

The Present
■ What are your skills?
■ Technical: knowledge of your specialist area; knowledge of products/services; knowledge of organizations; knowledge of outside organizations/competition
■ Practical skills
■ Communication skills: written, oral, presentation, visual
■ How well do you motivate yourself?
■ How well do you motivate other people?
■ By being firm, and giving clear directions?
■ By being fair, caring about each individual's development?
■ How well do you delegate?
■ How well do you organize others?
■ How well do you keep your eye on long-term aims?
■ How well do you plan?
■ How good is your analytical skill?
■ How creative are you?
■ How effective are your problem-solving skills?
■ Do you have empathy with other people's feelings?
■ How assertive are you?
■ How persuasive are you?
■ How accommodating are you?
■ How high are your standards?
– Have you met them? See **20.**
■ How consistent are you?
■ How loyal are you?
■ How energetic are you?
■ When do you work best?

The Future
■ What *should* you achieve over the next three months?
■ What would you *like* to achieve?
■ What training do you need?
■ What will you read?
■ Who will you meet to give you advice?
■ Which of your strengths will you enhance?
■ Which of your weaknesses will you reduce?
■ What is your potential?

 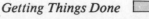

31 *Improving self-discipline*

Two types of people find it relatively easy to practise self-discipline: those who are exceptionally well-motivated – who will pay any price, deny themselves anything – to achieve their goals; and those for whom self-discipline is a well-established habit, quite possibly from childhood.

The rest of us are, at best, inconsistent. Because of unpleasant past associations, periods of self-discipline tend to be logged in the mind as programmes of unpleasant tasks with no light relief.

 Remedies

The self-evident cures for lack of self-discipline are first to break the vicious circle of regarding it as unpleasant; then to establish self-discipline as a habit step-by-step over a period. It cannot be rushed; you will fail if you attempt, starting tomorrow, to be more self-disciplined in every area of your existence.

This book is full of tricks for breaking the vicious circle of poor self-discipline – see especially **37** and **49**. In this section, the object is to look at the basic attitudes to life which nurture the condition.

Are you:

■ **The pleasure-seeker?** Do you privately suspect that opting for the comfortable way out will bring long-term happiness? Do you suspect that those who grasp uncomfortable options do so from suspect motives, such as the urge to be a martyr, or to compensate for generalized guilt?
Symptoms: watching TV rather than mowing the lawn; chatting with a friendly customer rather than selling to a tough one; working on a brain-teaser rather than doing your expenses.

■ **The defeatist?** You persuade yourself that self-discipline is only for successful people, not you.
Symptoms: you tend to enumerate everything that might go wrong on the next big project. The project never gets started and you log this as another example of your lack of self-discipline.

■ **The softy?** You accept too many of your own hard-luck stories, extend your deadlines and lower your standards.
Symptoms: you intend to work in the evening or at the weekend, but when it comes to it you tell yourself: "You deserve a break" – and never get started; you were going to jog every day, but "the cold weather makes it impractical".

■ **The parasite?** Your kind parents have done too much for you. Your instinct is to depend on others to make things happen for you.
Symptoms: in meetings you let other people do the hard work. If no one volunteers, you are willing to settle for communal inactivity; you grumble that no one in your organization cares about your development.

■ **The butterfly?** Your butterfly mind, always on the look-out for something new, takes you from one unfinished job to another.
Symptoms: before starting on an important job, you look through your in-tray, and when that is finished, it is too late to start the main job; you readily receive visitors, post, telephone calls and read relatively unimportant articles whenever they catch your eye.

■ **The sieve?** You forget what you wanted to do until it is too late.
Symptoms: if you cannot remember

these, you are an acute and probably hopeless case.

■ **The rabbit?** Thinking about what ought to be done frightens you. You act like a startled rabbit caught in headlights.
Symptoms: sitting, staring at a blank sheet of paper.

■ **The physical and mental wreck?** You don't keep fit; you are lethargic.
Symptoms: you don't do very much, particularly at weekends.

 Analysis

If you recognize that your self-discipline is not what it should be, you probably have no difficulty in recognizing one or all of these characteristics in your own make-up. They are not, in themselves, cardinal sins; but working in harness they are very effective blocks to being a self-starter, to concentrating on the mundane as well as the interesting, to finishing what you began – in short, to being self-disciplined.

People truly in the grip of these attitudes tend only to perform when forced to do so by superiors, or fear of the consequences. In some organizations, such people can make acceptable, even useful employees; they can even become managers and get away with it if they know their job and have appropriate back-up.

What such people never do is *achieve* in the sense of getting on top of their jobs, bringing something new to them, and fulfilling their true career potential.

Ultimately, improving self-discipline is a question of personal choice. It is a matter of how much you value life's pleasures, because of course once you have improved your self-discipline, you can enhance life's pleasures by doing without them occasionally.

The novelist Laurie Lee wrote:

> **❝One of the major pleasures in life is appetite and one of our major duties should be to preserve it . . . I think we should arrange to give up pleasures regularly . . . our food, our friends, our lovers . . . in order to preserve their intensity and the moment of coming back to them.❞**

If you really mean to improve your self-discipline, you will find this a sympathetic statement; if you don't, you will probably remain one, some, or all of the pleasure-seeker, the defeatist, the softy, the parasite, the butterfly, the sieve, the rabbit or the physical and mental wreck.

32 *Not one, but two brains*

> *Sitting at your desk, without thinking, you throw a piece of paper into the waste paper bin, the other side of the room.*
>
> *Someone watching you says "Well done, but I bet you a pound you couldn't do it again." You think: Fool! I've just done it. You accept the bet.*
>
> *Your head is suddenly buzzing with activity. You are analysing what you did to achieve the target last time. You think much harder than you actually did when you first threw it; considerations of speed, trajectory, position of the fingers, size and weight of paper, shape of the bin, all compete frantically. You also remind yourself that:*
>
> *You have not got a pound just now.*
>
> *If you don't get it in, which you probably won't, you will have to borrow a pound to pay the debt.*
>
> *You start to get irritated with yourself.*
>
> *A small crowd gathers.*
>
> *"Oh, no, come on . . . off you go. You'll put me off."*
>
> *They laugh. You get put off.*
>
> *Just as you throw it, you say to yourself "I'll miss it".*
>
> *You miss.*
>
> *Debit one pound.*
>
> *But you got it in before.*

Man has always suspected that he has not one, but two selves. We talk to ourselves, surprise ourselves and irritate ourselves by doing silly things: 'His left hand doesn't know what his right hand is doing.'

In the past 20 years, Nobel prize-winning work on the brain has gone a long way towards explaining these two selves. Sometimes working in harmony, often against each other, as in the waste bin episode.

1 ▶ Left and right brain

There are two sides to the brain; they have contrasting talents and weaknesses. In simple terms:

Left	Right
logical	creativity and fantasy
analytical	lateral thought
ability with words	deals in pictures
	controls what the body
	ends up doing

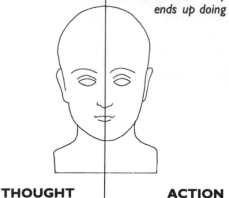

THOUGHT   **ACTION**

Unless you are meditating, you can only use one side of your brain at a time. When you are uninhibited, though, you can move from side to side in microseconds (it does not always feel like that, but you can).

A good example of this swift movement is humour. As you listen to a joke or watch a sketch, you are constantly switching sides.

It is an over-simplification to describe the left side of the brain as mainly concerned with thought, and the right with action – but nonetheless a useful one. Most people have a bias towards one side or the other.

Appreciating how the brain works helps not only in developing latent talents of memory and creativity, but also with: problem-solving **(51)**; confidence-building **(36)**; concentration **(37)** and communication **(83-84)**.

33 *Left and right brain: switching techniques*

It is essential to read **32** before embarking on this section. In **32**, much is made of something most of us feel instinctively: that we have two brains, or rather that the brain is fundamentally 'split' in its functions: the left side predominantly logical and verbal, the right side much less dominant, but nonetheless the seat of powerful skills including imagination, intuition, certain forms of memory, lateral thought and knowledge.

We tend to use only one side of the brain at a time; but we have the ability to switch backwards and forwards between the two in microseconds.

1 Genius

Take the two great stereotypes of genius: one a scientist, the other an artist. The scientist is popularly seen as working for days and months through carefully controlled experiments, sifting methodically through data and arriving at a brilliant conclusion as a result of this essentially logical power.

The artist, by contrast, is popularly believed to create from a mind in anarchy; the stock portrayal is of someone whose waking hours are deliberately undisciplined in order not to inhibit creativity.

Just how simplistic these archetypes are is being confirmed by contemporary research. The common denominator of all types of genius, whether scientific or artistic, is use of both sides of the brain. Scientists make discoveries through step-by-step analysis *and* creative, intuitive leaps. Painters have highly developed left brains, using the logic of draughtsmanship to structure their work and mix their paints.

We cannot all be geniuses; but we can move towards that condition by developing the ability to move quickly from analysis to creativity; to pacify the constant conflict between thought and action, emotion and logic, reality and fantasy; to switch more easily from left to right brain.

2 Techniques for switching

Techniques for switching between left and right brain amount to little more than prompts. They are easily applied, but to have maximum effect there are two prerequisites:

> To believe in left and right brain theory.

> To believe in the importance of relaxation.

If you can contribute these two small acts of faith, the following techniques will be easy to practise.

■ **Use pictures.** When you cannot sleep, your 'chattering' left brain is almost certainly in control. The time-honoured expedient of counting sheep amounts, of course, to nothing more or less than displacing words with pictures. Since you can only use one side of the brain at a time, the chattering left side is blocked for as long as the pictures are in your mind.

It is true that many people find the effect short-lived – and end up worrying about the sheep's money problems. But this is no reason to dismiss the picture method; merely a reminder of the dominance of the left brain and the need to develop skills that will put you in control of how and when you switch sides.

33

The use of pictures need not, of course, be restricted to sheep. Pictures of success suggested in **36.3**, can be a potent balance to anxiety and depression: picturing a peaceful scene can counteract stress and tension. Before speaking at a conference I combat apprehension by imagining a charmingly furnished, quiet, empty room; it has a view across a lawn through a gap in some fields to a lake. Think of your own equivalent.

■ **The nose and temple method:** Place the thumb of your left hand on the tip of your nose and the index finger of the same hand on the centre of your forehead above your nose.

Close your eyes and breathe through your nose.

Concentrate on the feel of your finger and thumb.

Appreciate your brain quietening down and feel the balance returning to your quietening brain.

■ **Self-hypnosis:** Hypnosis, in simple terms, is self-suggestion, and for its success it depends on displacing or suspending interference from the dominant logicality of the left brain. As everyone knows, some people are more susceptible than others; even if you are one of those who do not easily hypnotize, the following is a safe and effective relaxation method designed to improve control in switching between left and right brain.

■ Sit down; make sure you are comfortable and still.

■ Fix your attention on a light-coloured object in the room, say an ornament with the sun shining on it.

■ Concentrate on its image.

■ Occupy your left brain by counting slowly and deliberately from one to 20.

■ Your attention will switch from the object to the numbers.

■ Consciously switch your attention back to the object every time you stray and ensure that when you do listen to your left brain it is only to hear the numbers and not to listen to a running commentary on how successful or not you are being.

■ On reaching 20, close your eyes and concentrate on reproducing the image of the object in your mind's eye.

■ As you do this, tell yourself that for ten minutes you will relax and at the end of ten minutes your eyes will open and your mind will be quiet and still.

■ Tell yourself that though you would like to open your eyes during the ten mintues it will be impossible for you to do so.

■ Keep the image alive. Feel yourself relax.

■ Your eyes will open after about ten minutes and you will feel quieter and stiller.

As with many of the skills mentioned in this book that involve greater use of the right brain, the hardest part in regularly implementing them is overcoming scepticism – a function of the left brain. You will tell yourself that the techniques are cranky, and that they probably will not work for you.

My only advice can be: give them a chance. If you discover that they do not work, you will have lost nothing but a few moments of time.

34 *Slow down and perform better*

The British comedian Jimmy Tarbuck described in a recent interview how when a comic loses confidence he loses his timing. "The first thing that happens is he speeds up."

Pele, the Brazilian footballer, is widely acknowledged as being in a class of his own. Why? As one commentator put it: "Every time he has the ball, he seems to have all the time in the world to play it."

Good business negotiators seem to have much the same command over their own pace. The cool brain in a cool head is never thrown by other people's attempts to speed up the action.

It is no coincidence that "cool", "relaxed" and "laid back" are complimentary descriptions ascribed to successful people in all walks of life. Conversely, many people associate panic with pressure, moreover they see it as an essential, or at least an inevitable, factor. I suspect that this attitude develops through habit: 'When I'm under pressure I panic' turns without much effort into 'I am under pressure, therefore I need to panic.' Do you think Pele agrees with this logic?

Panic is a difficult habit to break. It is easier said than done to persuade yourself that you will perform better at your next meeting if you walk into the room coolly and smoothly, rather than apologetically rushing in at the last minute, shuffling papers. Or to wait until the best moment to speak, rather than blurting out the first thought in your head.

1 Breaking the habit

Panic is a difficult habit to break; but the everyday complaint of just dashing around, of being flustered rather than controlled, is easier to tackle.

I remember visiting a writer friend in hospital where he was recovering from an appendectomy. Instead of finding him morose at being bedridden, he was in excellent form. He said he had never felt so productive, fresh and clear-minded. He had written plenty of good material, and when asked if he knew why, he said that the stitches forced him to make every movement very slowly to avoid pain. Slowing down movement and having to control his body had, he thought, given him a much clearer mind.

I am not suggesting that you go out and break a leg in order to slow down; but I do think that this is a complaint that can be tackled by short, sharp, shock treatment. If you are caught up in one of those periods when life seems an unending rush, try dislocating the entire routine by packing your briefcase with a day's work, driving to a country hotel, and working all day without moving from an armchair.

2 Further action

■ Every day, make at least one conscious effort to slow down all body movements – not just limbs, but head and trunk as well. Make movements deliberate and slow.

■ **Don't move unless you have to.** Try to sense your mind becoming clearer.

If you can establish the habit of slow movement as a regular point of your daily routine, you could well find that the next time you feel the 'need' to panic, it will not be quite so overpowering.

35 *How to jump out of your skin*

No man is an island, but it can feel that way when things start going wrong all at once.

Andrew Miller's worst day (of last week)

Lost argument at home; many casualties.

Slammed front door, smashing glass.

Waited for glazier in hostile environment; bill comes to outrageous sum.

Late for meeting on day when chairman is picking on latecomers (Miller's suggestion at the last meeting).

Production manager, boss and staff belligerent.

Customers unavailable (luckily).

All edible lunches gone in canteen.

Monthly report takes all afternoon; no inspiration.

Raining. Puncture on way home.

No supper, enemy regrouped on high ground.

On days like that you feel beleaguered and embattled. Conversely, on days when everything seems to go your way, you feel spritely and invincible.

There are plenty of expressions to fit both situations. For instance:

High spirits
Jumping out of your skin
On cloud nine
Beside youself with joy
Filling the room with your presence
On a high

Down in the dumps
Need to pick yourself up
Brooding and inward looking
Flat as a pancake
Down and low

Sometimes it is outside circumstances that make you feel up or down. Sometimes it is your own physical and mental state. Either way, would it not be useful if you could control these feelings more effectively?

1 ▶ Reproducing good spirits

Look at the positive list: there is a regular theme of 'high', even to the extent of being 'outside' yourself. It is not impossible to create this sensation at will.

The English novelist John Cowper Powys made a considerable impact in the United States in the 1930s lecturing on positive attitudes to life. His excellent book on the subject, entitled *The Art of Happiness*, describes 'a motion of the mind which I call the Lothian Act because it bears a remote resemblance to the leap of a fish out of the water, into the air, and back again into water': what you might call jumping out of your skin.

> – Sit down and sit still.
> – Imagine that your brain is not in your head but somewhere in the empty space in front of you.
> – Every time a thought occurs to you, make sure it is out there and not in your head.
> – Give an image to these thoughts: perhaps a swarm of bees.
> – Move them around the room ('filling the room with your presence').
> – Don't let them jump back into your head and start self-analysis, brooding or introspection.
> – Imagine them becoming cheerful.
> – Make them go round in circles.
> – Concentrate on this movement, don't get bored and let them back into your head.
> – Gradually slow down this movement (and therefore slow down your thoughts and relax your mind).
> – Look back at yourself from outside. How tense are you?
> – Let yourself relax now that your busy mind is 'outside' your body.

This exercise really can help to revitalize both your spirits and your body. Try it when you are with someone you find dominating. Let your thoughts dance around them with impunity, uninhibited by their presence. However tense your body gets, let your ideas be free agents.

2 ▶ Picking up trouble

A similar exercise can stop the feeling of troubles getting 'on top of you'.

> – Sit down on a comfortable chair.
> – Begin to think of your troubles and worries.
> – As the first one occurs to you, imagine putting it down on the floor next to you.
> – Do the same with the next one.
> – Put each of your concerns or pressures on the same pile.
> – When you have finished, imagine the pile being crushed.
> – See and feel the pile getting smaller. Finally it is reduced to a ball.
> – Smash this into a powder and blow it away.

Notice how your body has become more relaxed. Do your concerns seem more manageable?

Warning

These two tricks put problems into perspective, give you back a measure of control. They don't make problems go away. Now take one practical step towards eliminating them.

36 *Overcoming fears*

> **❛❛** *The only thing we have to fear is fear itself.* **❜❜**

It is a hoary old saying, but fears are still one of the main barriers to getting things done.

Take something that makes most of us afraid: speaking in public. Whether to 1,000 strangers, or ten people whom we know well, the act of standing up in front of them neutralizes many of our skills.

You know your subject well. You stand up. A voice in your head tells you that you are about to be dull and boring; that you have not had enough time to prepare and it is the wrong time to speak.

The audience stares at you, apparently maliciously. Most audiences hope the speaker will succeed. But you are too concerned with your fears to give that thought a chance.

Quite soon you are the only person in the room not listening to what you are saying. You are listening to the voices in your head. They tell you not to look at the audience, because that only reminds you how boring you are being. So you stare at the floor, or occasionally at the ceiling.

The audience sees you give a sudden jerk as if you have had a small seizure. The voice in your head has just told you that you have missed out two key points.

"I'm sorry, this is probably sounding very muddled."

You pick up a marker pen. The audience rustles with anticipation, "He's going to write on the board – at last, visual stimulus." The voices, however, tell you that you cannot possibly write because your writing is a scrawl. So you slowly put the pen down. There is an audible groan from the audience.

Now you decide to peep at the audience. They don't spot you because now they ARE bored.

As a last resort, you tell yourself to speed up.

Speaking at your new speed, you realize that it is now impossible to stop; that you are approaching the same point for the third time.

Finally you are forced to stop – in mid-sentence.

"I'm sorry, that was probably very dull and boring."

Yes, it was. The fear cannot be put down to the audience though, who sat there hoping you would be good. It was all generated by the voices in your head.

They can start chattering any time: when you are writing a report, dealing with a difficult person – or doing anything about which you are uncertain or anxious.

▶ 1 Controlling fears

First of all, think back to when you were last working really well, when you surprised yourself by the quality of your efforts. How was your head then? Almost certainly, the adrenalin was flowing, you were keyed up, even nervous, *but your head was clear, your mind was quiet*. It is that kind of clear, quiet mind which you should be taking into these difficult situations.

▶ 2 Origins of fears

It helps if you think of fears as arising out of the divided nature of the human brain. In simplest terms, the brain has two sides – see **32**. One majors on logic and the use of words; the other on intuition, creativity and images. The marvel of the brain lies not just in its ability to be logical, not in its creative capacity, but in its ability to combine the two.

When you are anxious, you get 'stuck' in one side of the brain – usually the chattering, verbal side. You deny yourself full use of the brain at the very time when you need all the help you can get.

There are, in fact, times to listen to the chattering side of the brain, and times *not* to listen. You should listen *before* you do things (planning) and *afterwards* (reviewing performance). If you don't make enough time for these, you tend to listen instead when you are in the middle of doing the task: you hear the voices planning retrospectively ('You've missed out two key points') or reviewing in advance ('Probably going to be very dull and boring').

In other words, making more time to plan and review will reduce your chances of nervous failure.

▶ 3 Relaxation

Another essential aid to overcoming fears is of course relaxation, both physical and mental. Try these basic steps:

> **1** Taking deeper breaths and concentrating on breathing out.

> **2** Systematically relax each part of your body as recommended in **42**.

> **3** Picturing a clear mind. Pictures from the right brain displace words from the left.

> **4** Imagine you are a student of posture, balancing a book on your head. The book represents a quiet mind, as opposed to a chattering one: you must carry it calmly into the situation which you fear.

> **5** Visualizing success – a technique which many sportsmen are adopting. Replace the verbal description of likely failure with a visual image of a realistically successful outcome.

37 *Improving concentration*

B efore tackling this section, which is about concentrating on specific tasks, make sure you have read **31**, Improving self-discipline. (Section **53** would make useful further reading.)

Poor concentration tends to go in self-defeating spurts:

Get in the mood for going through a report by reading a serious article on a similar subject in the business section of today's paper.

Distracted by 'more urgent' task. Feel flustered because time has passed.

Get started: but the report is heavy going. Struggle on.

Re-read the last paragraph.

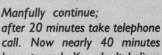

Miss points because you were thinking how dull it is.

Manfully continue; after 20 minutes take telephone call. Now nearly 40 minutes have passed. You don't believe you should concentrate on anything longer than that.

Stop reading in the middle of a particularly boring section. Persuade yourself that reading it in short bursts will reduce the pain.

Resolve to return to the report after lunch.

After lunch, the thought of going back to the report is even more disagreeable than before: you cannot bear the thought of that particularly boring section.

How can you break the cycle?

▶ Basic conditions

■ Choose a familiar place in which to work. Be wary of working somehwere unfamiliar, even if it is away from distractions. New places offer new sights and sounds to divert you. Do everything you can to shut off outside interference – telephone off hook, no visitors, or your secretary instructed to intercept calls.

■ All the better if the work place is well-lit, well-ventilated and not too hot or too cold.

■ Try and build up an association between place of work and work itself. If you regard the work place as somewhere you have worked successfully in the past, just entering the room can put you in a working frame of mind.

2 ▶ Getting started

■ **Assemble all the components.** If it is a report you have to read, get the previous report out too if you suspect you will need to refer to it. Have everything within arm's reach.

■ **Don't 'warm up'** – simply dive straight in. Actually starting work should be the warming up period: Work slowly but purposefully at the beginning. Alternatively, start work by reviewing the task for five minutes. This might involve recalling and writing down the main points in the last report so that you are attuned to related issues in the new one.

3 ▶ Further action

■ Anyone who is serious about their work should be able to concentrate for about 45 minutes, but if you are not in training, you will find this hard.

If you are not in the habit of concen-

trating this long, build up to it gradually over four days, concentrating for 10, 20, 30 and 45 minutes successively.

Far better to determine to concentrate for just 20 minutes than spend a whole morning on something that should take only 45 minutes.

■ Be ruthless with yourself about day-dreaming. Resolve to day-dream when the concentration period has ended.

■ Make notes of the key points.

■ Regularly recall what you have read, without looking at the notes. This challenge hanging over you should make you concentrate harder.

■ Allow yourself a five-minute break every 45 minutes.

■ End on a point of interest. The next concentration period will be easier to get down to if the last memory of concentrating was a pleasant one.

Concentration should be rhythmic, cyclic:

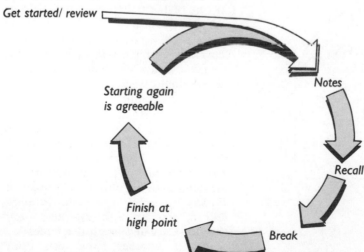

Get started/ review

Starting again is agreeable

Notes

Recall

Finish at high point

Break

38 *How to be more resilient*

No one, however talented or lucky, has a trouble-free life. Those who succeed have had at least as many adversities to overcome as you or I. Do you have the necessary resilience to carry you through?

What adversities could hit you next week? How could you overcome them? You almost certainly have ways of minimizing their effect; but the real challenge is combatting the depression they induce and their capacity to kill off the enthusiasm with which you embarked on a project.

▶ 1 Resilience: case histories

In 1835 the philosopher-historian Thomas Carlyle had an appalling, and indeed widely celebrated, setback: the manuscript of his first volume of The French Revolution: A History *was accidentally destroyed.*

His reaction was entirely unemotional. He immediately set about re-writing it without, it is said, a word of complaint.

More recently, a millionaire insurance broker lost his business overnight after an irresponsible remark of his in a public speech was reported in the press. No insurance companies wanted to be associated with him. "What did you do?" I asked him. "First, I felt deeply depressed. Then I said to myself: 'It hasn't happened, it's not true, I'm starting again.' He now has an even more successful business, started again from scratch.

From Jeffrey Archer to Jack Dempsey (who was knocked out of the ring in one of his fights and came back to win it), the list of people who make come-backs is endless. You will have at least one example from your own life where you have weathered a bad period to eventually succeed. Pinpoint when that was. Remind yourself of the details. Then stop and tell yourself that realizing this truth *is only the first stage.* You have to acknowledge in addition that overcoming setbacks is as essential a part of the top performer's armoury as drive, ability, salesmanship or any other business skill. Triumph and disaster are both imposters – and should be treated much the same.

Put it another way: you don't *deserve* success until you can overcome

38

set-backs. I always feel that 'bouncing back' is an unfortunate phrase in this context because it implies *immediate* recovery. My definition of a resilient person is one who knows how to nurse themselves through a set-back; how to maintain a low profile while regaining confidence, who comes back *in their own time*. Stephen Potter's humourous books (including *Gamesmanship* and *One-Upmanship*) offer an interesting perspective on the art of resilience. They are essentially about how to 'psyche' opponents, friends and colleagues into performing less than their best. A typical example of gamesmanship was shown by the BBC as part of a tribute to Potter when he died in 1969. Potter was playing golf. Just as his opponent was about to drive off at the first hole, he said to him: "When you've played the shot, I'll tell you what you're doing wrong." Needless to say, the shot was weak.

If Potter's opponent had been expecting the remark, his resolve would not have been so readily undermined.

The most damaging aspect of a set-back is its element of surprise; remind yourself regularly that set-backs can happen any time, and they become less difficult to overcome.

In addition, cultivate these qualities as a means of gaining greater resilience:

■ **Don't brood,** do something tangible to displace the constant rehearsal of the problem in your mind.

■ **Remember that what has happened is finished.** Thomas Carlyle perceived that anger was a waste of time; so he started writing again immediately.

■ **Separate fact from fiction.** Don't let your mind run away inventing further disastrous consequences. Use less thought, more action.

■ **Expect discomfort.** It *is* a shock when it happens.

■ **Don't feel sorry for yourself.** It never improves your condition.

■ **Don't accept too much sympathy** from others – it makes you feel sorry for yourself.

■ **Don't look for excuses** – it is results that count.

■ Rather than trying to bounce back immediately, try saying "It didn't happen" – not to escape from reality permanently, but to overcome the temporary obsession with your problem.

■ **Never have an objective that is not fully thought out,** eventually achievable, likeable and believable. Take another look at **5.**

■ **Know your natural strengths and weaknesses.** Look again at **19.**

39 *Intuition*

" Reason's last step is the recognition that there are an infinite number of things that are beyond it. "

– Pascal, 1670

What *exactly* is intuition? 'The immediate apprehension of an object by the mind without the intervention of any reasoning process' *(Oxford English Dictionary)* is, for the present purpose, an ideal definition.

Section **32** explains how we have, in effect two brains: logic and reasoning on one side, creativity, artistic appreciation, gut feel and intuition on the other. Only one side can be used at a time. For most people, the logical mind is predominant. It is sensible, reasonable, efficient at determining the building blocks of a step-by-step approach to thought. By contrast, the right side can make massive jumps forward in thinking through a problem, or sideways from subject to subject: can create frivolous fantasy, but also solve problems and invent. While logic is a convergent process, the scope of intuition is 'infinite'.

Brown and Root are construction engineers to the petrochemical industry. One of their off-shore engineers described in a recent trade journal feature how he sees the two sides of his brain working in his job:

"If I'm on an oil rig and the customer asks me 'How would this alteration to the design affect the completion date and how much would it cost?', I could telex the problem back to head office where it would be discussed, run through the computer, given to the estimating department, the results analysed and the answer sent back to me, say two days later. Alternatively I could look at the drawing, imagine the implications and give an estimate within an hour which in most cases would not be very different from the computed answer." Scientific methods are more popular than intuition these days; many people – not only business school types – belittle 'gut' feeling, when they ought to be using it in parallel with logical processes. Too many are ready to accept that the old-fashioned foreman with no degree must be wrong if the MBA says so.

Some jobs do still rely mainly on intuition. There is no computer to tell a jockey when to make his move in the Derby, or a stand-up comic the timing on which the effect of his lines depends. At the top of their professions such people attract adulation and large incomes mainly as a result of using intuition.

It is also significant that many inventions have been created through an accident triggering inspiration. Alexander Fleming discovered penicillin in 1928 while working on an unrelated subject. He spotted that a culture dish, accidentally left near an open window, had become mouldy, and this started the life-saving thought process. He wrote later 'If my mind had not been in a reasonably perceptive state, I would not have paid any attention to it.'

1 ▶ Reasons for mistrust of intuition

If intuition is so useful, why do we talk about having to trust it?

It is odd that a skill which contributes so much cannot be allowed out on its own.

Most decisions you make are not a matter of life or death, yet even with them you still don't trust your intuition as much as you might. It is as if the logical brain regards itself as the sole authority on all problems and looks down on intuition as second-rate. When confronted by an awkward situation, the logical side becomes noisy and dominant: it 'chatters'; its demands for sole attention are so insistent that you are prevented from using the right side. See **36**.

Over the years, your brain has been conditioned to associate sudden challenge with mental chaos; if you don't react 'dynamically' to a difficult situation, you suspect you risk a dangerous loss of 'control'. But in reality, a quiet and relaxed mind, allowing access to intuition as well as logic, would improve your chances of a successful resolution.

Intuition does, of course, have its dangers:

■ You cannot retrace your steps. Intuition allows no working papers.

■ You cannot explain intuitive reasoning to others or yourself.

■ It can be an excuse for laziness.

■ Like your logical mind, it is not foolproof.

2 ▶ Best applications of intuition

■ Interviewing: always mentally log your first intuitive impressions of anyone you interview or meet. They are insupportable by facts, but easy to look at alongside the logical analysis after the interview meeting is over.

■ Problem solving: when you are bogged down with facts, 'lateral' (see **51**) intuitive thought can transport you to fresh and potentially fruitful areas.

■ Planning: when logic tells you to move in one direction, but a nagging doubt warns that this could be a false move, follow it up; try and define what is worrying your intuition.

■ When you don't know which way to turn. Don't let logic take you round in another circle. Make a clean break with it. Simply leave the problem alone and do something different. This may not be any use at all, but at least it gives intuition a chance. The most you have to lose is a few minutes of thinking time.

40 *When to speak, when to be silent*

Most people have experienced a problem similar to Basil Fawlty's with German guests in his hotel, Fawlty Towers. The more he tries to avoid mentioning the two World Wars, the more he brings them up.

The situation strikes a chord because human beings have a universal tendency to say exactly what they should not when they should not. We are also afflicted by the potential to be struck dumb when events overawe. I believe that many more people have the first problem than the second, but the two are related, and are therefore dealt with together in this section.

Have you noticed how few top salesmen talk more than their clients? And have you ever gone into an appraisal with a well-rehearsed demand for a salary increase only to be reduced to apologetic chatter, simply because your boss has kept his mouth shut?

Do you find that however sound are the plans that you make in private, they sometimes fall apart under the pressure of face-to-face contact? Having this kind of problem is *not* a sign of inherent weakness, incompetence, immaturity, or advancing age. Its real causes include:

■ 'People think I'm weedy.'

A little voice tells you that you are weak and, what is worse, the person you are dealing with suspects it, too. Your objective becomes not to deliver your intended message, but to talk your way out of trouble. Most of your subsequent remarks are designed to change the other side's opinion of you. You are seen as protesting too much: your inferiority complex shows through.

■ 'This man's an idiot.'

You suspect that you are speaking to an idiot, which means you can discount them. They become an object, off which you can bounce your ideas. You become increasingly insensitive to their feelings and fail to notice their eyes glazing over.

■ 'At last, a friend.'

Confidentiality, tactical thinking and your long-term objectives are flung aside as your beguiling listener tempts you to be more and more indiscreet. Something he said, or maybe just his friendly manner, made you think he could be trusted. Your doubts flood in later, when it is too late.

> ■ **'She is impressed by me.'**

A flattering remark sparks off your ego, and the flood gates open. Even if the audience was impressed at the start, they are less and less likely to remain so as you monopolize the conversation.

> ■ **'This is my last chance.'**

Your overactive logical mind (See **36**) has worked out that failure is imminent. It tells you that your only hope is to talk your way out of trouble. You sign, or at any rate speak, your fate.

> ■ **'I daren't say a word.'**

Daunted by the danger of saying the wrong thing in high-powered company, you find yourself unable to speak at all. You inhibit yourself by fear of being hurt or of hurting others. Your tongue is released only when you feel safe again.

▶ **Remedies**

■ Remember, the more your speak, the less you gather. To communicate effectively with anyone else, you do need to know something of what they know. Work out exactly how much knowledge is shared by you both. Just this act of concentrating can release you from self-doubt and stop you talking too much.

■ When dealing with dominant, manipulative people, or critical meetings, deliberately say *too little* at the outset: try to draw their fire. Let it all come at you; be a model of humility. When the last shot has gone off, *don't* answer immediately. Let there be silent pause – it could well discomfort the opposition. Then smile, and say "Would it be possible to repeat the points one by one so that I can deal with them properly?" Make the opposition do the work of reiterating their arguments.

■ If you feel the "People think I'm weedy" scenario starting to develop, remind yourself that dominant people and power-seekers will often deliberately foster it. Cease talking abruptly at the next stopping point – don't tail off. An uncomfortable silence will follow: don't be phased. Look at your audience directly and pretend you stopped because you thought they wanted to interrupt: "Sorry, did you want to make a point?" If the answer is a curt "No", *don't* start talking again. Say "Well can you appreciate the point I'm making?"

Now the initiative will have passed to you; wait, in silence, for their answer.

■ If you are stuck for words, ask questions. This does not merely cover your confusion: it prevents you making controversial remarks.

■ See **73**, Controlling conversations.

Be a starter and *a finisher*

> **"** There is an old saying 'Well begun is half done' – 'tis a bad one. I would use instead – not begun at all until half done. **"**
>
> – John Keats, 1817

etting thing done involves both starting and finishing. Can you honestly say that you always get started when you want? And do you see everything through to the end? John Keats' adaptation of the saying was aimed at poor finishers – unlike the original which applies to poor starters. The two problems are quite different, and most people suffer from either one or the other. To help you decide which is you, consider these two acute cases:

Eric *'I'll-do-it-in-a-minute'*
Lyons: poor starter

Eric has great difficulty leaving home for work in the morning – he was always late for school as a child. But he can claim to achieve an enormous number of small, inconsequential jobs: he likes them because they enable him to postpone major pieces of work. His list of important outstanding jobs never runs to less than three pages, and he spends up to half a day each week re-writing it. He has perfected the art of avoiding detection by those to whom he owes work.

He can work for hours at a time without a break, often into the early hours of the morning if he has to, because he leaves so much to the last minute before getting started. He spoils much of what would otherwise be his free time by worrying about starting. He justifies himself by claiming he works best under pressure.

Tony *'It's-finished,-it-just needs-typing'*
Price: poor finisher

Tony starts a couple of DIY jobs at home before leaving for work every morning. They will remain unfinished for months. On the way in, he listens to the first of a series of 32 Spanish language tapes; tomorrow he will go back to listening to the radio. At work, his desk is covered with files, all started. He believes he is highly successful: he has only to start a job and he imagines it is finished. He buys more books than he reads; subscribes to several magazines, but rarely opens them.

He gets irritated with people who seem too interested in minor details (like having reports finished and typed, on their desk).

1 Poor starters

These people want the reward *before* the work. They build up such an alarming picture of the discomfort involved in actually working that they will do anything to avoid starting.

2 Poor finishers

Most are enthusiastic, but over-ambitious. Their expectations are greater than their capacity. Their attention span is short and their enthusiasm easily distracts them into other areas. They have vivid imaginations: their picture of the finished job is so accurate that they believe they are achieving, despite the fact that they have still to complete the work.

3 Compatible partnerships

Ponder the successful business partnerships you know. It is probable that most work well because the participants are opposites: a starter is linked with a finisher. Often, the starter is the salesman, the one whose enthusiasm lands the job, while the finisher, presented with a *fait accompli*, completes the work. Meanwhile the starter takes his enthusiasm off to generate more work, using his vivid imagination of what the completed work will be like to motivate the next customer.

You need to combine these two skills to make yourself a more complete operator.

4 How to treat poor starters

- Break the job down into stages for them. Give a strong reason to have the first stage in on time.
- Make them start at the earliest date.

- Don't accept excuses for missing that deadline.
- Put management time aside at the beginning of a project to get these people started. They need less time later to keep them going.

5 How to treat poor finishers

- Ask them how they intend to work through each project. Break it down into stages with them.
- Set dates for deliveries of each stage. Let them know what sanctions you will impose if these dates are not met.
- Don't accept excuses for not completing.
- Resist giving any praise until the whole job is complete. Only then show appreciation.
- Don't let them promise too much.

6 How to be a starter yourself

- Use day planning skills (15 and 16) and treat commitments to start times as absolute.
- Remind yourself that you do not do yourself justice by leaving a job to the last minute. You are only leaving time to survive, not to research, plan, revise and do your best.
- Use the 'banjo' concept (49).

7 How to be a finisher

- Don't celebrate, congratulate yourself or tell others how well you have done until *everything* is finished.
- Don't let other people praise you too soon.
- Enlist the help of people whose attention to details will ensure that the last steps are completed.

42 *Coping with irritation and anger*

In contrast to **34,** this section is about general self-control, particularly in terms of tackling anger and irritation, rather than overcoming fear of specifically stressful situations.

Exhortations such as 'Take a grip on yourself' or 'Pull yourself together' are not only well-worn, but misleading. They suggest the necessity of strain and tension in self-control.

If you have ever seen someone lying on a bed of nails, you will know that this feat of self-control is certainly not achieved through physical tension. Bio-feedback techniques in controlling blood pressure further illustrate the point. The patient is wired to a monitor that gives an immediate visual indicaton of blood pressure, then asked to visualize a peaceful scene. Whereupon, the blood pressure is actually seen to drop. When asked to think of current worries, the patient sees the reading increase again.

As shown in **36,** and explained in detail in **32,** the 'chattering' part of the brain has a way of dominating day-to-day existence. "Could I have my body back, please?" is the unspoken wish of many people as they drive themselves through their working days, conscious of nothing except a buzzing head. This condition is to blame for most outbursts of anger and irritation at home and work; a buzzing, chattering head denies access to the reserves of patience which everyone possesses in some degree. Many people think the only way out is to be above emotions – not to have them. This is at best a temporary expedient: the emotions, like blood pressure, are always with us; disassociation amounts to bottling them up.

In fact, the key to controlling irritation and anger is a closer relationship between mind and body.

▶ Body and mind

The senses are the bridge between the brain and the body:

■ **Use your eyes.** Have you ever driven home in the evening and seen 'nothing' on the way? Or have you been told by a friend that you 'snubbed' them in the street by walking straight past? These are extremely obvious signs of a chattering mind. When it next happens, make a conscious effort to use your eyes. Sit down for five minutes and look at your surroundings; imagine the eyes are the only part of your body that matters. When the brain races, it is possible to regain control via the eyes; the whole body can follow them back into line.

■ **Use the ears.** Try listening to the silence in the room. Even if there is some noise around, which there almost certainly is, listen to the parts of the room that are silent. As you did with your eyes, concentrate on using your ears. Don't let your verbal mind take you back into your problems. As you fight and win the battle against your thoughts, feel your head becoming quieter and your whole body more controlled.

■ **Hold your tongue.** Is your tongue really relaxed? Try relaxing it now: you will find it much more difficult to talk to yourself.

■ **Hold your hands.** Focus awareness on your hand movements: are they jerking around? Keep movement to a minimum: imagine the hands are big, heavy plates, incapable of moving from the arms of the chair.

■ **Keep still.** Sit comfortably and still. Don't move. You will experience sudden urges to move, but resist them. You are already developing greater confidence in your ability to control the body. See **38**.

When you return home from work, try lying down and concentrating in turn on toes, feet, lower leg, knees, torso, shoulders and so on up to the crown of the head, feeling each part come under relaxed control until your entire body is in a state of deep relexation. See also the mental relaxation techniques described in **34**.

▶ 2 Specific irritations

Relaxation techniques are an effective general expedient, but in everyone's lives there are individuals who are frankly provocative. Their talents for irritating or frustrating seem to be targeted directly on you. Try writing down in each case why they are such a problem to you. Does a pattern emerge? Every time you say "He makes me angry" or "She is so frustrating" you are in effect saying "I possess no rational way of coping with these people and therefore I let myself get angry or frustrated. I am angry and frustrated at my own lack of skills." Other people cannot *make* you angry; you do that yourself.

You can, of course, try counting to ten – but this does not address the underlying problem. It is more effective to identify the precise source of irritation in the other person, and the personal weakness of your own which it exploits; to act rather than react. Most confrontations involve ignorance on both sides; it is worth taking the initiative to work out how and why the ignorance exists. If you do, you will not only have the edge when you confront people who irritate you, but the means to enlighten them.

43 *Understanding inner drives and desires*

Everyone carries a set of inner motivations and drives that influence the way they behave much more radically than they realize. The better you can understand these, the better you will understand your everyday feelings and motivations, and the more fluently and naturally you will act.

What motivates you? Money? Promotion? Doing a good job? Having a happy family? Notice how all these are tangible *end* results; things that will be achieved, sometime in the future. We have to assume this, because if they were with us now, already achieved, they would no longer motivate us. Inner drives are buried deeper; are with us all the time, permanently influencing our behaviour.

Take money – the most common motivation of all. Clearly, the inner drive it represents can be security to one, freedom to another and to a third the exhibitionist's satisfaction of showing the world how successful they have been.

Motivation is complex; no single model does it justice. However, there is a useful, simplified view of motivation: as a series of stages. You go through each stage most times you change jobs; as the illustration shows, each stage depends for its stability on the previous one: take one building block away, and the whole structure collapses.

When each stage or block has been achieved, your main thrust is on towards the next.

Practically no one builds this structure without set-backs. The threat of redundancy, a colleague promoted ahead of you, rejection of an idea close to your heart: all too easily, these have the effect of taking you back one or two stages, whereupon you start the building process all over again. These drives really are *that* fundamental.

Attitude to the blocks
These drives may be fundamental, but different people pay differing amounts of attention to different blocks. Some take too much trouble on the lower levels: too much attention to details retards their growth. Others don't leave enough troops behind to guard what they have achieved: over-reaching themselves, they bring their achievements down through reckless decisions.

- Where are you now?
- What are the possible threats to your current status? How can you stop them retarding your progress?
– Are you unnecessarily preoccupied with one particular stage? Do you, for instance, care too much about what people think? Or the effect that one mistake will have on your career?

Remember:
- You have to be someone special to get to the top – ie yourself.
- You can work your way up there whatever your skills.

Stage Five – **Being Uninhibited**
Now you feel less restrained – not only by the need to avoid mistakes, but by what people think: you are, relatively speaking, free. Free to be yourself; free of the need to tailor your remarks because of internal politics; free to take bolder decisions. This is the 'plateau' everyone wants to reach in an organization. Getting there, and staying there, is considered in greater detail in **48.**

Stage Four – **Gaining Respect**
Now you have outgrown simply being accepted on others' terms. You want to be accepted on your terms. Whatever you perceive as your important attributes – being kind, being a tough negotiator, being a wit – you want others around you to respect you for it.

Stage Three – **Being Liked**
Now you are looking for signs that people not just tolerate your presence, but like having you around: "It's good to have you in the team" is what you are hoping to hear. When you have achieved this stage, you describe your job and your colleagues as "good fun" and "enjoyable". In extremis, you may try to be accepted on any terms, even as the departmental idiot.

Stage Two – **No Mistakes**
To make certain of a job, you quickly learn a set of ground rules: what will endear you to your new employer; what risks should be kept to a minimum; what conformities are essential. For some people this phase lasts a few days; others never leave it.

Stage One – **Survival**
Getting a job satisfies the obviously basic need to feed yourself, the family and to pay the mortgage. If you have ever been heavily in debt, you will understand better than most the power of this imperative. Once achieved its importance appears to recede – but in reality it is always present.

▶ **Inner drives, a closer definition**

Status	Key attributes
Being Uninhibited	*Not concerned by what people think*
	Freshness of approach
	Unhostile sense of humour
	Spontaneity
	Occasional need for privacy
	Acceptance of yourself and others as they are
	Compatability with reality of situations
	Problem-orientated, not self-orientated
Gaining Respect	*Wielding power*
	Manipulative politics
	Increasing influence through 'favours'
	Dominating to get respect
	Having your perceived talents recognized by others
Being liked	*Need for enjoyable relationships*
	Having fun
	Being liked
	Accepted into a group
	Wearing the 'right' clothes
	Adjusting to other peoples' standards
No Mistakes	*'Keeping your nose clean'*
	Protection of job
	Attention to details
	Avoiding disagreements
	Taking a lower profile
	Avoiding mistakes at all costs
	Knowing and keeping to rules (official and unofficial)
Surviving	*Protecting your family*
	Having somewhere to live
	Having enough to eat and drink

44 *Who's to blame? Not me*

Everyone has the instinct to preserve themselves, but some take it to extremes. Nothing is their fault. "The car broke down because my son didn't take it to the garage last week", or "My assistant left because he's so self-centred", or "I lost the order because of the slowness of the marketing department."

When I ask people why they cannot manage their time as well as they would like, the replies are all in the same mould:

> "It's my boss's fault."
>
> "My customers are impossible."
>
> "Not enough staff."
>
> "Poor quality staff."
>
> "Poor equipment."
>
> "Too much work."
>
> "Not enough business"
>
> "Too much travel."
>
> "Too many 'phone calls."
>
> "Smudgy blotting paper."

Psychologists call it 'externalizing' problems; and the irony of it is that failure is practically never all the fault of the individual. In reality, blame should be shared between you and external circumstance; or between you and others.

1 The Christmas card syndrome

Have you ever received a Christmas card with the message "Another year and we haven't seen each other; do call in some time." Should the writer not share the blame, rather than asking you to call?

It is easy to get into the Christmas card syndrome, but equally simple to avoid it. Either say nothing at all, or say "Aren't we both lazy for not bothering to get in touch?"

There are many work situations in which the same honest approach can be a positive virtue: an invitation to joint action in solving a problem, and a way of cementing relationships.

2 The dangers of externalizing problems

■ The more you avoid blame, the longer you postpone the problem. You can end up living in a fantasy world where everyone who surrounds you is incompetent – except you.

■ You make life frustrating for other people.

■ Consultants, and people in service businesses are particularly vulnerable to externalizing. Part of doing your job well is giving confidence to your customer and one way of doing this is to gloss over problems. The next step is to believe your own story. Before long, *any* problem can be eloquently explained away as not your fault. Eventually everyone sees through the explanations, except you.

Don't be your own worst enemy

The experience of childhood discipline remains with all of us into adulthood. It surfaces each time one says to oneself things like: 'You'll look stupid', 'You're no good at that' or 'Don't offend her by telling her what you think.' Such self-restraints usually serve the purpose for which they were intended: they stop you looking really stupid, help you to understand where your talents lie and prevent you being unjustifiably offensive.

But they can also be destructive: they tend to arrive without warning from the subconscious, where they cannot be controlled or viewed rationally. "You'll look stupid" can turn, for no good reason, into "You're bound to fail." Rabbi Kahler, an American psychoanalyst, describes these injunctions as mental tape recordings or 'miniscripts'; others have called them 'loser tapes'. Kahler sorts them into five groups, each of which is named after a type of parental admonition.

Be Strong

Examples: 'Be reliable'
'Be resilient'
'Things are boring'
'People can't hurt me'-
'I feel awkward with compliments'
'Don't show feelings'
'I'm not worthy of your love'
'I'm unappreciated'

Spends time: Being a no-nonsense, dependable producer of work.

Avoids: Putting self in a situation where one could be rejected.

Hurry Up

Examples: 'Be efficent'
'Life's exciting'
'I don't care about you'
'I'll be rude to them'
'Life is futile'
'I'm outside of the mainstream'
'I want'

Behaviour characterized by complaining, sulkiness, not listening, gabbled speech.

Spends time:	Doing as many things as quickly as possible; over-filling time.
Avoids:	Having spare time that could be used for reflective thought – thought that may destroy current values.

'Sort of . . . '
'Who is the real me?'
'Yes' when I mean 'no'

Spends time:	Smoothing over situations, being nice to other people.
Avoids:	Confronting own real feelings and those of others.

Be Perfect

Examples:	'Who's to blame?' 'I'm guilty' 'I worry' 'I'm not competent' 'Oh, me – I'm worthless'

Is organized, speaks in measured tones, itemizes points "A.. B.."; stiff, erect posture.

Avoids:	Having to widen narrow view of which people and values are acceptable.

Try Hard

Examples:	'Be persistent' 'You've failed' 'I'm going to be brilliant – next time' 'I'm potentially great' 'I'm bound to fail' 'I'm better/worse than him' 'I envy him' 'I start lots of things - but don't finish many' 'I'm puzzled' 'He was lucky/unlucky'

Please

Examples:	'Don't argue' 'Be nice' 'Be acceptable' 'I'm sorry' 'I feel so embarrassed' 'You know'

Spends time:	Concentrating on activities rather than objectives.
Avoids:	Completion – as this may bring punishment for failure or envy and jealousy for success.

▶ 1 Handling loser tapes

The more you can laugh at your loser tapes' extremes, the more you can limit them. Likewise, you can exorcise loser tapes by forcing on yourself the very experiences which since childhood you have assumed are not permitted.

Be Strong
Spoil yourself with regular treats; encourage yourself to do 'silly' things; be more open in your relationships, share more feelings; allow the concept of people liking and disliking you.

Hurry Up
Slow down; give yourself a quiet time each day to concentrate on your own needs and plans; don't be afraid to reflect on yourself and your qualities.

Be Perfect
Challenge your prejudices; try to understand the people you discount; meet people outside your accepted circle.

Please
Discover more of your feelings; say "no" when you feel it; imagine scenes where you are more honest that usual with other people.

Try Hard
Don't make excuses for your failures; try to win, risk envy and jealousy . . . yet don't worry about losing and being reprimanded; do your best.

▶ 2 Loser tapes are universal

Remind yourself that everyone has loser tapes running in their head. Think about individuals with whom you have difficulty coping. Which of the five groups mainly represents

them? How can you use the unblocking methods above to give them permission to be themselves?

■ Involve 'Be Strong' in a frivolous presentation.

■ Have regular thinking periods at a slow pace with 'Hurry Up'

■ Enthuse to 'Be Perfect' about not strictly acceptable people or ideas; introduce them to each other.

■ Make 'Please' commit him- or herself before you reveal your opinion.

■ Reassure 'Try Hard' that people can respond in a balanced way to failure and success – for example 'Sorry' and 'Pleased for you'.

46 *Thinking big*

Go back to **6** and remind yourself how you responded to the basic question posed in that section. *If* you decided that you would gain most satisfaction in life by closing the gap between your achievements and your ambitions, that you indeed want things to change, this section is for you. It is about the advantages of aiming high *from the start*.

Write down something special that you would like to achieve in the next 12 months: don't just have an idea – this is not sufficiently precise. Make it truly ambitious. Now list all the restrictions that could prevent you achieving it. Shortage of money, lack of talent and courage, opposition from other people: make the list as long as you can. Put the list aside.

Now imagine you were offered a large sum of money just to devise a stunt by which you could become sufficiently famous overnight to be a suitable guest for a TV chat show. All you have to do to get the money is *devise* the plan, not to implement it. You cannot choose 'streaking' at a sports event – that has already worked for someone else. Despite this, I think you will find that coming up with a suitable novelty is rather easier than you had initially imagined – especially if you bear in mind how desperate TV companies must be to find new faces and stories.

When you have managed to think up the stunt, reflect for a moment on how much more difficult it would have been to devise if, to get the money, you actually had to do it.

The object of this exercise is to show why people tend to think small. The threat of reality is a blight on our ability to expand and define our ambitions; so much so hat we find it difficult to state clearly, without qualification, the

best we can do. But if your basic thinking and planning is realistic, **(5)**, why not think big?

1 ▶ Why you don't think big . . .

The reasons, as usual, break down into the emotional and the logical:

– Emotional: you are afraid of failing; of looking stupid, of the unknown; you lack experience.

– Logical: you don't plan at all, or if you do, you plan too cautiously; received advice from other people limits your vision.

2 ▶ Raising your horizons

Solutions to most of these problems are found all through this book: See particularly **36, 47,** and **8**.

Two of the problems, however, are peculiar to thinking big when you do it for the first time:

■ Fear of what others might think. If this worries you, ask yourself: which is more important, their respect, or the issue itself?

■ You lack experience. Thinking big may well be a novelty; it may be perfectly true that you have no track record in this department. But which millionaire experienced earning their first million before putting it in the bank?

Earlier you wrote down a heady ambition, plus what input stopped you achieving it. Now, try challenging each of these limitations in turn.

Each one successfully challenged brings you nearer your goal; if you read **64**, about the art of taking calculated risks, you may decide to go ahead even if one or two limitations still remain.

47 *The power of positive thought*

The concept of positive thinking has been around long enough for cynics to be ready with knowing looks as soon as it is mentioned. They think it is naive, superficial, and worst of all, it implies extra work.

> *There is a well-known story about a manager who sends two shoe salesmen to a Pacific Island. Before they leave, the manager asks them to report back by telegram.*
>
> *One salesman goes to the north of the island, the other to the south. The first telegram back to base read: "Bad news, natives don't wear shoes." The other read: "Good news, natives don't wear shoes."*
>
> *Which salesman was likely to sell more shoes? Life would be boring if everyone was positive all of the time; but the sender of the second telegram, besides being more likely to sell shoes, would probably have been brighter company on a remote island.*

Positive and negative forces, around and within, need to be balanced – with a sensible emphasis on the positive.

1 Some causes of negative thought

■ You are 'stuck' in your left brain – see **32.**
■ People around you are negative.
■ You have discovered that negative thought can sometimes fire you into action: you do things 'just to prove yourself wrong'.

There are some real benefits of negative thought: realism; spotting dangers and pitfalls; but it is a short list compared with the benefits of being positive: feeling better; enthusing others; generating more ideas; spotting opportunities; giving yourself extra energy.

Perhaps the worst effect of negative thinking is loss of energy. Try comparing the ease with which you can perform a purely physical task when feeling positive against when negative.

2 Aids to a positive frame of mind

■ **Eliminate negative phrases** from your speech: this helps you identify subtle negative conditioning of yourself and others. Don't start off requests for help with "I don't suppose you can . . . ", or "You haven't got . . . "; this makes it easier for people to be negative rather than positive.

■ **Start with a smile.** When you meet people, don't dump all your negative rubbish on them. Be bright, positive, energetic and . . . smile.

■ **Be skilled at spotting negative thinkers.** It is easy: they tell more bad news (without helping you to avoid it next time) than good. Remind yourself that if you are not on guard they will sap your energy.

■ **Keep problem-stating until later.** Get all your good ideas out before shooting them down.

■ **Think positively about other people.** Who is perfect? Not you, for a start. Be particularly positive about your favoured colleagues and friends: it is excellent therapy, and helps you make best use of the talent around you. Don't begrudge anyone's success, nor be smug about their failures.

48 *Are you willing to be yourself?*

In his book *Going For It!*, Victor Kiam describes two very different characters.

> One is a Midwest salesman called Bob Englud, owner of a racoon coat. No matter how hot, Englud wears this stifling garment whenever he visits a store to make a sales pitch. Questioned about this eccentricity, he says "You know old Bob. I'm just a cool customer."
>
> Englud, of course, has sound reasons for wearing the coat, as Kiam discovered on meeting him. "So you think this is a fur coat? Let me tell you, it's not that at all. It's an ice-breaker." He went to explain how invaluable it was in getting the conversation rolling with new customers when, as usual, neither side can think of anything to say. Englud adds: "I'll tell you something else. There are about nine billion salesmen in this country. Almost every buyer we call on sees so many of us . . . that he can't tell us apart unless we have numbers on our backs. This coat is my number . . . "
>
> The second character is an executive employed by Kiam at Remington. Whenever he opens his mouth, he apologises for doing so. "I'm not sure you're going to like this, but . . . " or "Well, of course, this is only my opinion . . . " The irony is that the executive's ideas are always brilliant. Kiam carries on working with him because, as an entrepreneur, he does not "give a hoot how a concept is wrapped." However, Kiam also admits that because of the lack of confidence, he would never hire this genius to head a division in his company.

"Fur Coat", in effect, is a man who realizes his personality in his work – or at any rate a part of it. The diffident genius does not realize it at all, in fact he probably represses it.

Personality or 'self' is notoriously difficult to define; just how much of it can or should be realized when working in an organization is an equally grey area. Organizations' and individuals' needs are bound, to some extent, to be in conflict.

But it is also true that if personality is unduly repressed, it surfaces in some undesirable way.

Here are some run-of-the-mill symptoms of personality not being realized at work:

■ **Tension with colleagues and superiors:** Being unable to relax in their presence. This does not mean feeling free to put the feet up on the desk; it does mean feeling sufficiently at ease to express oneself well and to challenge concepts.

■ **No allies:** Everyone needs at least one friend at work with whom to share a conspiratorial joke. Friendship only flourishes when people can show their true selves; no self-realization, no friendships.

■ **Trust:** Do colleagues/superiors trust you enough to allow you occasionally, to work at home?

▶ **Remedies**

The bottom line, as Kiam would put it, comes down simply and solely to risk. There are no magic formulas for realizing the self, except the willingness to take a punt on it.

'Being yourself' is a slight risk the first time you do it: but the odds improve dramatically after taking the first plunge. The first time you challenge your boss's thinking will be a novel experience. The second time, he, and you, will probably take it in your stride.

Procrastination

"Three o'clock is always too late and too early for anything you want to do."
– *Jean-Paul Sartre.*

Procrastination is not merely a block to getting things done. It is a prime cause of extra worry, lost opportunities, increasing pressure from colleagues and waning self-respect.

For procrastination to flourish, there are two essential conditions:

1 Some spare time in the future (however imaginary) and

2 Something more pleasurable to do now (however unimportant).

De-procrastinating: basic methods

■ **The Banjo Method:** everyone feels better when they have achieved something; and about ten times better when they have achieved something horrible. Banjo stands for Bang a Nasty Job Off.

Every day, out of all the tasks you have to complete, choose the 'nastiest' and don't rest until you have completed it. You will find yourself far better prepared mentally to do the rest of the day's work, partly because you feel good from the sense of achievement, partly because you have proved that you are in control of yourself.

■ **Use silence.** If you did not have to listen to those voices in your head, you would be freer to get things done. So develop the ability to clear your mind (see **36**). And once you are working, maintaining silence in your head will keep your mind on the job.

■ **Do it:** like jumping into a cold swimming pool, the longer you leave it, the worse it gets. Jump in now; do something – make a start, even if it is not the whole task.

■ **Little and often:** people tend to leave nasty jobs to be done in large blocks. This makes no sense: you are far more likely to shy away from a day of misery than say an hour of boring tasks integrated with more stimulating work. Make a routine out of jobs which you regularly procrastinate. Set definite times at which you will start them.

■ **Positive thoughts about nasty jobs:** try to imagine yourself doing them with pleasure. It may seem improbable, but self-suggestion can dilute negative feelings. Reinforce positive feelings by reminding yourself of the benefits of having achieved the task(s).

■ **Give yourself a treat.**
Procrastination is about putting pleasure before pain. But pleasure is all the better if experienced after pain, as a contrast. Reward yourself with interesting tasks, or time off, after nasty ones.

■ **Get someone else to help:** people tend to assume too often that their nasty job is everyone's nasty job. If this applies to you, stop and reflect on how many people earn their living doing things you cannot abide.

Thursday

Have you ever experienced the lost weekend?

Thursday In the morning you say to yourself: 'I'll get these letters written at the weekend, and I'll read those articles.' During the rest of Thursday and right through Friday, you add more tasks to the list.

Friday

Friday evening You acknowledge that if you were sensible you would start tackling the list straight away. But a voice in your head says
'You've had a hard week, havn't you?'
'Yes', you agree, 'at least someone appreciates me.'
'Well, you have this huge expanse of time stretching out ahead of you called The Weekend, so pace yourself.'
'That sounds like a good idea.''
'So put away those papers, have a drink and enjoy yourself. You will do the letters quicker in the long run if you recharge your batteries first.'
You don't take much persuading.

Saturday

Saturday You wake up - not too late - but things start moving at weekend pace. A large, prolonged breakfast followed by essential shopping; a long lunch; television in the afternoon. But at five o'clock you start to get out your papers. 'Well don't start now', says the voice, 'you're going out at seven. You'll be putting it all away as soon as you've started.' 'Of course'', you say. 'Anyway, there's all of Sunday.'

Sunday

Sunday You wake up even later than on Saturday, have an even larger breakfast, and then there are all those newspapers. Then it is lunch time. Now it is mid-afternoon, and you can hear Sartre 'Hardly worth starting now you've wasted the whole weekend.'
'But you said...'
'Well, you don't have to listen to me, do you? Your trouble is, you have no self-discipline.'
Something to brood on for a Sunday evening.

50 *The now effect*

Too much time worrying about the past or dreaming of the future is unproductive. You must spend time actually doing things. But apart from the obvious value of producing results *there is an additional feeling of well being to be gained from concentrating on the present moment.*

Have you ever thought what a relatively small amount of time you spend concentrating on *now*? Worrying about outstanding jobs, concern over how you performed yesterday, and fears for the future, all tend to crowd out the obvious, everyday function of *now*. Concentrating on this moment in time, not the next one or the last one, can take effort; but it is effort that is rewarded not only by greater productivity, but by greater energy.

Tom is a successful man: a well-paid financial adviser, alert, quick-thinking, decisive, active and productive. Yet he has every reason to brood: 12 years ago his wife and daughter were killed in a car crash; he is left looking after his 13-year-old son, a small farm and a range of international clients. He is the best example I know of someone who lives in the present and enjoys it. He seems to derive much of his energy from spending the minimum of unproductive time in useless thought. He does more, feels better and is an inspiration to others. There is nothing particularly contrived about this frame of mind — and he certainly did not achieve it through heavy self-discipline — just the expedient of not brooding, of living in the present.

The 'now effect' is the same phenomenon as filling 'the unforgiving minute with sixty seconds' worth of distance run' (Kipling); it is narrowing the gap between thought and action –

see (section 3). 'Now' people can be irritating: but it is usually not their fault. When you are feeling jaded and slow, 'now' people are overwhelming. They seem to think faster, do more; they tend to trigger negative thoughts such as 'I could never be like them'. But have you tried?

▶ **Towards the now effect**

■ Do it now. Sit down and concentrate only on what is happening around you. What do you feel like *now*? Your toes? Your fingers? Your head? What can you hear and see? How does it feel? After a few minutes of keeping your thoughts on the present you should feel more energetic, freer, more 'together'. Practise this simple expedient daily.

■ Get out of bed. The obvious way of starting the day now is to get out of bed – when you first wake up. When the alarm goes off, open your eyes and get out of bed. Keep your head clear and concentrate straight away on the present moment. Enjoy yourself for the rest of the day.

■ Concentrate. Don't let your mind wonder. Concentrate harder than you usually do, and concentrate on one thing at a time. It will make you less of a prey to fears and worries. Enjoy life in practice, not in theory.

51 *Unblock your mind*

To solve problems quickly and efficiently, you usually have to use both logic and creativity. Easier said than done, of course: on the way to any solution, one encounters blockages.

1 ► Logical blockages

Symptoms
- Too many facts.
- Too long gathering material.
- A feeling that you still have not got a hundred per cent of the information.
- Uncritical gathering of material, regardless of its relevance.
- Making information-gathering the objective, not solving the problem.

Solutions
Engage your right brain by:
- Using an image to describe the problem.
- Describe what a successful conclusion might look like.
- Encourage yourself to produce silly ideas as a potential bridge to a feasible solution.

2 ► Creative blockages

Symptoms
- Leaving problem-solving to the last minute, relying on a past record of inspiration and thinking on your feet.
- Following hunches.
- Having no detail to re-examine if your initial hunch was wrong.
- Finishing off people's sentences for them.
- Making creative leaps and not explaining your thought processes.

Cures
- Ensure that the problem has been properly identified.
- Discipline yourself or use others to gather the optimum amount of information.
- Use checklists to avoid missing points.
- Write all ideas and thoughts down so you don't lose them.
- Slow down and relax your brain regularly.

3 ► Emotional blockages

These can be summarized under two headings, Confidence and Bias.

Confidence

Symptoms
- Lacking confidence in your own ideas.
- Not speaking up at meetings.
- Not writing down all ideas, dismissing some in your head.
- Feeling you are not 'creative'.

Solutions
- Regularly remind yourself of past successful problem-solving.
- Quieten down your critical mind (see **36**).
- Write everything down, suspending judgement.

Bias

Symptoms
- Dismissing ideas because of who presented them, or 'we've tried it before and failed'.
- Pre-judging issues politically or ideologically.

Cures
- List 'likes' before your 'dislikes'.
- Identify your fears and prejudices. Plan to avoid them.
- Put an embargo on your own and other people's 'butting in'.

52 *Taking notes*

Verbal communication is swift, direct and effective, but when it comes to recalling what has been said, there is no substitute for the written record. That is obvious; what many overlook is that keeping notes of key conversations not only improves the memory but boosts the confidence; that being able to recall, with the aid of a few notes, what was said when you spoke to a contact five months ago makes a favourable impression, helps you take and keep the initiative:

"Hello George. When we spoke in March I told you the building could be completed in six months. I am ringing to tell you we can improve on that provided you can accept a pre-fabricated roof."

or:

"Hello George. Do you remember talking some time back? Yes? About the roof. I can't remember what I said about the completion period but whatever it was I think we can do better now. Why? Well, if you have a pre-fabricated roof . . ."

1▶ Reasons for slow note-taking

If you don't have the note-taking habit, you probably feel that it is too slow a process to be much use in everyday speech, which rattles along at typically 130 words per minute. But note-taking need not be cumbersome if you devote a very little time to developing a personal shorthand. This is quite distinct from a fully fledged shorthand – no special training is required.

Slow note-taking is the result of two main failings:

■ You do not know what you want to write down.

■ You are making no effort to write notes – you tend to take dictation instead.

If you find it hard to accept the suggestion that you don't know what to write down, and if you don't believe that you make no effort, try these tests:

■ Switch on the radio, and find a station with a talk programme. Take notes for exactly one minute on what is being said. Leave your notes for an hour. Then look at the notes again and see if you can remember exactly what was said.

Now take notes from the radio for another minute – only this time concentrate on listening rather than taking notes. Pick out key words or combinations of words to write down. What can you remember with the aid of your notes an hour later this time?

■ Next, try to write down as much of the last-but-one paragraph as you can in 30 seconds. You probably got little further than halfway through the second sentence.

Now do the same, abbreviating any words which lend themselves easily to it; leave out words like 'the' and 'a'. What you write in 30 seconds may now look something like this:

'Switch on rad & find stat. with talk prog. Then take notepad & take notes on what said for 1 min. Leave notes for 1 hr. Look at notes again, see you remember what saying.'

With these notes you have recorded in 30 seconds not just the first sentence-and-a-half, but the entire paragraph.

2▶ Action

■ Before you start to take notes, think

what you need them for. Notes of a conference need, of course, to be more detailed than an *aide-mémoire* of a brief conversation.

If all you need is an *aide-mémoire*, take down only key words and phrases. Look for the important nouns (especially the subject) and what is being said about the subject – perhaps a single verb or adjective. For the previous paragraph, for instance, the notes might read:

'Notes – what for? Purpose dictates form.'

For more comprehensive notes, try to identify sub-headings and sections in the argument and lay out your notes accordingly. Indent each section below headings, and further indent sub-sections, start each new topic on a new line. Proper layout is important not only for easy digestion of the notes later, but for the note-taking process itself, because it forces you to concentrate on listening and understanding rather than note-taking.

The first step towards your own shorthand system is making the most of abbreviations.
– Using an abbreviated ampersan for 'and' and 'eg' for 'for example' are obvious instances. But there are many standard abbreviations and symbols which people overlook and which are easy to incorporate into notes:

. . .	because	cf	compared with
->	leads to	>	greater than
<	less than	=	the same as

■ Phonetic 'spellings' are also useful:

u *you*	**y** *why*	**c** *see*	**q** *queue*

Leave out vowels whenever the vowel missing is obvious:

vwl *vowel* **Amrc** *American*

■ As a final step, develop your own abbreviations for words and phrases that crop up frequently:

DIS for 'downturn in sales' or PO for 'production overheads'. Finally, remember that many words, especially the definite and indefinite articles, can be left out of notes altogether.

3 ▶ True shorthand

Secretarial and business schools have developed a wide variety of noting systems over the years, and each has its own merits and demerits. Conventional shorthand uses simple symbols to reduce letters into little more than dots and dashes and anyone fluent in it can write almost as fast as speech. The drawback is that it takes time and effort to learn. However, there are alternatives – a simplified shorthand system such as Gregg shorthand, or one of the alphabetic script systems such as Pitman Script. Both are much easier to learn, and can give writing speeds of 60 wpm or more after a little practice.

4 ▶ New technology

An increasing number of hard-pressed executives are dispensing with pen and paper for note-taking and coming to grips with Microwriters. The Microwriter is actually an electronic writing machine that fits into the palm of a hand, and has six keys pressed in different combinations to give all the letters and numbers. There is a small digital display at one end.

Most people can learn the basic principles of these machines in a matter of hours, and within a few weeks they have the prospect of writing faster than with pen and paper.

53 *Improve your memory*

How keen is your memory? Most people don't think they have an efficient memory: most acknowledge that if they could have confidence in it, they would perform more efficiently, waste less time.

A friend introduces you to a group at a party:

"I would like you to meet Graham, John, Maureen and George."

You reply:

"How do you do, how do you do, how do you do, how do you do?", smiling enthusiastically, and thinking: 'I shall never remember one, let alone four of their names.'

Most probably, you use the first few minutes in the group to sum people up, and to assess their friendliness and intelligence.

Only then do you wish you had remembered their names; a wish that can develop into an obsession; an obsession which means you are taking in very little of what they are saying.

You escape from the group, then later re-meet one of them and have to say "I am sorry I didn't catch your name."

You probably realize that this is likely to be interpreted as "I am sorry, but you looked so boring I did not bother to remember your name; now I am stuck with you I had better find out what it is." You don't wish to give that impression; but cannot avoid doing so.

As Dale Carnegie put it, the sweetest word in anyone's ear is the sound of their own name; provided, of course, it is not sycophantically repeated in the manner of insurance salesmen who think this is a certain way of winning your attention.

Besides names, you would probably find it useful to retain lists of advice and facts in your head for use from time to time. But how?

1 ▶ Why you don't have a good memory

■ Because you tell yourself you don't. Belief, or rather quietening this disbelief, is the most important step to a better memory. Because of your lack of belief, you don't try to improve your memory.

■ You use the wrong side of your brain. In section **32** you saw that the creative part of your brain is the most effective for developing memory skills. The part of your brain that doubts its effectiveness is also the part least effective in terms of memory.

2 ▶ Why do you remember things?

Think of what your memory has retained over a long period. It will include the:

■ painful	■ colourful
■ enjoyable	■ smelly
■ funny	■ noisy
■ sexy	■ interesting

This list can be the key to improving your memory. Whatever needs to be remembered you associate with one of the headings from the list by means of right-brain creativity.

■ **Remembering names:** When you are next introduced to someone, build a quick visual picture around that person's face involving one of the ideas in the list, for instance:

John
John Wayne

Jim
'Jim Lad' with a parrot on his shoulder

Jane
Just about to swing off with Tarzan

Marilyn
Marilyn Monroe

Eileen
A large eye on her forehead

It is important that these 'pictures' are yours; develop your own versions. Develop a list of such 'pictures' now, so you don't have to think too hard about them when needed. The face then becomes the trigger; you will recall the name every time you see the face.

If you think all this is ridiculous – it is, which is why it works.

The credit you get for remembering people's names will act as motivation to build on the system.

■ **Remembering important checklists:** Again, pictures are the key. Develop a story in pictures that highlights each point. For instance, here is a checklist for solving a recurrent problem:

– Define the problem – a problem child . . .

 – List ideal solutions – in a solution of custard

– Develop ideas – with a think bubble out of his head . . .

– List restrictions – restricted in a cage . . .

– Check each idea against the restrictions – put the custard through the cage

■ **Storing items in long-term memory:** First create a story in pictures, as in .2 above. Then simply put a note in your diary to re-run the story in pictures through your mind tonight, tomorrow, in one week, in one month and every six weeks. Spend two or three minutes doing this.

For an investment of a few minutes over one month, you can put a great deal into your long-term memory: names, informal talks, foreign languages, sporting facts, speeches.

How to develop ideas quickly

> "My brain froze."
> "I can't think of a thing."
> "I haven't got the
> imagination to think like you."
> "I'm not creative."

Every time someone makes this type of remark, they program themselves for failure; there is no such thing as a totally uncreative person, incapable of ideas. The human brain contains many more ideas and facts than its owner is conscious of at any given moment. Glimpses of the 'hidden' contents of your mind do occur, but they tend to be fleeting, and they ususally happen when you don't need the distraction. So what can you do to gain access *when you choose*?

In the next minute, write down as many uses of a pin as you can.

Typically, you would have got between one and six. You probably spent some of the 60 seconds staring into the middle distance, hoping that a list of pin usages would unfold like a pantomime song sheet; not the most productive use of our brain.

You may also have got half way to other uses, but discounted them. You may also have got bogged down in a mental cul-de-sac, spent some time telling yourself off for being uncreative; or you might have just got started when you suddenly remembered that you hadn't switched the kettle on.

Now, in the next minute, make a list of as many objects as you can.

This time you probably got between 15 and 30. Why so many more?

Because you were not constrained. You did not have to think about it. You were able to build on one object to trigger off another. You only had to write down single words.

Go down this second list again and you will see that there could be a use of a pin associated with each of your words, whether straightforward or a little silly. If you can't see it, then think again. If you still can't, ask someone else. *So you could have had a much longer original list.*

Here then is one way of being more creative: simply by getting ideas out of your head randomly, but quickly and comprehensively.

You can use the technique to write an original wedding speech; prepare for a meeting at short notice; to gather possible solutions to a problem. The barriers are:

– Not writing anything down.

– Panicking

– Being too logical

– Eliminating 'poor ideas' in your head

– Staring around, hoping for inspiration

Brainstorming – basic technique

Take a sheet of paper.

Write the objective in the middle, eg 'New product name for this year's catfood line.'

Randomly, without any attempt at order, put down as many headings as occur to you. Write them as single words or small phrases. Use sub-headings in order not to restrict the potential of headings which seem to cover too wide an area.

Now go round these headings and let them spark off further headings; mark them as satellites. Don't stare into space for inspiration – use what is already on paper.

When you have what looks like an impressive number of idea-headings, start moving out from broad headings, adding comments on the quality of ideas, ie 'useful if the spring promotion budget also allowed free gifts.'

Start to find links between topics and form subject groups.

Arrange these in a logical sequence, and write a linking narrative.

If you still need more ideas, use 'the method' once again. Also try using a totally unrelated word to stimulate thoughts and then relate these back to your topic.

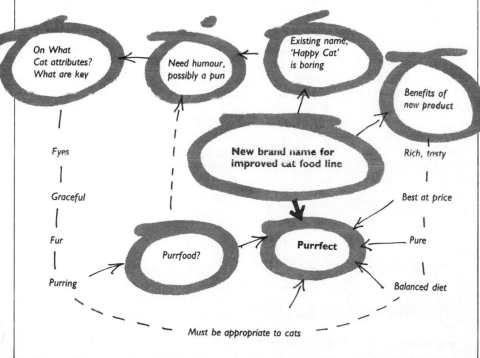

55 *Read faster*

An editor in a publishing house took a typescript to the head of the firm for consideration. The editor had spent hours reading the first three chapters, and come to the conclusion that although the work was competent, it lacked the insight which would make it competitive.

He expected the publisher to listen to his view, then hold on to the typescript for some days to read it properly.

As he was leaving, the publisher said: "Where are you going?", then started leafing through the pages, glancing at most of them for less than a second, pausing occasionally to read a whole sentence.

After less than five minutes, the publisher said: "It's competent, and covers the subject well, but it lacks insight. We won't take it on."

Reading large tracts of material quickly and *well* enough to make competent business decisions is less to do with whizz-kiddery than it might seem. Slow reading boils down to three simple failings, all of which can be tackled without resorting to special training:

> You are not *trying* to read fast

> You have a poor recognition span

> You have a poor vocabulary

If you doubt that this is true, try the following tests:

Recognition Span

Now take a pencil, and read the following lines, marking each place where your eye momentarily pauses:

Come live with me and be my Love,
And we will all the pleasures prove
That hills and valleys, dales and fields
Or woods or steepy mountain yields.

Effort

Turn to section **70** and read it at breakneck speed, trying simply to pick up the key points. Write them down. Then read section **71** in full, at your usual speed, noting the key points. Compare the two times. Both have the same number of key points.

Very few people perform significantly worse by deliberately reading fast provided they are trying to pick up key points only.

Docs your copy look like this?

Or like this?

A

*Come live with me/ and be
my Love,/
And we will/ all the pleasures/
prove
That hills and valleys,/ dales
and fields,/
Or woods or/steepy/mountain
yields.*

B

*Come live/with me/and be/
my Love/
And we/ will all/ the pleasures/
prove
That hills/and valleys/dales/
and fields/
Or woods/or/steepy/mountain/
yields.*

Reading word by word is not the natural way. People who do read this way often mutter or mouth the words under their breath, too. Sublocution, as this is properly called, slows you even more. The quickest, and most natural way to read is by visual recognition – not just of single words, but of groups of words. It is relatively easy to improve your recognition span, and equally easy to let it contract through neglect. Passage A above shows a respectable, average recognition span; passage B a below-average span.

Read these passages, trying to understand them both:

*Si fueris Romae, Romano
vivito more;
Si fueris alibi, vivito sicut ibi.*

*If you are at Rome, live in
the Roman style; if you are
elsewhere, live as they live
elsewhere.*

Of course, you had to read the Latin quotation word by word; and you probably went over it twice or three times to work out whether you could make sense of any of the words. With the English translation, your eyes quickly regained the ability to take in words in groups.

Unfamiliarity with words reduces reading speed.

55

▶ ▶ **Action**

■ **Read aggressively:** Try to read fast, and consciously brief yourself to note and take in the key points, rather than the details. A tip: in most paragraphs, there is usually one key point; it is often right at the beginning, but may also be in the middle, or at the end. It will be supported by details – in the form of facts, or arguments; but details they remain.

Go through the leading article of your newspaper every day analysing which are the main points. After reading, ask yourself what the leader was about. There are few more effective training routines to improve reading speed, and it can be done on the way to work.

■ **Improving recognition span:** This is as simple as trying to take in larger groups of words than usual. Once again, you will make progress simply by practising. Mentally rap yourself on the knuckles every time you lapse into sub-locution.

■ **Improve your vocabulary:** This, too, is easier than it sounds, but it is a long-term undertaking. Simply make it a rule to look up in a dictionary any word you come across which you do not honestly and fully understand.

3 Further action – skimming
The suggestions above are specifically for material you have to give your best attention. But there is also a mass of lesser printed material with which most people need to be familiar. Often enough, it is not written well enough to merit a detailed read; but it could deserve a skim.

■ First **assess material overall** for ap-

pearance, layout, and presentation. If it seems well organized, it is probably suitable for a fast skim, and vice versa.

■ **Take in the structure** before attempting to read. Every piece of written work has structure: a beginning, middle or end. Just by finding the key passages marking beginning, middle or end, the content can be usefully assessed. You will not of course get the whole content, or even an accurate idea of its value; but you will get something that is usually worth having.

The contents list of a book often does this work for you; read it together with the cover blurb to get the best quick impression.

It is surprising how many people forget this apparently obvious ploy under the stress of having to assimilate a mass of printed matter. If you have just a little more time, read say one or two chapters or sections of a book.

Similarly with newspaper and magazine articles: the introductory paragraph, or lead-in, is written by an in-house sub-editor whose job it is to summarize the contents – in other words to do your fast reading for you.

■ **Always admit to skimming.** Colleagues will respect you more for admitting that a little knowledge is potentially a dangerous thing.

56 *Controlling paperwork*

Despite, perhaps even because of the word processor, minimizing paperwork, and preventing it from submerging you and your colleagues, remains an essential skill. Somehow the paperless office promised by computer salesmen has not quite materialized; indeed office managers are the first to admit that vast amounts more paper are used once electronic printers are installed than in the days of typewriters.

There is plenty of conventional wisdom on coping with paperwork. I feel that while much of it is useful, most of it needs simplifying. This is a mundane area of office life; you don't want to have to think about implementing systems of any complexity; you just want paper control to happen – naturally.

Read this section in conjunction with **55** and **49**.

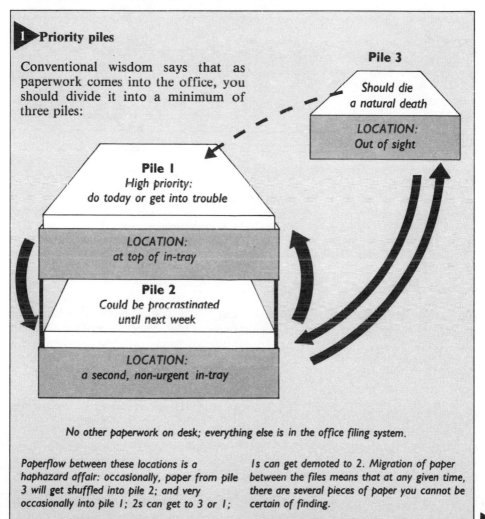

1 ▶ Priority piles

Conventional wisdom says that as paperwork comes into the office, you should divide it into a minimum of three piles:

Pile 3
Should die a natural death
LOCATION:
Out of sight

Pile 1
*High priority:
do today or get into trouble*
LOCATION:
at top of in-tray

Pile 2
*Could be procrastinated
until next week*
LOCATION:
a second, non-urgent in-tray

No other paperwork on desk; everything else is in the office filing system.

Paperflow between these locations is a haphazard affair: occasionally, paper from pile 3 will get shuffled into pile 2; and very occasionally into pile 1; 2s can get to 3 or 1; 1s can get demoted to 2. Migration of paper between the files means that at any given time, there are several pieces of paper you cannot be certain of finding.

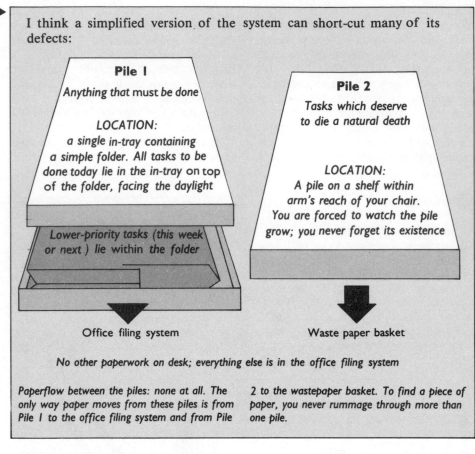

I think a simplified version of the system can short-cut many of its defects:

Pile 1

Anything that must be done

LOCATION:
a single in-tray containing a simple folder. All tasks to be done today lie in the in-tray on top of the folder, facing the daylight

Lower-priority tasks (this week or next) lie within the folder

Office filing system

Pile 2

Tasks which deserve to die a natural death

LOCATION:
A pile on a shelf within arm's reach of your chair. You are forced to watch the pile grow; you never forget its existence

Waste paper basket

No other paperwork on desk; everything else is in the office filing system

Paperflow between the piles: none at all. The only way paper moves from these piles is from Pile 1 to the office filing system and from Pile 2 to the wastepaper basket. To find a piece of paper, you never rummage through more than one pile.

I have found that this system works for many people who attend my courses. Dispensing with a low-priority pile makes people concentrate harder on the fate of paperwork. Pile 1 in my system is a much hotter place to be than the same pile in a three-pile system; pile 2 becomes a real rubbish bin, as opposed to a euphemism for a rubbish bin. You don't put paperwork in there lightly, and if you have a reasonably tidy mind, you will not like to watch it grow, either. Cutting it down to size becomes a periodic but satisfying routine.

It is of course important that you take the folder from the in-tray every day and extract paperwork which has become high-priority, replacing it, for attention today or latest tomorrow, on top of the folder, facing the daylight. Many people however find that not actually seeing a piece of paper has a remarkable tendency to make them forget its existence; in which case, use a transparent plastic folder rather than a conventional one made of card.

One refinement: whenever there is a high-priority piece of paper you cannot face handling, over which you have repeatedly procrastinated, take it out of the tray last thing at night and place it in the centre of your desk. Remove the tray to the far side of the office. Next morning, do not do any other work until that piece of paper has stopped cluttering up your desk.

▶ **Further action**

Once you have a truly workable system going, there is little anyone can tell you about minimizing paperwork. The following widely used tricks will be merely useful adjuncts to basic good habits.

■ Letting low-priority paperwork die is of course an absolutely basic way of controlling paperwork. The principle is that everyone is bound to receive unimportant or unnecessary requests which either answer themeslves in time, or become irrelevant. The wise executive spots these and places them in pile 2.

But there is an important refinement to this technique: when you let a piece of paper die, *tell someone*. Think out clearly why it deserves to die, and state your reasons to the person concerned, politely but firmly. This is a useful insurance policy.

■ Never touch a piece of paper once it is sorted into a pile unless you mean to take a step towards resolving it, or resolve it completely. Some time management theorists say 'Never handle paper more than once.' I think that is unrealistic; the goal should be try to handle only twice – once on sorting it into the pile, once when resolving it.

■ Minimize letter- and memo-writing whenever possible by hand-writing your reply on the letter or memo you received. Take a photocopy for your file. If you don't have the tact and commonsense to work out who will

and will not be offended by this shortcut, you should reflect on the possibility that you have been over-promoted.

■ Allow *some* letters through with typing errors or spelling mistakes. Retyping letters takes a long time. People with whom you correspond regularly and have an established working relationship understand that fingers can slip and some secretaries have difficulties using a dictionary. One or two such errors, corrected neatly in your handwriting prior to signing, never do any harm.

It should go without saying that all letters and documents to people or firms with whom you don't have an established business relationship should be letter-perfect. Word-processors make this simple.

■ Filing systems should be simple enough to explain to a new temporary secretary in less than five minutes. I personally think that executives should do their own filing – thereby ensuring it is done to their satisfaction, and that no one else is to blame when paperwork cannot be found. Sliding a piece of paper into a file is probably more economic on time than any other act of office life.

It is good practice, however, to ask your secretary to regularly sort all papers *within* a file into chronological order.

■ Standardize paper sizes for all documents and letters that will reach the filing system. Paper is much easier to handle and sort if it is all, for example, A4. If something will not fit your filing cabinet, go to the length of having it reduction-photocopied so it will fit. Special outsize files make nonsense of a system.

57 *Getting letters written*

J ust a few people in business get by never writing letters – and claim that once they have conditioned colleagues, this causes no problems.

Others – almost always in exalted positions – annotate the letters they receive, returning the marked original to the sender by way of reply, retaining a photocopy for their file. Others, again a select few, dispense with the apparatus of dictation and secretaries, answering letters promptly, by hand, with the briefest messages.

All of which proves that far from being avoidable and unnecessary, letter-writing has to be lived with.

Most people, in business or in private life, acknowledge this, and have little difficulty writing letters they see as essential or pleasurable to write: congratulations on the birth of a new child, or a step up the career ladder; communications which bring deals to an important next stage; reminders that money is owed. But there remain dozens of other letters with a lower priority rating which still have to be written.

1 ▶ Why letters don't get written

The reasons why letters don't get written are to some extent the same as why any other task doesn't get done; but they are also, to a large degree, peculiar to the nature of letter writing. Even in the age of the word processor, when in theory you could keep standard replies on disk to a large number of routine queries, actually getting down to doing the letters is harder than you think. So go through the following checklist, noting which reasons apply to you, and cross-referring to the corresponding action.

■ You cannot see a spare hour in the day; or if there is one, you won't be able to answer all the letters in that space of time, and it offends your tidy mind not to be able to finish the job; better leave all the letters until you have longer.

■ Before you can reply, you need information from another source. This is not readily available.

■ You don't mind writing the letters, but frankly, the pile is huge and you are, well, slow at composing; dictating would be the answer, but you are not sufficiently fluent: your secretary gets impatient and/or flustered because you keep making corrections; and you get into a mess talking into a tape recorder.

■ You don't feel like writing letters; the idea bores you, and you feel lazy today.

■ You would write the letters, but feel the time could be better devoted to something creative; the letters can wait.

■ This is perhaps the most common and justifiable reason for not writing a letter: you need more information in order to give an intelligent reply, and that information is not to hand. ACTION Reply to the letter anyway – NOW – saying the information is not readily available, but nonetheless surmising on the possible answers: i.e. 'if the cost per unit were less than x, we could give you the product for x; if it is more than x, our price to you will be higher.' If you don't want to commit yourself at this stage, say so. Some reply is better than none at all; the correspondent is kept in the picture and on the boil; your thoughts are crystallized; you avoid having to answer the letter at some later date when you will feel even less like doing so than now.

Another ploy in this situation is to invite the correspondent to share the no-information problem with you; often, this is justified because he has raised the question in the first place. Perhaps he can find the answer quicker than you? Perhaps your outlining the missing facts will help him answer his letter for himself?

■ These are basic time-management problems: see sections **12–16**. You cannot be creative every hour of the day and if creative work is conflicting with nuts-and-bolts tasks, your overall balance is wrong. Find the time of day when you can do creative work best – and do it then. Do letter-writing and mundane tasks at other times.

■ It is certainly important to reserve letter-writing for a time it deserves: many people find ending the afternoon or morning in this way is practical, having given their mind at its sharpest to high-priority meetings and conversations. On the other hand, you may well need to motivate yourself to write boring letters by saving up a more interesting task as a reward.

■ Be sure to read what follows in conjunction with sections **81** and **82**. Composing – writing – is a lifetime's art, and only improves with practise. If you draft slowly and painfully, your first aim should be to do much more of it.

However, there are, even in the limited context of letter-writing, some tricks to take some of the pain out of it. First, let your correspondent do some of the work for you. Have his letter in front of you as you write the reply. Deal with points in the order he raises them; don't try and structure the letter yourself. This has the additional advantage of ensuring you do what you set out to do – answer the letter.

Secondly, plan the letter in advance by listing every point you wish to make. Then write it, in rough, in one-sentence paragraphs, one paragraph for every point.

The sentence is the basic vehicle of expression; several sentences build up into a paragraph to present an idea or point supported by subsidiary arguments and facts. Making paragraphs only one sentence long forces you to make just the point you wish to make, without qualification.

57

▶ ■ You have delayed writing the letter so long that the mere act of responding at this stage is embarrassing and unpleasant.

■ Don't write a letter apologizing for not writing the letter. Give the person a ring, today, at a time when they are likely to be most at ease, able to talk to you. Say you are calling to apologize for your neglect, give them an interim answer to any question raised; find out what their likely future needs are likely to be. This is the short, sharp cure for the embarrassment you feel. It has the advantage of forcing you to pay the neglected person special attention – to consider their needs.

■ The letter(s) to be answered is/are hidden inside one of three piles of correspondence awaiting your attention; it would take you the rest of the afternoon to find them, and you have to finish a report for your boss before going home.

■ This is a paperwork, not a letter-writing, problem: you must read **56** before going any further. Essentially you need two readily accessible pending trays or folders, one for A-priority papers and one for Bs, Cs and Ds. In the trays or folders, all letters are stacked in strict order of urgency. Even if you only have five minutes spare in which to reply to a single letter, you waste no time in locating the paperwork. If a letter is personal – say a family matter – read **2** – perhaps this type of correspondence could be fitted into a magic hour?

2 **Towards cutting down correspondence**

■ Make use of the humble postcard to reply to letters. Letters on full-size company stationery, with carbon copies, take a large amount of time in relation to the result when you add in all the extras required to produce an acceptable finished result – including filing, re-typing and so on. If necessary, write postcards by hand, clearing a large volume at once, thus

short-circuiting the secretarial system. There are many circumstances under which colleagues and other business people appreciate a legible, personal note on smartly printed card as much as if not more than a formal letter.

■ Many C- and D-priority letters require simply an acknowledgement or a word of agreement; or a simple comment. Consider getting your secretary to telephone it, if necessary leaving a message with the correspondent's secretary. Mark the letter with a note of your reply, and the date, for filing purposes.

■ Work out a set of personal standards (see **20**) for answering letters. This could be: reply by return of post for A-priority matters; reply within two days for Bs; reply inside one week for Cs and Ds. Keep to the code, but be prepared to relax it temporarily due to absence from the office.

■ Learn how to use the office word processor. Playing with gadgets is fun, and can act as motivation to sit down and write. Get your secretary to type in – data capture – letters in rough; edit them yourself on the screen.

■ Keep a set of standard replies to letters which recurrently need the same answers.

■ Whose letter-writing style, in your business or private circle, do you admire the most? Analyse why. Copy the style.

```
          Mr David Henderson
          Computerspeed Rentals Ltd
          24 The Priory
          Brighton
          West Sussex    RG22   8BE

          Our Ref: LH777

          8th May 1987

          Dear Mr Henderson,

          Your invoice No. A285 dated 5th May.

          Fifteen of component A222 were faulty, and are returned
          with this letter. Amount overcharged: £15.00.

          The actual number of component B225 supplied was 225, not
          250 as ordered. Amount overcharged: £12.50

          Will you please be so kind as to issue a credit note for
          £27.50, plus VAT, as a refund?

          We will then settle the balance no later than 20th June,
          not, as requested on your invoice, by 10th June. This is
          because you delivered ten days late.

          Yours sincerely,


          Lyn Hector (Ms)
```

One self-contained point per paragraph
Queries dealt with in same order as they arose on invoice
Paragraphs follow in chronological order
Avoids pompous terms such as 'herewith'.

58 *Harnessing technology*

Businesses and organizations thinking about buying computers do so, more than for any other reason, because they think everyone else has one. This sorry fact was revealed by a recent Lancaster University survey. The reality is that only a small proportion of businesses actually use, or need computers.

Fear of being left behind in the technology race can sometimes be a valid reason for investigating the possibilities of computers, and many organizations invest tens of thousands in equipment for this reason alone. But the approach is fraught with dangers – not least the possibility that computerizing turns out to be a complete waste of time and money. It is estimated, for example, that perhaps a third of all business would receive little or no benefit from computers.

So the first question to ask if you are thinking of buying a computer for yourself, or involved in buying one for your company or organization is: do you really need it?

▶ Becoming computerized

Before you plunge into the computer shop, you need to examine your current working practice.

For example:
■ Does your business involve sending large numbers of statements, invoices and cheques accurately and on time?

■ Do you have a problem keeping track of stock?

■ Are hours of secretarial time spent drafting standard letters? Do you have a long mailing list?

■ Do you spend hours redrafting written material, especially reports including charts and graphs?

■ Do you regularly need to file and pull out details of, say, clients, parts or materials?

■ Do you spend a great deal of time calculating the effect of variable costs and income on net profits?

■ Do you have an enormous amount of information to handle?

■ Would you benefit from access to continuously updated sources of information?

■ Does your business spend too much time on administration and not enough on production?

If the answer to any of these questions is 'Yes', the chances are you would benefit from using computers. But it is important to remember that computers cannot save a badly-run business; indeed, imposing a computer on a system that is already a mess will almost certainly create an even bigger mess.

There are numerous books on the market offering advice in this area, and even more consultancy firms. Some consultants are helpful and well-informed; others are glorified sales people: before you accept their advice, ask them to put you in contact with an organization that has successfully used their services.

Before you approach any consultant, though, bear in mind that there are two major pitfalls that beset the all too many would-be computer users:

■ Failure to analyse fully the details of your current working system and to work out exactly what it is you expect the computer to do. A consultant can suggest how this major task is approached; but only you and your colleagues can do the work because only you know (or should know) your existing system well enough. Moreover, unless a consultant has been properly briefed – in writing – you have little comeback in the event of disaster.

■ Failure to consult all those who will be working with the computers, or will be affected by their introduction. Oddly enough, the last people managers often think about consulting are the secretaries who will actually operate them – and who could tell them instantly that such and such a system would not work.

Beyond this, you will probably have to come to an agreement with staff who may be justifiably worried about job prospects, training and potential health hazards. It makes sense to involve them right from the start, so that they have the satisfaction of putting in their own ideas, and you have some idea of just what is going to be acceptable.

Health hazards are a particularly controversial area, beset with rumour and confusion. VDUs do emit radiation, just as conventional TV screens – but in quantities below the safety level. It is generally accepted that pregnant women should not operate microcomputers, though no study has conclusively proved danger to the foetus. Other common complaints are eyestrain, headache and fatigue. See **59.4** for advice on how these can be minimized.

When working out the viability of computerizing bear in mind, also, the many hidden costs, beyond the basic equipment:

■ Extra wages to staff as 'sweeteners'.

■ Extra cost of trained operators.

■ Time taken for staff to train for and adapt to the technology.

■ Time lost through mistakes and breakdowns.

■ Regular supplies of new disks, printer ribbons and other essentials.

■ Maintenance.

■ New stationery, including new letter-head paper, envelopes, and so on. (Ignore anyone who tells you computers save paper – they consume forests' worth.)

■ New office furniture, including special chairs for VDU operators.

■ New lights.

■ Special wiring and new electrical sockets.

You can rarely switch overnight into full computerization: the new technology usually needs to be phased in gradually while maintaining the back-up of the old system in the event of failure.

Finally, a warning: many managers do not bother to learn how to use the new technology they have given their staff. This may make doing their job impossible.

59 *Staying in charge of a personal computer*

The arrival in the late 1970s of microcomputers, also known as 'personal computers' or PCs, made available enormous computing power at a price that individuals and small businesses could afford. Soon special program packages (software) were developed for PCs that allowed even those with little or no knowledge to use sophisticated systems to automate many personal and business tasks.

PCs are now so reasonably priced – especially the numerous inexpensive clones of IBM's PC – that you no longer need to go through extensive cost-benefit analysis calculations to justify purchasing one. You may decide to buy one for business reasons alone. But equally you may buy one for your own personal use in order to:

■ Acquire a new skill that may improve your job prospects.

■ Familiarize yourself with what computers can and cannot do – perhaps because your company (or competitors) are planning to, or already have, introduced them.

■ Overcome your 'technophobia'.

■ Simplify and speed up tasks such as writing letters and reports.

■ Improve your ability and willingness to make financial forecasts.

■ Rationalize your accounts.

It may, of course, be that familiarity with computers, or computers themselves, are of little use to you. Even in business there are some sectors where the technology will never have much impact. But for a great many people, familiarity with computers may in the long run be a skill that is taken for granted by employers.

If you decide that you could benefit from a PC, though, you may be put off because you believe it takes months of effort to learn how to use a computer – perhaps absorbing hours of your free time, or costing a fortune in training.

1 ▶ Learning time

It is a myth that learning how to use a PC takes a long time. It is also a myth that you have to go on extensive (and expensive) courses. Learning how to program a computer does take a great deal of time, and so does learning how to use a wide range of different software – which is why word-processing operators who need to be familiar with a range of different word-processing packages often have to go on lengthy training sessions. But most people using a micro for their own purposes only need to fathom out one (or perhaps two) software packages.

Many business software packages for PCs are now so accessible or 'user-friendly' that even a complete novice can find the way round them in a rough and ready manner in just a couple of days, and without special training. It helps to have a sound instructional book – not the maker's manual, which is almost invariably as thick as a breeze block, and about as penetrable too. But most people find that they are able to pick up the basics at speed. Although it may be many months before you have mastered all the subtleties, you can be *using* it inside the first week.

2 ▶ The jargon

Computer buffs and salesmen delight in displaying their repertoire of technical terms, buzz words and acronyms – usually at the expense of the poor 'computer illiterate'. Computer technology has spawned such a large vocabulary of new terms that there is no easy way to beat them at their own game; the best approach is not to play at all, and do your best not to feel inadequate. Remember, just as you don't need to know what a carburettor is to drive a car, neither do you need to know what 'parallel-interfacing' or 'OCCAM' is to operate a PC.

 Software first

When buying a hi-fi system, people always buy the equipment (the hardware) first and then the records (software). But with PCs, it is much better to approach from the other way round. You should generally choose your software first, and then find a computer that will run it.

Computer hardware is all basically similar, but software varies enormously – and while some packages may suit you perfectly, others ostensibly similar may be very difficult to use, or may not do what you want. The personal experiences of friends and colleagues with different packages are worth listening to – but you should take their opinions with a pinch of salt, since they may be familiar with only one or two packages.

There are three main types of business package available for PCs:

■ **Word-processing:** enables you to compose, edit and manipulate text on the screen, and saves numerous redrafts.

■ **Spreadsheeting:** the computer becomes an electronic version of the accountant's spreadsheet, with rows and columns for costs and income, for instance. When you adjust one figure, the rest of the sheet is automatically recalculated, thus allowing you to determine how changing costs might affect profit and loss.

■ **Data-base management:** a way of organizing, and retrieving, data automatically, like an electronic card-index. The advantage is that the program can rapidly select chosen items from each 'card'. From an address list, for example, you could quickly summon up a list of all the people in a particular town – so data-bases are ideal for mail-shots. They are also an effective way of storing complex data that must be constantly updated. Databases stocked with up-to-the-minute information on such topics as share prices or scientific research are becoming increasingly common.

 PCs in action

You can learn a great deal from reading the manual and instruction books, but the only way you can really come to grips with a computer is to try it out for yourself. Be adventurous, and have fun. Don't worry about pressing the wrong keys; you can do no harm to the computer whatsoever by pressing keys.

When using a computer:

■ Don't panic if the computer 'freezes' and will not respond to any key command. Simply switch the computer off and start again (after first removing the disk, if the instruction manual indicates that this is advisable). This trick, quaintly known as giving it 'a warm boot', will get you out of most ▶

59

▶ situations. The only problem is that you lose all material not already stored on disk – that is, all your 'live' file. This explains the importance of the next point.

■ Store material on disk frequently and regularly. If word-processing, for example, commit text to memory as you complete each page. This may cost a few minutes extra over the course of a day – but it will be nothing to the frustration of losing pages of material if something goes wrong.

■ Keep files small in order to minimize loss if anything goes wrong.

■ Beware of the 'disk full' trap. If the disk's memory is already full when you try to store a live file, you will probably lose the file. Check regularly on just how much of the disk capacity is taken up, and move to a new disk when it is about 85 per cent full – the last 15 per cent or so tends to be unreliable.

■ *Always* copy important material on to a back-up disk in case of accidents *as soon as possible*.

There are numerous different systems for backing-up disks storing material that is being constantly modified, and you must work out a system that best suits your method of working. One is to keep three generations (successive versions) of the disk, often known as grandfather, father and son. You work on the son, and copy the material on to the grandfather. Alternatively, you could have a separate disk for each day of the week, updated weekly.

■ *Don't* make back-ups at the end of the day when you are tired. Make them when you are fresh, early in the morn-

ing. It is a process which demands concentration if you are not accidentally to erase the current disk or copy an ancient version.

■ If you are using your disk for accounts, you *must* follow the back-up system or 'audit-trail' agreed by your accountant. If you don't, your accounts will be useless.

■ Most people have a disk for each subject, and work directly from it. But this is often quite messy, leaving disks cluttered with half-finished texts and back-up files. A neater system is to have a working disk which acts like an in-tray. Only finished work is transferred to the appropriate master.

■ Simplicity in operation helps minimize mistakes, and saves time. If the software only takes up a third or so of the space on the disk, copy it on to every working disk. If the software is on a separate disk, you will have to load two disks every time you switch on: the software disk and then the working disk. If the software program is on each working disk, you only have to load the working disk.

■ Pay attention to lighting and positioning. If light reflects off the screen it will put extra strain on your eyes, while an uncomfortable chair will be doubly uncomfortable, since you are staring at a fixed screen for long periods.

■ Many unions recommend that you should never work at a VDU for more than four hours a day. This is sound advice – but if you cannot follow it, make sure, at least, that you break for about ten minutes in each hour.

60 *Improving your own PR*

Nobody finds it easy to look objectively at the image they project to business contacts and colleagues. It is hard to know where to start; prejudice, vanity and self-esteem get in the way. Asking other people's advice does not necessarily help: as in the deodorant advertisements, there are some things even your best friends can find it hard to tell you.

▶ You the judge

Assessing your own public image – and improving it – is easier if you start by assessing others. Pick someone you have met recently in the course of work, and write down your objective and subjective views on this person's character, demeanour and efficiency. Start your list with a few black-and-white distinctions:

> Likable . . . Unlikable
> Efficient . . . Sloppy
> Business-like . . . Amateur
> Well-dressed . . . Shabby

When the list is complete, (you may find the list of personal styles in **65** a useful starting point) analyse why you have made each judgement, and write down the reasons. Don't shy away from apparently trivial criticisms – 'He never shuts the door behind him' is as valid in this exercise as 'He can't meet deadlines' because you are trying to list impressions made at first contact.

If you have been completely honest, you will admit that many of the assessments you made were based on aspects of your victim's character and habits that have no direct bearing on the way they work.

You may indeed find that the points which carry most weight are the feelings this person left you with after the first telephone call or letter, or after your first visit to their office. *Don't, however, dismiss your judgement as unfair or 'unprofessional'.* Remind yourself that the working environment is not like the family: no one is a special case; everyone, rightly or wrongly, makes surface judgements.

Now reverse the process: work through your assessments of the other person, applying them to yourself. Looking again at Self-appraisal, **30**, may assist the process, and also take into account:

■ **Your working environment:** Decisions about the office decorations tend to be made some way up the hierarchy, but there are still some factors you control. Your own desk is one: a completely empty desk may be even worse than a chaotic one ('Does he sweep the mail into a drawer when there is a knock on the door?'). Photographs often say more than you mean them to ('Are those his children? He must be older than I thought!').

■ **Territory:** Office life is highly territorial, and an astute visitor can usually figure out who is the dominant personality simply by looking at who controls the space, and the route each individual takes when walking across the room. How will the way you position yourself fit into a visitor's perception of your role?

■ **Staff:** Improving your own P.R. does not involve just you.

Anyone who has experienced the humiliation of being passed from one secretary to another because no one has the answer to a simple query knows that the "I'll connect you to someone who can help" syndrome makes everyone in an office look bad.

61 *Getting the most from training courses*

" *LECTURER — one with his hand in your pocket, his tongue in your ear and his faith in your patience.* **"**

– Ambrose Bierce, 'The Devil's Dictionary'.

Most people go on training courses from time to time. Attitudes towards them vary from one extreme to another: some feel they are a frustrating waste of time; others find them an effective way of developing knowledge and skills. If you want to get the most from a course, you must be in control: in control of events, in control of the preparation, in control of the learning and the implementation.

Training course: worst possible scenario

Duration: *one day.*
Location: *tacky hotel.*
Tutor: *not the person originally billed, though he did at least read up on the subject last night (which is more than can be said for the delegates).*
Participants: *as with the tutor, replacements for those originally intended to come.*

The course is due to start at 9.30. Most people arrive by 9.40. While waiting, the delegates are entertained by the lecturer (who had arrived at 9.25) fighting with the tripod stand as he tries to fix all three legs at the same length. Even before he starts speaking, the delegates decide they do not like him on account of his sandals: the day is polarized from the start into 'Him and Us'. This however gives a sense of purpose to those who have none (sent on the course to avoid a cancellation fee, they have no idea why they are there).

The first talk starts falteringly at 9.57, the trainer getting his own back on the audience with an hour-long introduction.

One delegate uses this time to complete the pre-course exercise (only to discover later that he alone has completed it, and thus it cannot be used).

Things look up with lunch, delegates noisily outdoing each other with inflated descriptions of jobs, budgets and status.

In the afternoon, the trainer builds his hopes on the support of the one positive delegate. This person excites the animosity of the others, and soon the scene for the final battle is set. The enemy forces, refreshed after sleeping off their wine, choose a point of minor importance over which to conduct vicious hand-to-hand fighting for one-and-a-quarter hours.

At 4.15, the morning's late arrivals begin to leave early to catch their trains. At 5.15, everyone else leaves, taking with them the large, impressive course binders that will adorn their office bookshelves, never to be consulted.

This, of cours, is an extreme example, but you will encounter elements of the same farce on any training course. By adopting the following code, you can avoid, or exploit the situation as appropriate in order to ensure that your day, at least, is not wasted.

1 ▶ Remedies

■ Before you go, ask yourself:
- Why are you going?
- What are your personal objectives for the year?
- Does this course meet them?
- What other media or expedients could meet your needs? Books? Cassettes? Videos? Talking to experts? Working in another department? Working on a project with colleagues? A computer program? TV or radio courses?

■ How much time should you devote to training this year?

■ How will you prepare?

■ Is there pre-course work? If so, how will you plan your time to get the best out of it? (Don't do it over breakfast on the first day, or hope that others have failed to do it, too.) If there is no pre-course work, ask the course organizer for a brief resumé of the content so that you can start thinking *before the course.*

Give yourself a period of quiet before the course in order to free yourself of day-to-day worries.

■ **What 'course objectives' can you set yourself?**
- To fix your mind on key points?
- To make the best use of new contacts you will make?

■ **Have you organized things so that:**
- You will only be interrupted during talks in a real emergency?
- You will not miss any of the course?
- You will not worry about what may be going wrong at the office while you are away?
- Staff will benefit in the same way?

■ **At the course:**

- Will you maintain a positive attitude?
- Are you sure you are not going to try to criticize just because you feel like making trouble?
- Will you be assertive with trainers if you feel they are not giving you what has been promised?
- If an object of the training is to demonstrate your weaknesses, don't make excuses. Don't say: "That's not me"; say "Well if I'm like that, how can I improve?"
- Ensure you get advice on implementation of ideas.

■ **Take notes.** See **52.**

■ **Ask for further reading** and advice on further development.

2 ▶ Afterwards

■ **Assess:**
- How well you met your objectives.
- What you need to do next.
- How successful the course was: make the strengths and weaknesses known to the course organizers and your company.

■ **Constantly revise:**
- Look again at your action/key points on at least two days each week for at least the next six weeks. This virtually ensures that you will make some changes as a result of the course.

■ **Help others**
- Encourage those around you to follow the same code.

62 *Stress: the warning signs*

Stress is unavoidable, and, in moderation, it actually contributes to enjoyment. Sportsmen and women savour the stress created by the will to win, and the chance of losing; and the working day can be very boring indeed without some measure of tension.

Much of this book (and particularly sections **7, 10, 12, 14, 21, 26, 29, 33** and **34**) is directly, or indirectly, about how to keep stress to that moderate level, and about how to minimize the destructive effects when it does get out of hand. See especially **22, 23, 26, 28 and 29**.

However, stress can manifest itself in subtle and insidious ways. If you always knew when it was developing you could adapt to it better. Here are a selection of the most typical symptoms: all are capable of masking an underlying problem.

1 Psychological reactions

■ **Regression:** Stress frequently brings out childish or infantile aspects of behaviour which experience and maturity have taught us to repress. The children of especially dominant parents may become domineering and bullying. The individual with an insecure childhood sometimes responds to stress by becoming obsessively tidy, or by being neurotically anxious to perform.

Don't expect such rituals to be obviously quirky: they tend to develop so gradually you are hardly aware of them. What begins as a nagging worry about lateness turns into a feeling that unless you are sitting at your desk *exactly* 15 minutes before 9 am, the day is bound to turn out badly. Or perhaps you are finding yourself taking unusual care about locking doors, windows and drawers?

■ **Sublimation:** This is perhaps the commonest reaction to stress: "No, no, everything is fine at work; I just got promoted. The thing is, I am anxious about how my son is doing at school." The stressed individual admits to worrying, but seeks the cause of anxiety anywhere but at the root of the problem.

Anxiety caused by stress in one context is thus 'displaced'. This can be particularly damaging in a family context, because the stressed individual interferes unnecessarily in perfectly satisfactory situations; family life deteriorates as a result, and this adds another layer of stress.

■ **Worrying:** Perhaps this seems too obvious to list, but it is worth looking at exactly what the word means, and what distinguishes worry from rational and constructive analysis. Worrying is characterized by fruitless repetition of a patern of thought; whereas analysis is a thought process that leads to a conclusion; after which the problem is put aside.

■ **Fatique** is often used deliberately as a cover-up for stress: an excuse for ill-temper, neglect of tedious routines or tasks and a way of procrastinating the evil moment when the source of stress has to be confronted.

■ **Drug dependence:** chain-smoking, alcoholism, and drug abuse are obvious, but 20-a-day, one-too-many, and heavy reliance on prescription mood-altering drugs are signs of developing, or established drug-dependence that often go unnoticed.

2 ▶ Physical symptoms

Like their psychological counterparts, physical reactions to stress can take many forms, ranging from subtle to extreme. Stress can be implicated in all of the diseases in the diagram – not as sole causes, but as exacerbating factors.

Relaxation techniques described in **34, 35, 36** and **38** can all be used to combat stress.

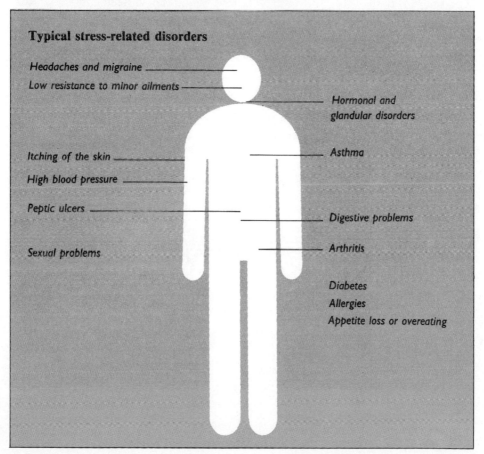

Typical stress-related disorders

- Headaches and migraine
- Low resistance to minor ailments
- Hormonal and glandular disorders
- Itching of the skin
- Asthma
- High blood pressure
- Peptic ulcers
- Digestive problems
- Sexual problems
- Arthritis
- Diabetes
- Allergies
- Appetite loss or overeating

63 | *Can you perform well* **all** *day?*

Are there times of the day at which you perform your best? Do you feel jaded at a regular time each day? Do you obey the signals your body sends you about when to eat and sleep? If you have never considered these questions, you will probably benefit from this section.

Your body is governed by a 'biological clock' which probably keeps much better time than you ever will. You need to be aware of it, take advantage of what it has to tell you; be capable of adapting if the clock has be reset.

Man is set to live on a circadian cycle of roughly 24 hours – try as you may, adjusting to any other cycle – 12 or 18 hours for example – is highly disorientating. Shiftwork, or flying across time zones, upsets your biological clock: its timing may coincide broadly with the coming and going of light, and the rise and fall of temperature, but it is controlled from within by hormone and blood sugar levels, oxygen intake rate, urine excretion and so on.

Your work rate is directly correlated to your physiological cycle. Just as you become hungry or sleepy at certain times, so you have daily peaks and troughs of acuity.

Most people are at their most accurate between 10 am and noon, with a gradual fall-off throughout the afternoon. Six am is the time of least acuity. Many people claim to be natural 'night birds' – capable of concentrating into the small hours. It is unlikely to be true. It makes sense to plan the key tasks of any day around the best two hours of the morning, and to reserve less demanding work for the afternoon, especially as the afternoon fall-off is to be compounded by drinking at lunch. The body breaks down alcohol slower between 2 am and 2 pm, so the effects of drink take longer to wear off between these hours.

 Fast or slow?

Although everyone must in theory live by a 24-hour cycle, it seems that many people's body clocks run fast or slow compared with the standard.

If, for instance, you tend to find rising an ordeal, but can stay awake easily until late at night, your body clock would be considered slow. There is probably nothing you can do about the sleep deficit built up in this way, except to be aware of it and pace yourself accordingly. The weekend lie-in is, for such people, more a necessity than a luxury.

If you tend to be sleepy early in the evening, and can wake early in the morning with little trouble, your body clock probably runs fast. This sounds much more convenient than a slow internal clock. But in fact such people are continually under pressure from the environment: their body feels the day should be coming to end, whereas environmental factors such as light and temperature suggest that it still has plenty of time to run. Some psychological tests indicate that people adjusted in this way are shyer and more anxious than their fast clock counterparts. The sleep deficit built up by these people is best compensated by an afternoon nap or occasionally going to bed early.

64 *The art of taking risks*

John Robinson, director of an ailing computer software company, was introduced at a party to a man who impressed him as a brilliant computer scientist – a software whizz kid with a near-legendary reputation for writing financial management programmes. In particular, he had written a mathematical model of the commodities market for his previous company, which had risen from an 'also ran' to number two in its field

However, as the evening wore on, John began to see another aspect of the computer scientist's reputation: his drinking.

The boffin sank into an alcoholic fug and had to be sent home in a taxi.

But before the mist descended, the two had an interesting conversation: the scientist revealed that his current contract was shortly to expire, and that he was open to offers.

On the way home, John tried to weigh the benefits of taking on the scientist. If he came up with the goods, John would be hailed as the saviour of his ailing firm. If the drinking got worse, John could see himself being dragged down with him. Would the risk be justified?

1 ▸ Calcultated risk

The simple answer is that risk is never justified – unless it is calculated. You should no more dream of taking a business risk than overtaking on a blind corner. You must be able to calculate the chances: you don't take your passenger's word that the road ahead is sufficiently clear for overtaking; you judge for yourself; likewise in business. Never take a risk on the basis of received information.

You must therefore ask, and answer, all the crucial questions for yourself. How long do you have to wait before the pay-off? When the gamble succeeds, will anyone remember that it was you who put your neck on the block? In concrete terms, such as cash, can you estimate the maximum and minimum rewards? Can you compare their levels to others achieved by not taking the risk?

2 ▸ Calculating the odds

The consequences of failure is the last factor to consider, and the most difficult. Will you personally be marked if the gamble fails? How damaging is failure like to be?

In assessing the consequences of failure, attitude is the key. Identify your fears at the outset, and admit to yourself what frightens you most. Imagine the 'worst case scenario' and decide whether it would be a total disaster, or just a setback.

If the consequences of failure are disaster, ninety-nine times out of a hundred you should not take the risk.

Usually, though, failure means no more than a temporary setback; but have you risked company money recently, and failed? If so . . .

3 ▸ Laying off the odds

When you are overtaking on a short straight stretch of road, you don't hang back. You change down and stamp on the accelerator. Likewise, you must be capable of total commitment once a risk venture is under way.

Conversely, you must know where you can pull back and cut your losses. Identify these points at the outset.

Did John Robinson hire the scientist? After introducing the scientist to a fellow director, John raised the matter at the next board meeting, taking the opportunity to hint at the man's weakness for the bottle. Then he suggested that the board offer a short-term consultancy contract linked to results and renewable six months hence. The scientist's retainer was to be paid in the usual way, but he was also to get a results-linked bonus if his software products did well.

John got it right: the incentive alone was enough to keep him off the bottle.

65 *Know your personal style*

Everyone has different styles or, to be precise, a combination of styles; and everyone can improve on them. Use this section to understand your preferred styles and to identify on which aspects of style you need to concentrate.

When you are an infant, you learn how to get what you want. Some learn that the only way to get what they want is to scream. Others learn the opposite: that screaming leads to a painful experience, and for them the only way is to develop a low profile.

These contrasting styles become second-nature; they are modified by the process of growing up, but essentially, some people still 'scream' for things as adults; just as others keep a relentlessly low profile.

These extremes are, of course, hopelessly inadequate for dealing with the diverse types of people and circumstance that come the way of the average adult. Most people have a range of styles at their disposal which I find helpful to break down into four basic types. At one end of the spectrum is, of course, the adult equivalent of screaming – 'telling and being forceful'; at the other is the equivalent of the low-profile approach – 'delegating/avoiding'.

Telling/being forceful

When you first come into contact with people, you need to tell them exactly where they stand. Later, you may also need to 'tell' some people 'off'. Lack of clear direction from yourself is potentially demotivating; at times you need to be able to spell things out.

Selling/manipulating

It is a poor use of your time, and insulting to colleagues, to 'tell' all the time. You need to persuade people to develop their own initiative; plant your ideas in other people's minds; to say "Do you think it would be a good idea if you went to visit the design department next week?", rather than "Go there on Wednesday morning." You are still getting your way, but others are invited to believe they have some choice in the matter. This style naturally develops other people's confidence in themselves; the next stage follows it naturally.

Accommodating/participating

The first two styles are about you getting it all your own way. However there comes a stage in every working relationship when the other side has developed a degree of self-confidence. In response, you need a more open style: one that invites contributions. You need to be prepared to adapt your own plans when others come up with potential improvements. They cannot do this unless you encourage participation.

Delegating/avoiding

When colleagues/sub-ordinates have really got on top of their jobs, you need to know how to stand aside. This has the obvious benefit of reducing pressure on your time, and it motivates others to develop more control over their lives. Once you have managed to stand aside, you have to know how to resist the temptation to interfere.

 Advantages and disadvantages of each style

Each style is potentially useful, but each has its negative aspects.

	Advantages	**Disadvantages**
Telling:	*Confident* *Assured* *Unwavering* *Clear instructions*	*Pig-headed* *Domineering* *Stubborn* *Inflexible* *Insensitive*
Selling:	*Confidence-building* *Persuasive*	*Cynical* *Transparent* *Time-consuming* *Long-winded* *Not direct enough* *Selling for the sake of it*
Accommodating:	*Interested in and* *respectful of others* *Wide range of ideas gathered* *Good for two-way* *communications*	*Blowing with the wind* *Uncertain* *Directionless* *Time-consuming*
Avoiding:	*Trusting* *Able to manage large* *projects* *Good developer of people*	*Abdicating responsibility* *Responsibility* *Silent at meetings* *Insular*

2 ▶ Natural style

Some of these styles will come more naturally to you than others. Try to asess which are your instinctive styles, the ones that you find no difficulty in using and conversely the ones that you have to try hardest to use. In reality, you won't have just one style; you will operate by combining the styles.

	Advantages	**Disadvantages**
Tell/sell	*Good for people* *joining a team –* *they know where* *stand*	*Claustrophobic, does not* *help people to develop* *Fearful of losing* *Fearful of seeming* *weak* *Disdainful of others'* *ideas*
Sell/accommodate:	*Encourages* *others, a builder*	*Dislikes telling people* *off – might rock the boat* *Cannot resist getting involved* *Your group sometimes* *appears cliquish to outsiders*

Accommodate/avoid:	Trusting of others Willing to listen Patient with problems	Too sensitive Too trusting of others Not direct enough Reactive rather than proactive (see 14)
Tell/avoid	Strong, yet trusting boss Likely to protect trusted colleagues	Loner Will tell people once only
	Gives clear direction, then leaves alone	Will not tolerate fools No patience or skill to help people develop

 How to develop your weakest style

All styles are necessary. Pick out your weakest one and try to build it up.

■ **Tell:** Are you over-sensitive to how others will react if you 'tell' them? Try to hedge your bets here, and to trust to sensitivity to get you out of trouble.

■ **Sell:** Do you think manipulation is a dirty word? Or do you tend to see arguments (of which you have more than your fair share) in terms of black and white? Try and see why the other side is motivated to take their particular line; and seek out common ground. Sell the benefits of your ideas:

this is not a sign of weakness, it is a step towards *effectiveness*.

■ **Accommodate:** Do you really think you are 100 per cent right all the time? Or do you fear being shown up as inadequate if you ask others for their views? Open up your meetings; if you are asking the questions, you are in control anyway; listen to the responses – they may contain free advice.

■ **Avoid:** Can you try talking less? Don't always feel you have to have to have your say. Your staff will never develop skills that will benefit you if you don't let them learn.

Now see section **67**.

		WORKING WITH		C O N T R O L L I N G
T R U S T I N G	PARTICIPATE/ ACCOMMODATE		SELL/ MANIPULATE	
	DELEGATE/ AVOID		TELL/ FORCEFUL	
		SELF-RELIANT		

66 *Do you make things happen?*

Y ou want to make things happen. If you could make things happen fast and effectively, you would have more time to make even more things happen.

When things happen as you predict, you feel good. Occasionally, things happen simply as a result of good luck; but most of the time you have to make them happen.

Try analysing your attitude to making things happen:

1 ▶ Ten ways of making things happen

Once you know what you want to achieve, use the steps below to ensure that you succeed.

■ **Be willing to feel temporarily uncomfortable.** Don't try and escape from problems. They always come home to roost, even if only by weighing on your conscience.

■ **See disagreements objectively.** Don't get drawn into emotional encounters or allow disagreements to develop into a battle of wills, a war of attrition. Try and find common ground. Persist in developing this common ground to achieve at least part of what you want. If someone says "No", don't take it as final. Ask why: seek a compromise.

■ **Take control of situations before you are asked.** You don't feel comfortable in leaderless groups, nor does anyone else. You will help everyone concerned by taking responsibility rather than waiting for it to be thrust on you.

Do you:
■ Expect things to happen?

■ Expect people to do what you ask of them?
■ Treat other people more gently than yourself?
■ Want other people to feel comfortable and cosy?
■ Have a benign view of other people?
■ Find other people don't do what you ask of them?
■ Tend to dream about things happening rather than making them happen?

■ Like to feel comfortable and cosy?
■ Prefer to keep a low profile?

■ Feel that making people do things is imposing on their liberty?
■ Do what others tell you to do?
■ Have a grudge against bullies, but do what they tell you?

■ Feel you don't have the power to get things done?

■ Fear that asking people to do things risks hearing "No"?
■ Need a more powerful position before making things happen?

■ Feel powerless in the company of some personalities?

■ Wait to be asked to take control?

■ Not use your power unless you are irritated?

■ Feel that power is often abused by some people?

■ Expecting things to happen is of course the appropriately positive approach. By anticipating failure, you invite it. Don't programme yourself to fail. Expect to succeed; take setbacks as only a battle lost not the whole war.

■ **See your instructions through to the end.** You don't have to be irritating when checking up on how people are progressing with tasks you have delegated. Don't say "Have you done it?", say "How is it going?"in a sympathetic manner that shows your concern with *their* feelings, and *their* progress, rather than from impatience to see it done. People usually do what you inspect, or enquire about. If they don't think you will check up, why should they bother? See also **9, 84** and **85.**

■ Remember that **people respect strength.** Do you prefer weak or strong people? Saying "No" can be constructive rather than obstructive.

■ **Believe in your own power.** Few people are totally powerless; remind yourself of your strengths, and think how you can use them. Remember that a successful salesman can start with no power at all over a customer, but may still make a sale.

■ **Don't be overawed by strong personalities.** Strong personalities often make others feel small. If this happens to you, it is not enough simply to remind yourself of your skills and past achievements. You need, in addition, a cool approach. Give away as little information about yourself as possible. Allow the strong personality to do most, if not all of the talking. Indeed, try to get them, by your reticience, to talk too much. People who talk too much normally give away something interesting. Make use of silence – see **40.** Be unresponsive, without being sullen. Although a strong personality probably will not show any sign of disturbance at these tactics, they will have an undermining effect. Anyone who seeks to dominate overwhelmingly can only do so in the long run by understanding what motivates their 'victim'. Deny them that knowledge.

■ **Overcome 'insurmountable' problems.** Some very humble people achieve great things. Don't brood on problems, try to solve them. If you try you might succeed, if you don't you won't. Give yourself the luxury of listing creative, even ridiculous ways round a problem. Choose one and give it a try.

■ **Have a better view of people who make things happen.** If you have bad feelings about them, reconsider; or at least think of someone you know or have heard of who shapes events, and who does it in an acceptable manner. What do they do that you don't? Why not risk using one of the skills they use?

67 *Other people's style*

This section is the counterpart to **65 – What is your personal style?** In order to have productive working relationships you need not just a run-of-the-mill understanding, but real insight into how your boss, colleagues or staff are likely to react in situations. How, for instance, will your boss treat a new idea? Will your assistant see a long project through to the end?

Use these outlines to identify likely responses.

1 Superiors

The four extreme types outlined here are combinations of the Tell/Sell model described in 65. Which one is your boss?

The controller
An excellent boss in your early days at a job – someone who will spell out clearly what he or she wants. This is a management style helpful for developing your confidence in yourself; but the condition is always that you work on things your boss chooses, not on your own ideas.

This type of boss does not often ask for your opinion: "Next month we will look at that idea of yours; in the meantime can you . . . ?"

He or she feels that asking for ideas is long-winded, a waste of time because staff are not as bright as them. They particularly fear losing control of situations and therefore they try to dominate meetings.

You need to:
– Reassure them that they have ultimate control.
– Minimize any threat to them in your new ideas.
– Negotiate more freedom.

– Persuade them that meetings need not be a waste of time.
– Remind them that if people working for them really are not up to standard, then more delegation is the quickest way of developing them.
– Tell them how respected they are.

The wheeler-dealer
Puts much emphasis on team leadership and team work. "I motivate my team down at the pub, we're a closely knit group." Very strong on building confidence within the team; holds regular meetings to gather ideas which they will act upon.

This type of manager can seem cliquish to new starters. He or she sees no need to explain things at the start. "We all know the routine; we're very open here; you'll soon pick it up." They often spend too much time persuading people instead of coming to the point and being direct. Delegating is another weakness: they cannot stand back.

You need to:
– Demonstrate that you would rather they were more direct with you. You need to indicate that knowing where you stand would not make you dislike them.
– Remind them that the team will be more successful if it is allowed more independence.
– Tell them how popular they are.

The truster
"My people are intelligent, I wouldn't insult them by telling them how to do things, and certainly wouldn't try manipulating them."

Here is someone who is too sensitive to their staff. An excellent manager, with a listening ear and sincerely intent on giving freedom to act; but you do sometimes wish you were told where you stood. "In a crisis we all stand around looking for direction."

The truster keeps too low a profile with new staff and is not clearly identified with required standards of work. He or she can fear that speaking critically will create unpleasantness: unpleasantness which, incidentally, they have the sensitivity to handle. You need to:
- Request more direction.
- Explain that intelligent people know they are wrong sometimes and need criticism.
- Tell them you would appreciate some occasional jollying along when you are flagging.

The independent
Here is someone who gives clear direction, but only once. If you don't listen first time, you will not get a repeat. "Well, I have an indifferent team; I'll tell people once but I haven't got the time to waste telling them the same thing over and over again." In other words, they lack the skill and patience to coax people through the learning stages of a job. The independent expects people to motivate themselves. Those who are self-sufficient they leave alone, only giving firm direction when needed. You need to:
- Weather their irritation if you do go back for clarification.
- Assure them that you want to stand on your own feet.
- Show how spending more time with the team could pay dividends.

2 ▶ Subordinates

When you find someone who works for you irritating, and when you cannot get them to do what you want, it is healthy to blame yourself; but you should also consider whether they are stuck or blocked at a particular stage of their development.

Is it, for example:

First stage block
Do they need to be told everything? When you say "Don't you think it would be a good idea if you . . . .?" do they reply "Yes", then do nothing?

Are you sure you made a good recruitment decision?

Second stage block
You can persuade them to do things, but if you ask them in for an idea generating session, the only ideas generated are your own. They sit in silence until you come up with something and then say "Oh, that's a good idea."

Third stage block
The most common blockage of all. This type is happy to come up with ideas, but when you say "That's a good idea, why don't you go away and do something with it?" they dodge the issue. "Well, it's not really up to me, is it? I thought you just wanted ideas." They are in effect loading work on to you, rather than helping.

Motivating others

There is no trick to motivating other people; no secret formula known only to a few. True, the Pied Piper of Hamlyn had a special talent for leadership, as did Adolf Hitler, and you will always come across people with unusual magnetism. Such special cases are usually red-herrings: motivating others is essentially a down-to-earth, easy-to-learn skill; a matter of behaving in such a way that people are likely to want to help you.

 1 What demotivates you?

None of us can work at our top performance level all the time. Try listing what makes you feel less willing to work hard; what 'switches you off'. Then compare your list with the examples below, all of which are contributed by people on my courses.

'Don't feel very well.'

'Working in a noisy office.'

'When I've got a worry on my mind.'

'When I've got too much work to do.'

'When work is repetitious.'

'When I don't know why I'm supposed to be doing something.'

'When I don't know how I'm going to be judged – what standards I'm working to.'

'When I feel that there's no chance to develop further.'

'When I keep failing.'

'When I don't know what's going on.'

'Nobody ever thanks me.'

'No one ever asks my opinion.'

'When I'm new in a group.'

'When I'm bored.'

'When a job isn't explained properly.'

'When I'm a small cog in a large wheel and feel insignificant.'

'When I haven't been properly trained.'

'When people keep criticizing me.'

'When there's a bad atmosphere about.'

'When I'm not criticized but deserve to be.'

'When I don't like the people around me.'

 2 There really is no trick . . .

I have asked the demotivation question to thousands of people and the answers I receive are always combinations of the list above. Try it on other people you know; whatever their job, it is bound to be a similar set of answers.

Every time they give those answers, they are telling you how to motivate others.

If you could ensure that none of your subordinates or colleagues ever have to suffer these irritants, or, if they are beyond your control, that you were able to limit their damage, then you would be the perfect motivator.

3 ▶ Firm and fair

Firmness and fairness are the two basic ingredients required to ensure the irritants in .1 do not occur.

Be firm enough to tell people what they ought to be doing, how to do it, what standards you expect and by when you expect it done. Be fair enough to spend time talking to people. Tell them how they are doing, listen to their problems and think about their future.

Be firm enough to:

■ **Give clear direction.** Often through lack of time, or lack of thought for others, you will not describe what you want done clearly enough. Some people feel that it is an insult to intelligence to spell out what ought to be done. This is not usually the case. Everyone needs a simple structure to which they can work and no set of instructions, especially for a complex undertaking, can be clear unless they are simplified. But you must distinguish between the need to give clear direction and the method of giving it. You will obviously switch people off if you talk to them as if they are educationally subnormal.

Think about the last job you asked somebody to do for you that was completed unsatisfactorily. Did you explain it clearly?

Take a few extra moments to put the job in perspective, to explain how it fits into their future, what benefit they might derive, like learning a new skill or meeting some new people. Put yourself in their shoes: make yourself identify a benefit for the person who is going to help you; suggest it, deferentially, don't sell it too hard: people like to think they know best what is good for them.

■ **Ensure it can be achieved.** In moments of panic it is all too easy to give somebody an impossible task. You don't have to think out every detail, but you do have to think about what might go wrong. Will it be a bank holiday in France? Will no one be in the Paris office? Will they have enough money to pay for spare parts? Apologizing afterwards does not make up for the frustration of working hard on a task which cannot be completed due to the boss's oversight. It usually means subordinates are less enthusiastic next time you ask for something to be done.

■ **State the standards.** Why do you want it done? Resist saying "As soon as you can", say instead by what time and on which day. Also be scrupulous about how much they may spend. I once met a manager in an airline whose unclear standards led to his persuasive secretary organizing a special flight to take a document abroad. Her boss blamed her for over-reacting, but ultimately it was his fault for not giving clear spending limits. Try and define the quality of work you expect. Specify exactly how much detail is required.

■ **Stretch people.** Nobody likes being bored, so don't expect to gain popularity by giving people undemanding jobs. Equally, don't stress subordinates by failing to consider whether they have the time and the skill to complete the task.

■ **Let people control something.** People deprived of all control over their time or the way they do a job soon become frustrated and/or lose interest; sometimes they will buck the system altogether to regain control.

Set the important parameters ▶

68

yourself, then let people choose how they will go about organizing themselves. Make sure you delegate authority as well as responsibility. Don't, for example, ask someone to gather information for you without their having authority from you.

■ **Create variety.** Monotony is an insidious demotivator. As far as possible, swap jobs around. Ensure that the essential but boring jobs are done by a variety of people. Give some thought to making dull jobs more interesting. But remember that a boring job to you may be stimulating to somebody else. Find out who likes what.

■ **Communicate regularly.** Don't let people have to say "We hear things on the grapevine long before we're told officially." Make it your duty to tell people around you what is going on *before* they can hear it from anybody else. Make sure others tell you what is happening so that you can pass it on. A manager once told me: "There are only two problems with this place. People above me never tell me what's going on, yet people below me keep asking for piffling bits of information that should be obvious to them."

Expect to be told, and expect to tell, and you will kill off the grapevine.

Be fair enough to:

■ **Give recognition.** Never mind who gets the credit. Say thank you for work done, even if you have some minor criticisms. Don't only speak to people when you want them to do things for you. Notice other people around you as they go about their work. Asking "How are you?" (and waiting for the answer) helps others to feel part of the team.

■ **Encourage participation.** Ask for other people's opinions and ideas. This not only draws people into the team, but makes it probable they will suggest improvements on your plans from time to time. If people feel they are involved, their commitment will rise. You obviously have to make sure that useful suggestions from below are implemented, and seen to be implemented.

■ **Train and develop people.** Take opportunities to ensure that people regularly learn new skills. Some subordinates may not want to go further, but everyone likes to learn more about other areas of their organization, its new directions and new products or services. Let people know you are thinking about this and talk about it with them.

■ **Tell people how they have done.** As soon as possible after a job is complete, tell people what they did well and what they did badly. *Don't do one or the other, do both*. If you only praise, this becomes cloying. Everyone knows they are not perfect and many would suspect that behind their back you say something else. If you only critize, they will lose respect for themsleves and possibly you too.

Encourage people to work on their strengths and not to become self-satisfied. Explain how their weaknesses let them down. Get them to tell you how they are going to improve.

Go down the list above and pick out the one area in which you feel you are weakest. Start putting this right today.

See also section **86 – Delegating Well**.

69 *Persuasion – against the odds*

You don't have executive authority over your boss; and you probably can't give orders to your husband, wife, neighbour, nor difficult colleagues either. Most days of your life, though, situations arise in which you want to persuade them to change their attitudes or actions. You can't 'tell' them (see **65**); so you have to 'sell' them.

1 ▶ Selling is not a dirty verb

The art of selling is too often associated with the negative aspects of manipulation: salesmen are seen as inhabiting a sinister, secret world full of tricks which act like anaesthetic on the innocent customer. Some people approach selling in this way; some of them are in prison.

Most successful persuaders are, however, decent men and women whose motives are no more sinister than to provide a service to others and a living for themselves. Some of the best business training is given to salesmen, but there are many more, in addition to full-time sales people, who would benefit from these skills. This section, and the following eight, outline the basics of salesmanship. All are cornerstones of achievement.

2 ▶ Raise your standards

A year ago you tried to persuade a colleague to take a different approach: you saw that he was on a course for disaster. You argued your case, became irritated with his intransigence, and gave up.

A year later, someone reports to you that disaster did strike and that business has suffered. "I told him a year ago this would happen", you say. How would you take it if the response

to your comment was "Oh, so it's partly your fault for not persuading him"? You would probably resent it. But should you?

If you really believed in your advice, perhaps you had a *duty* not merely to give advice but to persuade the colleague to take it. Put it another way: would you not prefer a doctor who puts himself out to persuade you to take advice when it is essential to your well-being? Persuading does not have to involve pleading or tricking; putting a point of view in such a way that the customer takes the best course of action for himself or herself is more effective, and more ethical.

3 ▶ Symptoms of failure

> *"You don't know my boss, I've tried 20 times to persuade her."*

– Probably 20 times in the same way: the wrong way. It is not the effort that counts, it is results. Use more ingenuity.

> *"I've spoken to them about it; I'm hopeful they'll change."*

You have done all the spade work, but not taken it the final step and asked for commitment. See **76.** It has been left hanging.

> *"I've argued my case."*

Reflect on past experience, and consider how productive you have found arguments to be. Arguments involve two points of view. Like parallel railway lines, they tend to meet only when there is a nasty accident.

> *"I give up."*

Stamina and persistence are essential. Easier said than done, of course, but see **38** and **96** for thoughts on recovering from setbacks.

> *"He can come and see me if he wants to talk."*

'I'm staying here, determined to deny myself the opportunity persuade.'

> *"I'm too busy to talk it over."*

Is it really that unimportant?

 Basic skills of persuasion

The key is a mixture of sensitivity and firmness:

Sensitive enough to:
- Listen.
- Have patience.
- Put yourself into the other side's shoes.

Firm enough to:
- Keep moving the discussion forward.
- Keep to the point.
- Spell out the benefits of your case clearly.
- Ask for, and gain, agreement.
- Overcome objections.

5 **The stages of persuasion**

When you successfully sell an idea to someone, you will almost always have gone through each of the steps listed below. You may not be conscious of all of them, and some of them you may have given little attention; but somehow you will have gone through them. Think of a recent failure: you should be able to identify the step that let you down.

Set objectives.

Positive attitude, the desire and belief to succeed.

Identify decision-makers and those who will influence them. Know how receptive they are likely to be.

Build rapport, get on the same wavelength. Build trust and confidence.

Gain an element of control over the meeting.

Discover the personal and organizational needs of those to whom you are speaking.

Relate your case to meeting their needs.

Ask for agreement.

If you are rejected, don't necessarily give up.

The steps follow the same sequence every time; some will take much longer than others to pass through; each is explained in much greater detail in the sections that follow.

70 *Preparing for persuasion*

I sometimes worry that I am reminding people of the obvious when I say that before going into any meeting with the intent to persuade, you must prepare by asking two questions of yourself: 'What exactly do I want to achieve?' and 'Do I believe I can achieve this?'

Yet remarkably few salesmen can honestly admit that they make the questions a habit. Surprisingly often I am told by a salesman that deciding such issues in advance "cramps their style", or that they "like the flexibility of an open-ended discussion." I suspect that this attitude is one of the surest signs of an average salesman. The most successful persuaders can tell you clearly the range of their objectives before the sales pitch; indeed they have probably written them down. The questions are not just important in themselves; the art of *clearing the mind* on these two intimately related issues is a kind of flexing of the muscles; rehearsing the answers to the questions leaves the mind free to cope with the complexities of communicating with the person to be persuaded. It is, incidentally, not an attitude of total commitment or 'do or die', like the kamikazi pilot's: it is a positive, balanced attitude, tilted towards success.

David McGregor, a production department cost controller, had an idea that would increase productivity and profit margin on a certain component produced by his engineering company. It did, however, involve persuading his boss to take on an extra member of staff. He had thought about the feasibility for months; but he had not thought at all about the tactics of winning his case.

He knew that his boss did not want to increase the head count for the department, although he was always looking for ways of increasing profit. McGregor did not like his boss; he found him "bigoted and arrogant".

Just before he went in to try out his idea, McGregor had a 'helpful' pint with two colleagues. "I know what's going to happen. He'll agree to the idea, but with me doing the extra work; he won't take on the extra person; he's impossible."

McGregor shuffled into the meeting and then stumbled on to the subject. At the first mention of an extra person, a frown appeared on his boss's face. McGregor's left brain immediately started chattering: 'Failed again. He's the worst boss I've ever had. This company is pathetic.' He retreated as quickly as possible, a bitter man: bitter with himself.

His boss felt pleased that he had effectively guarded the company's guidelines on manpower levels. And he also felt confirmed in his view that McGregor was essentially a backroom person with plenty of ideas, but no management potential.

The idea was never implemented. Everyone in the company lost out.

▶ Why did McGregor fail?

■ His objective *looked* clear – but in fact it was not properly *rehearsed*; it was clumsy. Knowing the nature of his ▶

▶ boss, he should have worked out what was the *least* that he would have settled for: an opportunity, perhaps, to present his case in more detail with others sitting in as well as his boss? Instead, he had rehearsed only the best possible outcome: instant agreement.

■ As a result of the above, he had programmed himself for failure – a program reinforced by his negative attitude towards his boss.

As it was, he did not really start thinking through his objective until he was in the middle of his sticky meeting. Under such circumstances, objectives usually focus on personal survival. The frown on his boss's face told him that his idea was not worth his boss's disapproval; his 'best' objective suddenly became to get out alive.

2 ▶ Room for manoeuvre

'Least' and 'best' objectives take the win/lose out of situations. They give you room for manoeuvre without compromising your main aim. McGregor could have gone in and asked for his idea to be considered at a second, more democratically composed meeting.

Least and best objectives help you:

■ Plan.

■ Steer yourself through a meeting and keep it to *your* objectives.

■ Identify opportunities in the conversation that will help your case (and ignore red herrings).

■ Review your success afterwards.

Writing down 'least' and 'best' helps you to be clear about them; just attempting to remember them means they remain vague.

Review 'least' and 'best' regularly, asking whether you have set them too high or too low.

3 ▶ A positive frame of mind

■ **Belief:** Don't arrange a meeting until you can see at least a glimmer of likely success. Then condition yourself to *expect* it, but not to *count on* it.

■ **Don't describe failure to yourself:** it makes your left brain say 'Told you so' at the first sign of difficulty.

■ **Desire:** Do you really want to succeed? Are you so busy that life would be easier if you failed? If so, you may subconsciously contrive failure. If necessary, re-plan your workload before you go to the meeting.

■ **Do you dislike the person you are attempting to persuade?** Would persuading them mean you would have to work alongside them? If so: either try to see their positive points so as to increase your tolerance of them; or, if you cannot, and the issue is important, should you consider getting someone else to go in your place?

71 *Identifying decision-makers*

You have read **69** and **70**. Now you are ready to actually present your case. But are you going to present it to someone who can decide?

No one wants to spend time with people, however good at listening, who have no authority to decide or to buy. Failing to speak to a decision-maker means that you are, in effect, training someone else to do your selling for you; each meeting becomes not only a sales operation but a training course. Non-decision-makers may put over your case reasonably well, but how will they handle objections?

1 Who are the decision makers?

People with the budget, the authority and the ability to say "yes" to your case: but don't, using this bald definition, discount *ability* to decide. You have almost certainly met directors who have the authority but not the guts to decide; and conversely young turks who wring every ounce from their limited authority.

For complicated proposals, there are usually several decision-makers in an organization of any size: someone who controls the budget, a production department which must have its say over quality, a sales force which will determine the quantity, an accountant who can dictate payment terms. Then there may be the board as a final hurdle. These are the 'seen' decision-makers. To them you must add the unseen – the influencers.

Influencers can be within an organization, or outside. They are people whose council is taken because of their intellect, power or friendship. If you want to succeed in getting proposals accepted, you must recognize and foster such people. A simple outline of your argument to an influencer 'for your information only' can be half the battle won.

■ **Take a look at the whole organization structure.** However well you know it, a fresh look can make you concentrate on who might be the key people for *this* proposal.

■ **Probe.** If you are unsure you are talking to a decision-maker, say "If you're happy with the idea, what's the next stage?" If you hear "Well, of course it's not really up to me, you can save your breath," start looking again.

■ **Spot the rising stars.** In all organizations, people go in and out of favour. Someone who enjoys current favour, but who cannot say "Yes", may still be a useful person to have on your side.

2 Is your boss a decision-maker?

Some tell-tale signs that he/she is not:

■ **He/she is rude about his/her boss:** "I can't do anything about your salary/new desk/holiday entitlement. I'm sorry, I tried as hard as I can."

■ **He/she is an envoy.** "Accounts have asked us to present these figures again. We'd better do it to keep them quiet – even though they'll probably never use them." This means, in effect, that your boss lacks the decisiveness to tell accounts to stop wasting his/her department's time.

■ **The Black Hole:** "Leave it with me, we'll talk about it later", may well be someone with the authority and budget who is too disorganized to make decisions. You must either persuade them to be a decision-maker, or go to someone who can apply pressure.

72 *Building rapport*

S peaking to deaf ears is not a pro-
fitable or pleasant way to spend
your time. You want to know that your
message is being received. You need to
develop rapport; mutual confidence
which will enable both you and the
other side to communicate honestly
and openly.

Yet building rapport is often treated
as a luxury to be discarded in moments
of panic. Some think it is a specialist
skill – the province of the silver-
tongued. But:

■ Do you plunge into meetings without
the initial courtesies that are good
manners and make you more likely to
succeed?

■ Are you the boss who, in a hurry,
bursts into your assistant's office blurting out staccato instructions (no time
even to use complete sentences), then
dashes out again? Have you ever looked back to see how puzzled is the person you left behind? *Result:* strong
possibility of a poorly completed job.

■ Are you the friend who blurts out
the particular problem on your mind
without checking how your listener is
feeling? *Result:* acute embarrassment
when you hear later that they were har-
bouring an even worse crisis; you gain
a reputation for being self-centred.

■ Are you the person who telephones
someone, rushing straight into your
topic without checking first whether
they can talk? *Result:* at the first
pause, a stiff voice says "I'm in a
meeting". The more intimate the topic,
the more likely it has been broadcast
over the conference facility.

Do you also find that when you are
asked by a sceptic to explain yourself,
they sometimes appear even more
bored or doubtful at the end than the
beginning?

What you actually said in all these
cases is less likely to have been the
cause of the communication block than
the manner in which you launched into
the exchange.

Compared with the brain, computers
are simple. Yet it is impossible to link
two different computers unless they
share a common 'language', and use a
modem. Human beings need similar
aids to communication.

Jot down which words you connect
with the term 'holiday'; then 'marketing'; then 'politics'. Now ask other
people to do the same. It is very unlikely that you will get the three same
answers.

Pick any three objects around you.
Jot down which you see as the odd-
one-out and write down your reason.
Offer the same choice to others and ask
for their reasons. You will eventually
get each item chosen as the odd-one-
out, and the reasons will vary
considerably.

Most people cherish the fact that
humans are individuals and dislike
governments, organizations and other
individuals who ignore this. Yet the examples above illustrate that we all have
a tendency to expect others to think as
we do; that we expect people to be
automatically receptive to our ideas,
and to take them in at the same speed
as we explain them.

Before reading the sub-section opposite, have a look at **78 – Understanding body language.** The first signs of
failure to build rapport are often to be
seen in posture and facial expression.
Worse, some of us – even at the best of
times – are capable of irritation when
people fail to grasp our meaning as
and when we speak.

▶ Steps to better rapport

You don't need to be a psychologist or possess special gifts. You already possess this talent: all you need to do is consciously use it in every encounter, whatever the pressure.

■ **Do more asking:**
"Can you talk?"
"How are you?
- and listening:
" – Oh, when's a good time to catch you?"
" – I'm sorry to hear that, is it better now?"

■ **Do more putting yourself into their shoes.**

■ **Use the motivation checklist** in section **68**. Make it a priority.

■ **Don't feel vulnerable,** or be in a hurry; don't feel negative about yourself.

■ **Sympathize** with the other side's cause, even if you are going on to persuade them of an opposite position. Whatever your case, you still need to understand why their brain is thinking as it does.

■ **Don't make definite statements of opinion early in an encounter.**

■ **Do and say things that will develop trust** and confidence in you. Smile.

- Don't repress your natural inclination to care about other people, and be interested in them. *It is not unbusinesslike.*

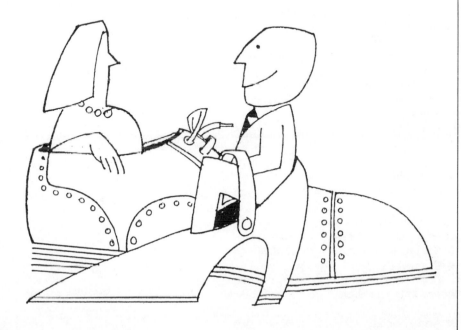

73 *Controlling conversations*

Mismanaged conversations are one of the most insidious barriers to persuading others and to getting things done: not just a waste of time in themselves, but a sure way of diffusing thought about objectives. This section is about never coming away from a conversation or a sales pitch with the feeling that more would have been achieved had the encounter never taken place.

The other party may be just as much at fault as you, even totally at fault; but the means of effectively managing conversations can be – must be – yours. In this area, there are no prizes unless you take the initiative.

> He came in, shoulders drooping, eyes moving from carpet to ceiling.
>
> She thought: *He's either leaving, or he's been sacked.*
>
> He said: "How are you?"
>
> She said: "All right." She meant: "Get to the point."
>
> He said: "Good, that's very good. Fine." He froze. He thought, *I've blown it.*
>
> She thought: *He's blown it.*
>
> He said: "Will you marry me?"
>
> She said: . . .

An absurd example, perhaps, of how not to obtain a conversational goal. The key point, though, is that although he was under pressure, this was no real excuse for failing. Things worth having always carry a price, and that price often includes uncomfortable dealings with other people.

Poor conversational control means, in the long run that:

■ Some, or all, of your ideas will not be agreed.

■ You are less and less use to friends; you cannot help them get to the root of their problems – their anxiety paralyzes you.

■ You do plenty of talking, but get nowhere.

'Control' in this context does not mean bossy domination. It means coming out of an exchange with a good result, or at least on equal terms. 'Good result' means anything from prevailing with your own point of view to gaining a fair hearing or, at least, respect.

The five ways of controlling conversation listed opposite are well known to us all, indeed they are more or less innate skills. But very few people practise them deliberately; most forget they exist when they need them most. In order to summon them more readily when needed, you may find it helpful to memorize the simple visual reminder below.

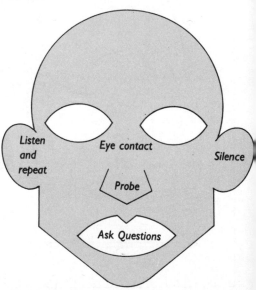

Listen and repeat

Eye contact

Silence

Probe

Ask Questions

> **Five techniques for controlling conversation**

■ **Establish eye contact.** Hypnotists gain control via the eyes. You don't have to be a hypnotist, but ensure you gain eye contact at least at the end of making a point or asking a question. Develop more eye contact while listening.

■ **Ask questions.** When you are nervous, or too sure of yourself, you are likely either to talk too much or to dry up. The moment you ask a question, two changes occur:
– You gain the chance to learn something, if only about the other side's attitude.
– You gain control; it may be momentary control, but however good the other side may be at fielding your question, or ignoring it, their self-possession suffers a degree of setback, and you have the chance to re-establish your edge.

■ **Probe.** Being sensitive to the other side's finer feelings is good, but don't overdo it. Be a little brash; dig down to find the real issues, then handle those issues with sensitivity and understanding. The other side will find a combination of blunt probing and sensitivity quite disarming. Don't accept monosyllabic answers from anyone; dig down to obtain the quality of answer you need:

"What's the matter?"
"Nothing really."
"That implies something. What is it?"
Silence.

■ **Use silence.** See **40**. Silence is not only golden, but a vacuum, often very useful for making questions penetrate and drawing out the quality of information you require. The catch about silence is that the vacuum can draw you in first.

"That implies something. What is it?"
Silence, lasting what seems to be an eternity.
"I'm not trying to be nosey. It's just that you looked unhappy after I came in from a difficult day . . . boss awkward . . . feeling irritable . . . traffic jam . . . "

Now it is the questioner who has lost control, sucked in by the vacuum of the other's silence. If someone uses silence on you, the most prudent course is to take the heat off by asking another, less prying question, which demonstrates once more your ability to control. Return to the main issue later.

■ **Listen and repeat.** These are the most difficult to practise and are covered in more detail in section **72**.
Discipline yourself to listen to what comes out of the other side's mouth – not just to what is going on in your head. The best way to do this is to incorporate the other person's words, phrases or sentiments in your replies:

"As you said . . . "
" . . . in fact, to use your words . . . "

74 *Look for the hot button*

A recent survey of people's motives in giving up smoking contained an important message to anyone interested in sharpening their selling skills. By far the most common reasons for kicking the habit were 'to save money' and 'to improve my health'. The least popular reason was 'to please someone else'.

Most people do things to satisfy, indeed to please themselves (which is why some are tempted to smoke in the first place). Important as they are, the moral consequences of this piece of common sense are outside the scope of this book. The practical consequences, though, are central: namely that the essential mechanics of persuasion are *first* to discover the customer's motives – their hot button – *then* to demonstrate how your proposition will satisfy their needs.

Obvious? In theory, yes; but not in practice. When it actually comes to selling, all too many make life difficult for themselves by *arguing* their case; they say, in effect, that 'It makes logical sense to buy this product or adopt this plan; do it to please me.' Never let a customer think that he can please you.

To persuade someone else successfully you must appeal to their needs, and to do this you must understand their nature. A simple but useful definition is that needs fall into two categories: logical and emotional. Indeed, you could describe them (32) as left and right brain needs.

There is evidence that feelings and emotions play the major role in decision-making, and that, contrary to some people's instincts, logic takes second place. Dispassionate, logical argument may be the common conception of how persuasion should take place; but it does have certain intrinsic weaknesses.

■ It relies on 'logic' and nothing else. If logic fails, it has to be repeated again and again: this becomes boring, and destroys rapport.

■ It tends to involve 'argument' – and this can lead to a war of attrition.

1 Identifying emotional needs

Section **43** defines in some detail the universal emotional needs – the 'innermost drives and desires' – of people at work. Although the combinations are extremely varied, you don't need to be a psychologist to recognize them: unless you are socially inadequate, you are already instinctively tuned to such needs. You don't, for example, try to build up a good relationship with a nervous, security-orientated neighbour by suddenly suggesting that you go free-fall parachuting for a laugh. You take pains to build up conversation in a reassuring way.

2 Logical needs

Obviously, you must research the facts of the case. If you want to persuade another manager to take one of your people on secondment, he has to have a manpower need, a logical reason for agreeing.

Establishing logical needs often rests simply on skills of controlling meetings (see **90**): there is a limit on the time you have to probe for facts.

3 Develop energy

The most successful sales people are those who know how to press the hot button: who can develop, out of basic logic and feeling, the energy and excitement in others to take the required action.

How to identify emotional needs

People's emotional needs come across not as simple, out-front statements, but in their choice of words and phrases. You need to know what these 'key words' are, and to listen for them.
For example:

Basic need	Verbal clues
Survival	'Keeping my job'; 'Not being hurt'; 'Not risking the savings'.
No mistakes	'Might be wrong'; 'We need more facts'; 'I'll give you detailed instructions'; 'Let's check it one more time'.
Being liked	'We'd look stupid'; 'People will think . . . '; 'I like him, he's friendly'.
Gaining respect	'I'm in charge'; 'You owe me a favour'; 'I'll see you alright'; 'I'm pretty good at that'; 'I'm important.'
Uninhibited	'Let's get it to work'; 'I don't care if it's difficult, it's the right way'; 'The figures are improving'; 'Let's stay successful'.

Listen for these, and similar key words, but remember people's needs change: don't be fooled by someone who appears to be stuck at one stage of the scale; nor by people who appear to be climbing consistently towards 'uninhibited'.

Don't take people around you for granted, listen for their *current* needs.

This is done by getting the customer to add the facts to the feelings for themselves: you contrive to make them think that 'buying' is not your idea, but theirs. People love their own ideas as much as they love themselves.

For instance, your objective is to gain agreement from your boss for an extra assistant:

FACTS: You know that your boss is committed to meeting all of her budgets this year.

FEELINGS: She likes to be popular.

Develop energy by asking a question that makes her confront the facts and the feelings: "What will happen if we don't meet budget?" As the answer is thought out and given, the energy is developed within your boss to *want* to meet the budget. 'Well, I won't be very popular; everyone else seems to be on target, and we'll all stick out as the only failures.'

Developing the energy takes both patience and brazenness. The answers to the questions that you must ask to develop the energy are often blatantly obvious; but you must wait for the answer – resist the temptation to race on to the next stage. Ensure the point is understood *and* felt.

The next stage is covered in **75.**

75 *Relating your case to the customer*

Y ou are probably familiar with these situations:

> You visit a shop to buy something you really want, perhaps a compact disc player. You have the money and motivation to buy. The shop has plenty in stock, but you still leave without buying.

> You are at a cocktail party. You are asked what you do for a living. You enjoy your job, and are quite proud of it but by the end of your description, your listener's eyes have glazed over.

What went wrong? Almost certainly, the burden of failure lay, in the first example, with the shop staff, and in the second with you. Both were guilty of ignoring the interested party. The shop assistants didn't put themselves out to help; and you failed to ask questions of your listener to maintain her interest. I am assuming that in presenting your case you have followed the steps explained in the last six sections: you have created rapport, gained control and used both to gain an understanding of the decision- maker's needs. But it is still possible to switch off a customer, and you have to avoid this at all costs.

1 The switch-off danger point

Why does your case so often collapse when you start to relate it to the listener?

■ Because you feel 'I've waited so long to speak, I'm not going to be interrupted now' and you speak for much too long.

■ You are bored with what you are saying. You have heard yourself say it, or rehearsed it, too many times.

■ You don't believe what you are saying.

■ You are inhibited: 'I'm no good at putting things over'; or 'I'm boring'.

■ You don't adapt what you are saying to what you have been told. You were not listening, you were waiting for a gap to speak.
In other words:

■ You lacked the self-esteem required to be interesting.

■ You didn't appear interested enough in your listener's problems.

 Features and benefits

The surest way of overcoming this problem is to make a conscious effort to convert the features of your case into benefits to the decision-maker.

What are the features of a table knife? It has a bone handle and a stainless steel blade: in themselves, boring. But the benefits: you could eat a meal with it; you could tighten a screw with it; or you could threaten someone with it.

If you were selling the knife to someone you would be most successful if you concentrated mainly on the benefits, rather than the bone handle and stainless steel blade.

Benefits are *personally* interesting.

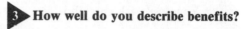 **How well do you describe benefits?**

A simple way of ensuring that you convert features into benefits is to add 'which means that' or 'therefore'.

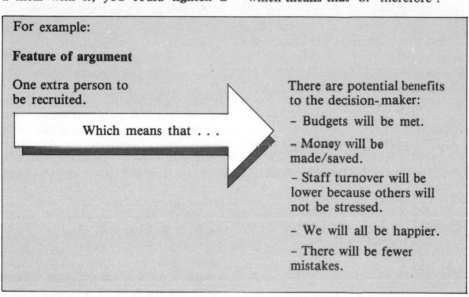

For example:

Feature of argument

One extra person to be recruited.

Which means that . . .

There are potential benefits to the decision-maker:

- Budgets will be met.

- Money will be made/saved.

- Staff turnover will be lower because others will not be stressed.

- We will all be happier.

- There will be fewer mistakes.

■ Questions are the essential means of getting to people's needs, but the asking should not stop there. As you describe your case, you should ask questions to check understanding. Spell out the benefits: don't leave their interpretation to chance.

■ Don't be too definite. Once you have turned features into benefits, it is tempting to state them too definitely. For instance, "The only way forward is to take on a graduate" runs the risk of hearing "Oh, I didn't think you meant a graduate; no, that's totally out of the question." This leaves you with some uncomfortable back-tracking.

Avoid this situation by stating the benefit as a possible approach: "One way of overcoming the staff turnover problem would be to take on a graduate" gives you the option of proposing a less qualified recruit if needs must.

76 *Gaining commitment*

There are two main reasons why people don't say "Yes" to you as often as you would like:

> 1 You don't ask in the right way.

> 2 You don't ask enough times.

The outstanding characteristic of the good salesman is an ability to ask for the order. A recent study of successful computer salesmen produced the significant figure of 3.5. This was the average number of times that the most successful asked for agreement in each meeting. Lesser salesmen had lower figures, and the most unsuccessful had a figure of 0.

(But note that this only holds true if you have prepared the ground as suggested in the seven preceding sections.)

1 Why don't you ask?

Asking for agreement is the moment when you hand over whatever control you had to the other side; the moment of truth. Reflect on some of the things people say when they have failed to ask:

> – *"It's not quite the right time."*
> – *"I don't want to spoil the relationship I'm nurturing."*
> – *"They might say 'No'."*
> – *"I think he got the message anyway."*

Most of the time, these are no more than excuses; the real reason for not asking is fear of rejection. It is emotional, self-centred and perfectly natural. No one wants to hear "You selfish inadequate. To think that you've been chatting to me about my family and my job just in order to ask for a rise. I should have kicked you out long ago." Of course, they are probably not thinking that, but you suspect it. Fear of rejection is deep-seated, probably stemming from childhood. Pause and reflect how many times since then you have experienced total rejection. Not many? Could that be because a child's wants are, well, childish, and that they can hardly compete on equal terms?

Whatever the reasons for fear of rejection, the best way to overcome it is to reflect on what happens if you don't ask:

■ You get little, or nothing, agreed.

■ You probably appear timid.

■ You excite people about your ideas, but leave them unfulfilled.

2 ▶ The right way to ask

"Can I have an extra person or not?"

"No."

That is the wrong way. Don't ask that final closed question until you have tested the water: until you have used what salesmen call a trial close. You have to disguise a test of commitment as an innocent query. For example:

■ **Offer alternatives:**
The well-worn example is

"Your pen or mine to sign the order?" – said as a joke.

If trying to persuade your boss to take on an extra staff member, it might be:

"Do you think a graduate, or someone with experience?"

The answer will indicate whether the listener is moving towards "Yes":

"Well, if we take someone, they should have experience";

or: *"Hang on, we've not agreed anything yet."*

The second response is negative – but at least it is not *"No"*.

■ **Build on assumptions.** You are persuading someone to change in some way. Most change is, at least, a little threatening. Assumptions enable you to soften the impact of difficult decisions involved in saying "Yes".

"If you agreed the extra person, where would they sit? – Should they report totally to me? – What shall we call them?"

As well as testing acceptance you are helping the decision-maker build a mental picture of how the change would translate into reality; and that can make the final decision less 'cold' and daunting.

Overcoming resistance

You have gone through the preceding eight sections, from setting objectives to asking for commitment. At the end, your 'customer' comes up with a reason why they will not buy. Your heart sinks and the whole discussion grinds to a halt. But need it? If your case is right, should you let it go?

Persuading someone to do, buy, or agree involves them in change. Staying the same is easier. You should not be surprised that they resist.

People put up two main types of objection – logical and emotional.

1 ▶ Logical resistance

> *"Can't afford it."*

This objection should strike terror into your heart, but not for the reason you might think. It is, in effect, an indictment of your selling skills.

> *"Well, how much is the change of plan going to cost?"*

You reflect that the true cost is about £30,000, but that you can't say this, because your boss will go through the roof. You resolve to ask for £20,000.
"£20,000."
She frowns, you experience mild depression and therefore add: "I'm sure we could get it cheaper."
"O.K. then, go ahead at £15,000."
Have you succeeded? No, of course not. You have sold yourself a good deal of trouble and stress. Anyone can persuade people by giving things away.

Hearing "That's too expensive" is hearing "You haven't made me excited enough", which is why it is an indict-

ment of you. You have not spent enough time on the customer's needs, adding facts to feelings to create energy (see **73.3**) – enough energy to spend £30,000.

■ **A real weakness in your case:** Every proposal has its drawbacks. If it did not, it would sell itself. Too often though, a weakness mesmerizes the customer. You have to ensure that it does not get out of proportion. Try to devise a single sentence in which you can set all the positives off against the one or two negatives. If you have spent enough time reflecting on how to turn the features of your case into benefits (**74**) and on energizing your customer (**73.3**), putting negatives into perspective is easy.

Don't get dragged down by negatives; expect them (but don't invite them); be ready to put them in their place.

■ **Customer grasps wrong end of stick.** If the customer makes a statement indicating radical misunderstanding of your case, act quickly: misinterpretation can lead to an entrenched position.
– Don't just hope the misunderstanding will sort itself out in the end.
– Don't treat the customer as the stupid one. If you are doing the talking, it is your fault if you are misunderstood. Explain the case in a different way.

2 ▶ Emotional resistance

The symptoms are familiar enough:

■ **Prejudice:** If a customer is prejudiced against a good case, they are ignorant of the facts. But resist the temptation to point out the silliness of prejudice. Don't score points; instead, remorselessly feed in the facts.

■ **Lack of confidence in you:** Perhaps you have gone through your case with unguarded enthusiasm, failing to build in regular assurance?

■ **"We'll look at it next month":** Don't show irritation. Seem to consider the possibility as a serious and sensible option, but then, equally seriously, point out that the cost of action taken later is usually more than that of acting now.

■ **The decision-maker lacks self-confidence:** There will be times when you need not only to persuade your boss but almost to push him or her into action; sometimes, decisions are too good to be left with an inadequate decision-maker. In these instances, accept that you will need to do all the work. Build up your energy level and carefully structure your questions to elicit "Yes" at each stage:

"Good day?"

"Yes."

"We need to get sorted out don't we?"

"Yes."

"I should take the responsibility for it, shouldn't I?"

"Yes."

"You should be in the clear if anything goes wrong?"

"Yes."

"Sign here?"

"Yes."

3 ▶ Is it really an objection?

"It's so expensive."
"It won't fit into the new office."
"George will never agree."

Objecting can be a buying signal. The customer could be saying: "I'm tempted by your proposal, but now I consider it carefully, whoops, I've seen a snag. If you can persuade me that it's relatively cheap, will fit the office and that there's a way of persuading George, I'll buy."

Often, such 'negative buying signals' present the perfect opportunity for a trial close (**76.2**): "If I can show you a way of persuading George, you'd agree to it, wouldn't you?"

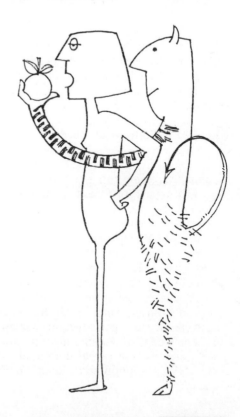

78 *Body language*

Great little mover

After conscientiously weighing the advantages and disadvantages, a departmental head and his personnel manager decided that a promising young executive would benefit from a move to a new department. The executive was called in and, after no more than a moment's hesitation assented to the move, saying she thought it a good idea too. Administrative details were then discussed and finalized.

But, as the executive got up to go, the personnel officer said: "You're not really very happy with this move, are you?" Soon it emerged that there was considerable personal antagonism between executive and sales manager – the move would have been disastrous.

 ew people doubt the importance of being sensitive to unspoken feelings; but what does it take to refine one's perception to the level of the personnel manager?

1 The limitations of words

Poor sensitivity to unspoken feelings is caused by relying too much on words and not paying sufficient attention to visual clues.

Everyone sends out a continuous stream of silent signals with their bodies, both consciously and unconsciously. They comprise fleeting glances and expressions, gestures, movements as well as the more obvious external pointers such as clothes and hairstyle. Some experts reckon that up to 70 per cent of communication can take place as non-verbal communication (NVC) – popularly called body language.

If you doubt the importance of NVC, think about how often people you have only spoken to on the telephone or heard on the radio turn out to be completely different in the flesh.

2 Better perception of NVC

■ **Practice:** Over a pre-determined period, pay particular attention to NVC in anyone you meet.

Build up a list of body-language signals which your regard as especially revealing. Evolve your own perceptions, rather than trying to use received knowledge. The list on the opposite page is a starting point only: body language perceptions you can rely on are the ones you have evolved and tested to your own satisfaction.

■ **Don't stare** at people's bodies; simply pay a little more attention than usual.

■ **Learn from the television:** select any chat show, turn the volume down to zero and try identifying as many body signals as possible. Use the chart opposite as a guide; the interpretations given are not exhaustive – meaning can vary quite widely from individual to individual.

3 Leaks

Resist the temptation to blow someone's cover publicly if you detect them 'leaking' their true feelings via body language. If someone has taken the trouble to try to conceal their feelings, the situation is almost certainly more complex and/or problematic than you realize. Try to understand their motives and, if it is your duty, or in your interests, broach the truth in private.

Physical gesture

Foot-tapping
Impatience, anger, need for comfort

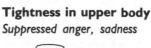

Touching face frequently
Anxiety, discomfort

Rubbing nose
Anxiety, wishes to hide

Tightness in upper body
Suppressed anger, sadness

Body leaning forwards
Concerned, interested or anxious

Stroking face, neck or hand
Anxiety, self-pity, compassion

Elbows on table, hands forming steeple
Confident, secure.

Body leaning backwards
Detached, confident, playing games

Arms or legs crossed
Defensive, vulnerable

Hand over mouth
Playing, wishes to hide, anxiety

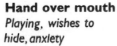

Upper crossed leg nearest person to whom one is speaking
Distrusting

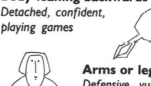

Upward gaze, head tilted
Remembering

Upper crossed leg furthest from person to whom one is speaking
Trusting

Downward gaze
Remembering emotions

Pupils dilated
Sexually attracted

Avoiding eye-contact
Anxiety, distrust, discomfort, hiding
Seeking eye-contact
Wants emotional contact anger, sympathy

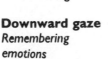

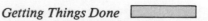

79 *The art of listening*

> **"** *The reason why we have two ears and only one mouth is that we may listen the more and talk the less.* **"**
> – Zeto of Citium, Ancient Greek philosopher.

Most of us acknowledge that listening is as crucial to communication as speaking; but that we devote much more effort to making ourselves *understood* than to making ourselves *understand*.

A common excuse for failure to listen is simply pressure of time. It is certainly true that when the pressure is on we tend to stop listening and start rushing around. But effective management involves not only issuing instructions but absorbing information as well.

Executives are exposed to other people talking for about 40 per cent of their working hours: in board meetings, at interviews, on the telephone, at conferences. Failure to listen effectively, therefore, not only increases the chances of acting on poor intelligence, but is actually an enormous waste of time.

▶ Why people do not listen well

■ They simply cannot hear.
below.

■ They are not interested in the subject or the speaker.

■ They are not paying enough attention because:
– They have other things on their minds.
– They would rather be at home/in the bar/on the golf course.
– They are distracted by more attractive sights/sounds.
– They are distracted by the discomfort of their chair.
– They are tired.

■ They do not understand all that is being said.

■ They disagree with what is being said.
■ They are mentally trying to outdo the speaker.

■ They forget what has been said afterwards.

2 Better listening

It is not enough to hear most words; you should never have to strain to hear every word clearly. If it is the speaker's fault, never be embarrassed to ask him to 'speak up'. If you are arranging a meeting, you owe it to everyone present to arrange the furniture so that people can hear: if necessary, move heavy furniture. Don't sit behind a large desk if you frequently find you can't hear. Also, sit facing the speaker so that you can follow mouth and eye movements. Establish eye contact; the feedback from you will help the speaker vary his/her delivery to ensure that you have heard and understood.

If you really have no interest in either the speaker or the subject, it is worth asking yourself whether you *should* be interested. Is the message interesting, even if the delivery or speaker is not? If the message isn't interesting, you should ask yourself if the information could be obtained elsewhere. If it can, then leave the meeting or spend the time thinking about more important matters.

That your mind wanders when you are listening is hardly surprising when you consider just how much spare mental capacity is left over. Most speakers talk at a rate of 100-150 words per minute, while a practised speed reader can absorb perhaps 500 words per minute. Consciously direct your thoughts towards the speaker/subject:
■ Mentally summarize what the speaker is saying as he/she goes along. Take notes – See **52**.
■ Develop counter arguments.

There is always some loss of understanding between speaker and listener, but the good listener can reduce this to a minimum. Do some homework, even if this means just running through the subject for a minute or two, or digging out the relevant file and glancing through it briefly.
■ Look for clues in the speaker's voice and gestures, listening for special emphasis and hints as to the way he/she has organized the material.
■ Don't hesitate to communicate your lack of understanding to the speaker. A puzzled look may be enough, but you may need to ask the speaker to slow down or repeat or explain a phrase. If you feel reluctant to show your lack of understanding so obviously, remember that it will be that much more embarrassing if it is revealed inadvertently at a later date.

It is important not to let your own ideas and prejudices cloud your understanding. See **51**.

It has been estimated that one forgets at least half of what has been said in any five-minute conversation within eight hours, and that after three days one remembers less than ten per cent of any conversation. There is thus plenty of scope for improving retention. See **53**.

80 *The dangers of poor communication*

A journalist, anxious to meet a deadline and needing to know the age of Cary Grant, sent a telegram to the actor. It read: HOW OLD CARY GRANT? The reply came back promptly: OLD CARY GRANT FINE. HOW YOU?

Communication breakdown can be amusing; it can also be frustrating, time-wasting and productive of nothing, except further layers of confusion. It is a symptom of many of the time-wasting tendencies described in this book, especially inadequate day planning (15, 16) and over-reliance on the chattering left side of the brain (32).

Communicating unambiguously is easy if you have sufficient quiet controlled time in which to rehearse your thoughts. Communicate effectively, and you deal with problems more efficiently.

1 Have they got the message?

If you have experienced any of the following problems, it may be that you need to communicate better:

■ Subordinates/suppliers tend to miss deadlines.

■ Subordinates/suppliers often deliver material that is not quite what you wanted, even when they seemed to absorb your briefing.

■ People don't take your orders as seriously as you would wish.

In theory, communication is a two-way process, but nobody has time, let alone patience, to instil this ethic into the large number of people they encounter in working life. You must rely instead on your own ability to communicate – for there is indeed a great deal you can do to improve the flow.

2 Remedies

■ **Subordinates/suppliers miss deadlines.** Don't just name the date: *also* say *why* the date is important. If you don't, suppliers can play the 'warehouse closed early' trick: ("Our lorry arrived at 5.15pm on the 24th, but your 'goods in' manager had gone home. The driver had an equally urgent delivery the next day, so he had to postpone yours until the the 26th").

Remember:
date (+ time if appropriate) + reason for date and time = no confusion and no excuses.
Example: 'Delivery before 4pm on the 24th. Our warehouse staff leave at 4.30, and need at least half an hour to process arrivals.'

■ **Work is delivered not as you wanted it.** Were you fooled by "Yes"? Everybody loves to hear that word: it is the easiest answer; it saves them and you the trouble of further thought and questioning; nobody then looks foolish for failing to understand. Possibly the person you are briefing has already formulated their idea of the task; if it does not coincide with yours, they would rather face up to the confusion later when they have already done it their way.

Solution: ask them to summarize the task. Don't be patronizing: just say "OK, shall we just go over it again?". Then be silent: let them fill the silence with a demonstration of whether or not they have listened – and whether you have explained clearly.

Also, make a habit of backing up complex spoken instructions in writing.

■ **Your orders are not taken seriously.** Of course, there are many reasons why this should occur: see also **Motivating others (67)** and **Delegating well (86).**

If poor communication is implicated in failure to motivate, the underlying malaise could be serious. It could, for example, mean that a colleague/subordinate has failed to signal to you that he is not fully capable of the task you are delegating – or that you have failed to read the signals he did send to this effect.

Such signals can be difficult to read. Asked to devise a marketing campaign for a wholly new product, someone unsure of meeting the challenge can suddenly gain remarkable insight into information that is lacking, or back-up which is unavailable, in order for them to successfully achieve.

Good communication means not only expressing yourself clearly; it means being clear yourself about a colleague's status or ability; your organization's expectations; a customer's probity, purchasing power or needs.

The classic way of receiving distorted information about colleagues and organizational policy is the grapevine. Not everyone is in a position to kill it off (see **68.3** at **Communicate regularly**); if you have to live with the office grapevine as an information source, ALWAYS cross-check received information with another source. This invariably enlarges your overall understanding of people and trends; and reduces the odds on poor communication.

81 *Effective writing – basic steps*

What would you think of the sender of each of these memos?

> **'Phil** – *the production short-fall in February means we cannot meet all of our export orders. We must meet tomorrow (15th March) to discuss alternatives. Regards,* **Tom.'**

> **'Dear Phil,**
> *We are anticipating a possible fulfilment problem with our overseas customers. This is on account of the problems we have been having recently with production. I think we should meet urgently to talk about it.* **Nick.'**

You would probably say, with justice, that Nick's whole style suggests an indecisive, pedantic manner – and that he has left out two essential pieces of information. Tom on the other hand, seems much more on the ball, and his memo covers all the ground briefly and simply. If asked who would make the better manager, you would probably have little hesitation in choosing Tom. Yet both suggested exactly the same course of action.

People make judgements about you from the way you write even the shortest memo. And, of course, sloppy, ineffective writing can cause all kinds of misunderstanding; the damning evidence is preserved long after the event, too.

Effective writing does not mean creating literary masterpieces; it is about getting thoughts into a clear and concise form of words on paper as quickly and efficiently as possible.

1 ▶ Why people write ineffectively

Effective writing is not quite the natural talent you may imagine it to be. Failure to write effectively can usually be put down to a combination of simple problems, each of which anyone can easily overcome if they put their mind to it:

■ You don't have all the facts and ideas at your fingertips.

■ You have failed to marshall the material into an accessible form.

■ You have forgotten why you are writing.

■ Your ideas are poorly organized.

■ Your style is poor.

■ You fail to check closely everything you write.

Most of the remedies suggested below apply to longer pieces of writing, such as reports, rather than brief memos. For tips on writing letters and memos, concentrate on **2.5** and **2.6** below and for further advice on letter-writing see **57**.

2 ▶ Remedies

2.1 Is your knowledge of the subject sufficient? Failure to come to grips with all the material *before* writing is possibly the most common cause of writing difficulties.

An incomplete knowledge of material is easier to rectify than you might think, provided you identify the problem, *before* you write:

■ Spend ten minutes making a list of all the topics you expect to cover, paying no particular attention to order, but giving close attention to the pur-

pose of the piece (see also **2.3** below). Do this as quickly as you can.
- Decide on four or five main headings into which the piece can be divided, and allocate each item on your list to one of these headings. Take your time over this.
- Spend a further five minutes filling gaps in the list.
- Ask yourself, searchingly, are there any major topics that you may have left out?
- Now note briefly what you are going to say about each topic. Again, do this as quickly as possible.

This exercise should pinpoint any area where you need to do additional research.

2.2 Sort the material: Too much research can be as detrimental to effective writing as too little. It is all too easy to become bogged down by a large number of facts and find yourself unable to write; likewise to cram too many facts into a short space. If your research material runs to dozens of pages, you need to rationalize it before you can begin to write. This is probably worth doing even if your research is relatively brief.
- Run through your research notes, underlining the key points in red pen.
- Write the four or five main headings you thought of before you started research (or new ones if appropriate), each at the top of a separate sheet of paper.
- Go through your notes transferring each point marked in red to the appropriate head sheet. Write any that don't fit on a separate sheet.
- Reorganize, or, if necessary, re-write your headings to accommodate the points that don't fit your original structure.

2.3 Keep the reader in mind. As you write, try to be constantly aware of the ultimate purpose of what you write.

In essence, this means:
- Reminding yourself who is the reader.
- Telling the reader all he/she needs to know.
- Not telling the reader what he/she already knows.
- Not telling the reader what he/she does not need to know.

It is always better to err on the side of brevity rather than length. Stand back when you have finished writing, take a deep breath and go through the text, editing whenever you have used two or more words when one, or at any rate fewer, would do.

2.4 Keep it simple and *active*. Compare these:

> *'Soaring iron ore prices world-wide are cutting profit margins in the steel industry today. British Steel say jobs in older plants may have to go.'*

> *'At the present time, net returns on sales after cost in steel manufacturing are being curtailed by the rapidly ascending price of the basic raw material – that is, iron ore – in every source country across the world, and, according to British Steel, there is a possibility of redundancies in the more antiquated establishments.'*

The second paragraph says exactly the same as the first – but the first is much easier to understand, is less than half as long, and is more interesting to read. It is active: something new appears in each sentence.

82 *Effective writing – refining the craft*

Writing is a personal art: the best way to learn it is to – write. The advice in the preceding section is essential to competent self-expression. Here are some suggestions for improving your written style as you go along:

1 Sentences and paragraphs

Too many people think that words alone are the building blocks of language: sentences and paragraphs are just as important, and the most comprehensive vocabulary in the world is useless unless it is harnessed to an understanding of, and skill with, sentences and paragraphs.

■ Sentences need to be *complete* sets of words, adding up to a statement, a question or a command. Obvious, perhaps, but for many the temptation to leave them incomplete, or to overload them, is irresistible. The best course is to consciously aim for medium-length sentences. Dickens' convoluted sentences had an average of 32 words; modern quality newspapers average 26-28 in their more elaborate articles. Tabloids tend to have as little as 16 or so. A happy medium might be around 20. Once established, this habit is one you can break in order to introduce changes of pace.

■ Start sentences with concrete concepts that require no prior knowledge. This means, for example, beginning with a noun:

'Going into all the ramifications and complications of the Midas project and thinking about the overall feel of the product, I think Mr Goldhawk is not the man for the job.'

Difficult to read, simply because one is more than half-way through the sentence before one knows what it is about.

'Mr. Goldhawk is not the man for the Midas job because . . . ' would be a much better way to start.

■ Naturally good writers have an instinct for the paragraph. A paragraph is a link in a chain: it should contain just one idea, point, or stage in a story or an argument. This can come at the beginning, middle or end; the rest of the material in the paragraph corroborates or amplifies the point. If you resist the temptation to make more than one main point in a paragraph, your paragraphs will automatically be limited to a reasonable length.

2 Generally:

■ Use full stops and commas (and occasional dashes). Avoid using more complex forms of punctuation such as colons and semi-colons unless you know exactly how they should be used.

■ Avoid complex, and especially Latin-derived words, where simple words will do just as well. Prefer 'about' to 'approximately'; 'after' to 'following'; 'let' to 'permit'; 'use' to 'utilize'; 'make' to 'manufacture'; 'plant' to 'facility'.

■ To keep your writing dynamic and direct, use verbs in the active mood rather than the passive, and avoid using 'there' as much as possible. For example:

'There has been a call for improved conditions of employment by workers on the factory floor'.

This sounds considerably less to-the-point than:

'Factory workers have called for better working conditions.'

■ Don't use metaphors, similes or other figures of speech which are often seen in print. Your reader will be tired of them.

■ Never use a jargon word or phrase, or a foreign one, if an everyday word in your own language will do.

■ Don't over-use slang ('Roger really hit the big time') or be too chatty ('So far so good', or 'surprise, surprise').

Common abuses of language

'Strike action'	*Just 'strike' gives the meaning.*
'Business community'	*'Businessmen' means the same.*
'Large-scale'	*'Big' means the same.*
'At this moment in time'	*Means 'now'.*
'To fund' long-term debt at fixed interest	*A financial term meaning to turn floating debt into long-term debt at fixed interest. Do not use it when you actually mean 'finance', or 'pay for'.*
'Vital'	*Means 'life depends on it'; don't use where you mean 'essential'.*
'Earnings'	*Don't use when you mean 'profits'.*
'Get'	*Is a work-horse word, but don't over-do it. A colleague should not 'get sacked'; he 'is sacked'.*
'Plane'	*A tool, or a surface; if it takes passengers, it is an airliner.*
'Presently'	*Means 'soon', not 'at present'.*
'Healthy'	*If it is useful or desirable, say so; don't claim it is physically fit.*
'Verbal agreement'	*Very few agreements are not verbal; if it is not written down in a letter or contract, it is oral.*

83 *Giving persuasive talks – what you say*

This section examines how to put a talk together; the next how to put it over.

When you plan a talk, a speech or any formal address, do it with continual reference to the complaints that could possibly be made about your performance.

"It was boring"

Almost always a result of using too many words, thus limiting the appeal to the audience's left brain. Build in pictures: plan to use visual aids, and don't restrict yourself to conventional items. Use anything that will do the job, from a jug of water to a Second World War helmet. At the very least, use word pictures.

"It went on a bit"

Be ruthless with your material. Only put in items that make or support your case. An extra tit-bit might be interesting to you and nobody else. Rehearse against a clock to make sure it does not over-run.

"It missed the point"

Are you sure you are planning to talk about what the audience expects, or about what you want to say? The art is to do both, but you must address the expected topic first.

"He talked down to us"

Always check on the education, status and attitude of the audience; make the content appeal to human beings rather than a defined socio-economic or professional group. Eliminate jargon, unless everyone understands it.

"He was on his hobby horse again"

If you have already spoken on the same subject to the same audience you can still keep up their interest by giving it a different treatment.

"He lacked confidence"

Don't build in apologies and self-derogatory remarks.

"There was no involvement"

Build in a question or questions.

"He didn't sound sincere"

Put your speech into your own words. Don't say what you think is expected of you; say what you believe.

"I didn't warm to him"

Build in an ice breaker. It need not be a joke; try an interesting, but controversial, anecdote to which everyone can relate. Initial rapport is essential.

"I didn't follow the logic"

Plan a sequence building up to your key point. Don't make the steps plodding and deliberate; add frills, but let the progression shine through.

"He just filled in the time"

Every time you get the chance to speak, you gain the chance to influence people. Don't waste it. Have a definite purpose, rather than deliver 15 minutes' worth of words.

"The equipment failed"

Check it beforehand, and have a spare of everything possible. Be prepared to deliver the talk without mechanical/electrical aids.

"He dried up"

Have a couple of extras up your sleeve. You may need to fill in a gap or add spice at an unexpectedly dry part.

"He wasn't funny"

Don't plan to be funny if you are not confident you can pull it off. There are other ways of being interesting.

"It won't change things"

Don't just tell people to change. Put some positive advice into the talk about how and when they can act.

"I can't remember the slides"

Vary the images by using diagrams, and changes of colour. Eliminate poor exposures. Ready-made cartoons are widely available, and introduced at key points they can be the making of illustrated talks. Don't use too many slides.

"He's always a bad speaker"

Get someone else to give you ideas, or write your script. Don't keep repeating the same mistakes; do something different; you can't get any worse.

84 *Giving persuasive talks – how you say it*

M ost audiences are on your side, but you would not think so to look at them: they usually look aloof and miserable. If you find this surprising, imagine you are a nervous airline pilot. Before take-off, you look down the rows of passengers. Would they be waving, giving you thumbs up signs and wishing you good luck? Yet they, like the audience, certainly want you to succeed.

"It was boring"

If you think you will be dull, you probably will be. Lift your voice and your spirits up a few notches before you start. Start with a smile. Make yourself move around; aim to be animated, but in a relaxed way.

"It went on a bit"

Put your watch on the table if you cannot see a clock. Never overrun, unless you are invited to do so.

"It missed the point"

Emotional response to audience feedback, favourable or unfavourable, can make you lose concentration. When a remark goes down well, don't dredge your memory for similar *bon mots*; you will lose the audience. Likewise, don't speed up as a reaction to the disappointment of failing to get a response. See **36 Overcoming fears.**

"He talked down to us"

Your attitude to the audience as you address them is absolutely essential. Don't 'creep', and don't patronize, whatever the status of the audience, or you will develop a 'him and us' feeling. See them as equals, however hard that may be.

"He was on his hobby horse again"

When you have to make the same point or speech several times, there is a real danger that you will fail to concentrate on delivery. The remedy is to make a benefit (see **75**) out of the repetition. "What am I going to say? Why? Because nothing's changed . . . "

"He lacked confidence"

Always relax, and quieten your mind, before speaking (**34, 36**). Imagine success. Ensure that the butterflies are in your stomach and not in your head.

"There was no involvement"

Don't talk *at* people, include them. Speaking ought to be like a tug of war which you must win. Pull the audience to you with the use of questions, even if they are only rhetorical. If you can get them thinking about the answers to your questions, you will have successfully involved them.

"He didn't sound sincere"

Contemplate your audience as soon as you can fasten your gaze upon them. What do they want? Care about them, and it will probably come across in your voice.

"I didn't warm to him"

Don't wait for the audience to relax you. Brighten yourself up before you start. Feel warm towards the audience.

"I didn't follow the logic"

Use regular pauses to allow the audience to digest your key points. Unlike you, they are hearing this for the first time.

"He just filled in the time"

Keep your end objective in mind *together with your finishing time.* Ensure that everything you say builds up to the main point. Ask the audience for some action, even if it is only that they "go away and think about it."

"The equipment failed"

If the worst happens, remember that the audience will stay on your side if you move on smoothly to your alternative method of delivery.

"He dried up"

Pauses can be effective if you are in control of them. If you do dry up, ask a question like "Any questions so far?" to give you time to gather your thoughts. Quieten down: drying up is caused by a 'chattering mind' (**36**).

"He wasn't funny"

When you make a joke, never wait for the laugh: it can be a very long wait.

Always move on; let the laugh interrupt you.

"It won't change things"

Build up the energy in the group to want to change (see **74.3**); look as though you believe they can.

"I can't remember the slides"

Don't let the commentary smother the images. Use a maximumn of 20 words per slide, preferably five to eight key words. A hundred slides is plenty for a single sitting – don't be tempted to swamp the audience.

"He's always a bad speaker"

Ask someone else to honestly appraise your style; or look at a video recording of yourself speaking.

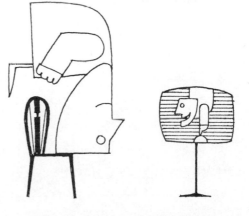

85 *The telephone – the enemy within*

If you were saving someone's life, or proposing marriage, would you answer a ringing telephone?

Of course not. You would decide that the job in hand was more important.

Yet every day you are probably doing exactly that, only in a less obvious way. You answer too many calls, and spend too long even on the important.

This section can help you get more control over incoming calls, and improve your general telephone manner.

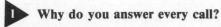 **Why do you answer every call?**

■ Out of curiosity? Perhaps because it might just bring good news, or an opportunity?

■ Because you believe that you are so indispensable that no one else is capable of answering for you?

■ Because you have never trained anyone else?

■ For fear of what might happen to you if you don't?

■ Because of a feeling that you are out of control of events?

■ Because it must be more enjoyable than what you are doing at the time?

■ Out of a sense of duty?

■ Out of habit – telephones are always answered by you?

Then remind yourself
Who answers the calls when you are :

■ At a meeting?

■ On holiday?

■ On the telephone to someone else?

Also

■ Do you end up re-routing some calls after you have discovered the real problem?

■ Are some calls for the same sort of information each time?

■ Could you provide a better, speedier service to people who telephone?

■ Do you answer the telephone when someone else is with you?

2 ▶ Telephone control

You know that by taking more control over incoming calls, you can give yourself uninterrupted time for creative work and improve the quality of calls when you do take them. BUT this is easier said than done: you need to exert control over the telephone in at least seven different ways:

■ **Delegate more calls.** Try to use staff who answer your calls when you are away.

■ **Do important creative work in an office without a telephone,** or someone else's office.

■ **Devise a rota** for handling calls.

■ **Resist the temptation of listening to your call being answered** – you will end up taking it.

■ If you have no one to whom you can delegate calls, **use the switchboard to take messages;** ask a friend; or use an automatic answering device.

■ **Develop the habit of setting aside a time of day when you want to do your telephoning.** Outside this period, tell a secretary to inform callers when you will be available, or, better, when you will call back. Name a precise 'time window' such as "between 3.30 and 3.45". This often has the effect of making the other person wait for your call. (But make sure you return all calls when promised: delaying tactics don't work more than once.) Use this system, and you will find fewer people telephone you.

■ **Don't take any calls when you have a visitor.** This really says to them that your call is sure to be more important than they are.

3 ▶ How to shorten calls

■ If you have a regular caller who cannot come to the point, tell them in a positive way about their bad habit.

■ If you don't think honesty is best, try these: "I've got an international call on the other line." "I'm in the middle of a meeting." "Hello, hello. Are you still there? Hello?" and then put the receiver down. (But when the caller says "I can hear you", don't say "Well I can't hear you.")

4 ▶ Giving a better service to callers

■ Keep all information you need up-to-date and near at hand, for example in a card index or on a computer screen.

■ Plan every important or complex call; make a list of points you want to bring up; do the same with points made to regular callers.

■ Ask callers to be properly prepared for their calls to you.

■ Don't pour out your problems and pressures to callers. They are your problems, not theirs, and may demonstrate that you are out of control.

■ Don't be afraid of offending by terminating the call when its usefulness to you both is fulfilled.

Delegating well

N o point in reading this section unless you have first read **68 – Motivating others.** That sets out the basic essentials of delegation: giving clear direction, making it worth the subordinate's while, ensuring the task is achievable, and so on. This section looks at delegation – perhaps the hardest single thing a manager has to do – at a more sophisticated level.

 The nature of delegation

The goal, the purpose, of delegation is to leave you free to manage: to

> - Assess work, solve problems.
>
> - Think about the relationship between tasks and those who undertake them.
>
> - Create new products/services, expand contacts and plan the future.

In order to be free for these all-important functions, you have to off-load work. What kind of work? Obviously, work which others can do just as well as yourself.

One thing delegation is not: an escape from work. Although you can delegate work, you cannot delegate responsibility for it. Delegate, and there will be many difficult, tedious, unrewarding tasks that will no longer bother you on a day-to-day basis. But if they go wrong as a result of poor delegation, sorting out the mess can be far more work than doing it yourself.

Delegation is, therefore, risky; it may not – should not – remove you from control of work – but it does remove you from immediate control. It

means that you are never free from anxiety about what might be going wrong. Worrying about a task you are actually performing is no holiday, but at least you can ease the tension by *doing*. The manager who has delegated a task has to wait and brood.

Delegation is paradoxical: you must do it in order to free yourself to manage; having done it, you enslave yourself to a higher order of tension and anxiety. It makes life difficult, but, like any difficult game, it has its rewards. One of my definitions of a person with high-level management potential is that they can handle the extra tension, *and* enjoy the rewards.

 Selling the task

Of course the person to whom you delegate must be trustworthy, and of course they have to have the aptitude, and intelligence, to fulfill the task.

You would not be a manager unless you knew how to recognize these essentials. But to delegate with flair, and effectiveness, you must not only match the subordinate and the task; you must *sell* the task.

Selling a task to someone in one's own organization seems unnatural to many managers. It should not be necessary, they say; the salary package plus the threat of dismissal should be enough to ensure orders are obeyed, and obeyed properly. Why should managers have to nurse subordinates into doing their jobs?

The simple answer is that our goal is not just delegation, but motivation; humans, being humans, get stale and need fresh motivation.

Even a boring, routine task can be delegated well, as opposed to averagely well, by adding motivation. Look at the two examples in the box.

It is company sales catalogue time again:
a horrible task, customarily delegated to
someone of plodding ability in the sales
department . because it involves endless
checking of figures and updating product
information. You judge, correctly, that the
new assistant has the ability to do the
task, and would benefit from the chance
to learn in some detail about the whole
range of company products. Which version sells the task well, and which sells it
really well?

Manager's sales pitch
"I've chosen you to do the catalogue this
year. You've not been with us long, but
from the way you checked the warehouse
reports, I don't think I'll have any complaints about accuracy. But do remember,
this job is not worth doing unless every
price, and every product description is
checked and updated to the end of next
quarter with each department. Try and do
the first six pages by the end of the week,
then we'll go through them together. That
will leave you a further fortnight.

"I know this isn't the most interesting
job in your department, but everyone has
to do it sometime."

"You don't need me to tell you that the
catalogue is a tedious job; but it will give
you a detailed knowledge of every product
line we sell and that can give you an opportunity to think about the direction in
which you want to develop. Too many
people in the sales department know only
about their particular product. Will you do
it? Good. I'll make sure you get something
more interesting next.

"Here are some notes I wrote last year
on how to go about it. Let me know if you
can improve on them.

"Come back to me with the first six
pages at the end of the week; if you need
longer, let me know by tomorrow."

Comment
Not bad; the confidence implicit in
"You've not been with us long but . . . "
can be quite motivating to some people,
and bringing in relevant previous work
makes sense of the request. The job is
well-defined, too, and the deadline clearly
stated. The subordinate now knows, or is
going to know, exactly the standard required, exactly his level of responsibility
within the task, progress reports he must
make, help he can expect and problems
he must refer back.

The only flaw is the parting shot: every
preceding effort to motivate is given a
hollow, insincere ring by the blunt admission that the newcomer has drawn the
short straw.

Here, the manager has chosen to come
clean at the start – and to do it in a way
that will not insult the subordinate's intelligence. Then, he sells the job by suggesting, rather than stating, that even this
dreary task can be relevant to the subordinate's development – his career plans.
People always like you for that.

Several other ingredients lift this sales
pitch out of the ordinary: promising
something better next is a nicely under-
stated hint of your appreciation of the
subordinate's worth; asking for advice on
the notes could well increase commitment; using a written briefing is perhaps
more appropriate to the task than a verbal
one; and offering an extendable deadline
makes getting into the task that much
more comfortable.

87 *Be available – with fewer interruptions*

If you have people working for you, much of your time is probably taken up sorting out their problems at the expense of your own.

It is 4.30 and you are up to your eyes in work. One of your team pops her head round the door. You affect a smile on the outside of your face only. "Have you got a minute?" You think: 'Got a minute? I've got a minus two hours. Go away, you are pressuring me. But I can't say that; she'll be hurt, she'll call me unapproachable'. So you say "Yes, come in."

She settles into her chair: "I'll just give you some of the background." While she goes through the background, you tell yourself again how pressured you are. After a quarter of an hour, with the prospect of listening to the 'background' for another half-hour, you say: "Look, give it all to me, I'll sort it out."

You have added to your workload; suffered tension and stress; and will probably let down your visitor by not completing her work.

It need not be like that.

Remedy

A sales manager had six sales representatives working for her; they were in the middle of the pre-Christmas launch – easily the busiest time of year. Not only were the representatives out on the road, but the manager was out at meetings most of the day too.

To each representative she said:

"If you have a problem, ring me, or come and see me, wherever I am. You can interrupt at any time, or in any meeting, however important – UNLESS it can wait until tomorrow.

"If it can wait until the next morning, I'll be 'phoning you anyway."

First thing every morning, the manager telephoned each of the six representatives in turn. They soon learned to be by a telephone at the appropriate time.

In one move, the manager ensured:

■ Unnecessary interruptions would be reduced, or eliminated entirely. The representatives were obliged to think for themselves whether they would be bothering her unnecessarily.

■ The representatives would report to her at a predictable time and in a structured way – each day's problems had to be noted and remembered for the next day's conversation with the boss.

■ The manager could herself give more of her time – and better quality time at that – than if the representatives had come at her with random problems at random times.

The system can of course work with anyone with whom you have regular contact, including service departments and even customers.

88 *Telling people off*

Receiving complaints about ones work is de-motivating and unpleasant: suggestions as to how one might improve, or avoid a mistake in future, can be reassuring and motivating: a sign that one's boss cares enough about one's role and work to view it in future perspective. Concentrating on the problem, not the personality, is actually a simple skill, and it enables the person doing the complaining to get more done in the long run.

If you are in any doubt about this, consider the following comments:

> a "You idiot. Go and do it again."
> b "It's all your fault."
> c "I've told you a hundred times before."
> d "Give it to me and go away."
> e "That didn't work, did it? How will you avoid it next time?"

The only statement that tackles the problem rather than attacking the personalities is of course e. It is positive, looks to the future, and yet it does not hide from the fact that something went wrong.

1 Complaining, face to face

■ Plan any encounter in which you have to complain about someone's performance. Get all the facts. Be sure you have a clear idea of the problem, not necessarily the solution.

■ Seek to jointly agree the problem. Pin down the objective threatened, be it a deadline, a budget, or a harmonious relationship. It is results that count, so don't waste time on blame or other minor aspects that will detract from the main point. Don't try to find solutions yet.

■ Explain how the problem affects you. Don't assume an understanding of the consequences. No two people think the same way. Explain both the facts of the case and your own feelings, but do it factually, not emotionally.

■ Ask why they think the problem has occurred. Listen when they explain. Remember the key facts and phrases that you can build on when helping to find an agreeable solution: "I didn't have all the facts/don't have enough people/don't like/find the task difficult". Help them to explore all the areas of the problem. Ensure they are not externalizing the problem (see **44**). Ensure they are covering both the positive and negative aspects. You want them to leave with enthusiasm – but not with their head in the sand.

■ Understand: understanding is not necessarily agreeing. Don't have a closed mind, clinging to your preconceived solution.

■ Agree achievable action. Discuss the past only long enough to agree the facts. Don't go on about things. Build on the comments they have made to encourage them to develop a situation: "I agree you seem to dislike parts of the job, so how can you overcome this?" Encourage them to sell *their* solution to you. They must own, and believe in, the cure. Expect the cure to be measurable by quantity, quality and by specific dates.

■ Monitor the agreed action. Give immediate feedback on success. Pick up on a further failure the same way.

■ Praise when they succeed, but resist the temptation to say: "Well, luckily you've got it right this time."

89 *Meetings – are they necessary?*

> *"I've got nothing done all day – I've been in a meeting since I arrived."*
>
> *"I'm sorry, I can't reach the managing director – he's in meeting."*
>
> *"It's not my fault – I just sit on the committee that made the decision."*
>
> *"I'd love to help you, but the selection panel met yesterday, and they won't be convened again for a month."*

Familiar words; who has not, at some stage, questioned whether meetings are necessary at all?

The frustrating but unavoidable answer is that sometimes meetings are the only practical way of making decisions. In a job interview, for example, four people at least usually need to be involved. Of course the candidates might be seen individually, but if there are dozens on the short list, this itself causes an explosion of meetings.

1 ▶ Why meet?

In a company with a perfect hierarchical structure, there would not be any need for meetings. Everybody's responsibilities would be clearly defined, and decisions would be possible without constant reference to a group of other people. Decision-makers would be supplied with information from lower down the organizational pyramid, and with policy guidance from above. Unfortunately, life is not that simple. Peter Drucker acknowledges this when he describes meetings as 'a concession to organizational imperfection'.

In other words, essential meetings are those which enable decisions to be made that would not be taken in isolation.

If, in your part of your organization, you apply this rule rigorously over the long term, you will cut down on unnecessary meetings but probably not without some squeals.

■ Someone suggests a meeting to discuss production schedules; it would be useful to compare notes from various colleagues on which manufacturers have had the best delivery record. You ask: "Do we need to take a decision?" If the reply is "No, but it would be a helpful discussion", insist that an alternative way is found of pooling the information.

■ If you are in the position of having to attend a regular meeting at which you suspect your presence is unnecessary, try deliberately missing it for some cast-iron reason such as sickness or a missed plane. Come to that, try missing out on a regular meeting regardless of whether you think it essential to be there.

2 ▶ Crisis meetings

These meetings are usually called at extremely short notice by people who insist that you drop what you are doing in order to attend. Look back over your diary, and note who called crisis meetings over the last few months, and what action was taken at the meeting. Did you find that it was just one or two individuals with a tendency to shout 'Help!', and that the 'crises' were resolved easily?

People who will insist on meetings often want to spread the blame for a developing crisis on to several people rather than carrying it all themselves.

If they are offered help and reassurance, the desire for a meeting usually fades as rapidly as it arose.

3 ▶ Committee meetings

The committee is generally a special kind of meeting: it makes recommendations, and it is the domain of people with specialist knowledge of several different areas. It provides the decision-makers with the information they need to do their job.

Besides the specialists, committees need probably no more than one person with a broad perspective who can put the issues into context. If you are neither a specialist nor a co-ordinator, your time in committee meetings is probably being wasted.

4 ▶ Psychological value

"It's the only time we all really meet as a team; it makes me feel that my role is needed. If we did not have our weekly meeting I would probably feel that if I went under a bus they would have someone new in my desk within hours."

Meetings do have a motivational benefit. In your enthusiasm for eliminating unnecessary meetings, don't destroy an irreplaceable aid to keeping a happy team. It may well be possible to upgrade a meeting of dubious value so that it becomes a tool for decision-making.

Alternatives to meetings

Star memos
Send a copy of a discussion document to every person who would otherwise meet, request comments.

Advantages: relatively quick response; everyone gets 'stroked', because they have had an individual copy.

Disadvantages: many copies; comments duplicated; much work needed in summing up; no interaction of ideas.

'Ring' memos
Circulate a copy of a document for comments – 'Tick your name and pass it on to the next one on the list'.

Advantages: one copy; comments made only once; easy to summarize; one comment inspires another: ('I agree with Joe's remark in principle, but . . . ').

Disadvantages: slow; recipients don't get stroked so much, so memo is not a priority.

Telephone conference
Many telephone networks now offer the facility to link ten or more extensions together.

Advantages: instant response; plenty of interaction of ideas; some of the positive features of a conventional meeting without physically getting together in one spot.

Disadvantages: not always easy to set up; hard to chair the meeting.

---

90 *Making meetings productive*

The following well-known (and probably apocryphal) anecdote is worth repeating if only because it illustrates how attitudes towards time management have gradually softened since it started circulating about a decade back.

> The chief executive of a large corporation was becoming impatient with the slow progress of the regular monthly planning meeting. He had a large digital clock made and set it up in view of everyone at the next meeting. When the chief executive (normally a very precise man) was asked why the 'clock' showed the wrong time, he replied that the display showed the cost to the company of the combined salaries of everyone present. As the digits clicked by, the meeting proceeded at record speed.

These days, progressive organizations try not to make such simplistic equations between money and people. This section explores some less abrasive ways of facing up to the underlying reality that meetings are among the most extravagant uses of staff time.

1 Advance planning

■ **Timing** is crucial. Early meetings – just after lunch or first thing in the morning – have a tendency to drag on interminably. On the other hand, urgency concentrates the mind wonderfully: a meeting scheduled for an hour before lunch, or late in the afternoon, can be concluded at breakneck pace.

■ **Duration:** Never arrange a meeting without setting a time limit. It does not matter if you have to go into 'extra time': it is wise in any case to allow an extra half-hour as a contingency. If you go into extra time, let everyone present know of the concession.

■ **Interruptions:** *never* allow them. Arm a secretary with fool proof reasons why the meeting cannot be interrupted. If a crisis threatens to occur during a meeting *either* delegate the authority to deal with it in your absence, *or* don't go to the meeting.

■ **Preparation:** Time is invariably wasted unless everyone comes prepared. Make sure that copies of essential documents are circulated and read.

■ **Agendas** need to summarize not just what will be discussed, but also the point of the discussion. 'New paper production plant – schedule' invites a rambling discussion. Much better would be 'New paper plant: building now five weeks behind schedule due to builders' strike. Estimate for recovering lost time: £65,000.'

Always put the most important items in the middle of the agenda. Trivial points should come at the beginning, so that late arrivals don't miss anything important. Try to end the meeting on an 'up' note, or with a vote that you know will be unanimous, so that everyone goes away with a satisfying feeling of something accomplished.

■ **Numbers:** the best number for a meeting is four. Ten is possible, 12 generally the upper limit. Cutting down on numbers is not always easy, because attendance often carries status – however illusory. If there is a fixed list of departmental heads who are invited to attend, many will come even if they have nothing constructive to add, and will speak because they fear that to stay silent shows lack of enthusiasm.

To prevent this spoke-in-the wheel mentality, invite only essential staff, but circularize all interested parties with the agenda, plus a note saying they are welcome if they have something specific to contribute. Ensure that these same people also receive a record of what went on at the meeting.

 Chairing a meeting

The blame for unfocused and unproductive meetings usually lies with the chair. If you are chairing the meeting, you have several jobs:
- Gently but firmly guiding the discussion in the planned direction.
- Eliminating digressions and gently cutting short dialogues that exclude the majority of those present.
- Watching the clock, and making sure that everyone is aware of time passing: 'We're about half-way through, so we had better move on to the next item.'
- Sum up briefly at the end of each discussion: nothing is more embarrassing than a chairman who likes the sound of his or her own voice.
- If you sense that two people are veering towards a serious conflict, try not to avert the crisis too dictatorially – this often inflames the parties to the extent that a collision occurs anyway.

3 **Obtaining agreement**

The principal purpose of a meeting is to take decisions, and if you are in the chair your energy should be channelled into making this happen.

Ideally, decisions should be unanimous because then they are, in theory, implemented with greatest conviction. If you cannot secure unanimity, explore whether the proposal can be altered to eliminate contentious details without altering the substance of the motion. Often it is best to obtain some kind of general agreement and to return to details at a later date when the heat is off.

If a meeting really cannot agree, ask yourself why. Don't simply say "We'll come back to this next week/later on/at the next meeting" and pass on to the next agenda item.

Consider especially:
- Is one individual taking an extreme position because he or she feels backed into a corner? If so, some gentle persuasion is probably needed outside the meeting.
- Lack of information: if you have prepared thoroughly, this should not be a problem. If it is, defer the decision, and get the facts together before the next meeting.
- The decision depends on circumstances or events beyond the control of the meeting: this indicates a poor agenda. Ask someone in the meeting to restructure the proposal, eliminating imponderables.

 The written record

The minutes of a meeting are absolutely fundamental. Their most important function is to record not what was said but the decisions that were made. Always highlight the decisions in some way. Brief minutes need record only the decisions themselves. If the meeting cannot agree, minutes should record the views of individuals, or the names of dissenters. Don't leave minutes to the least responsible person in the group. They should be taken by someone who can grasp the nuances of all the agenda items, and who knows each of the participants.

91 *Dealing with powerful people*

David beat Goliath and the tortoise beat the hare, and you will not get enough things done if you don't stand up to powerful people. However, it should not turn into a fight.

Heeding the advice in sections **40, 48** and **69 – 77** can make a useful contribution; here also are some specific pieces of advice to help with your campaign.

■ Do you really know what you want? Can you boil it down to simple, rational terms? Or do you get so irritated that you allow yourself to think only of scoring points? For example, your boss insists you turn up at weekly meetings at which you have no useful function. When he refuses to listen to reason, are you tempted to turn up at the meetings just to see how many you can go to without speaking? Festering in this way is a waste of time and energy for you and your boss. Far better to think your case out again, put your reasons into words and write a note saying why you should not attend. If you don't get a reply, don't attend - but have a watertight alibi.

■ Be optimistic about changing your boss.

Many people see their boss's superior fire power, the power to fire them, as overwhelming: the "I can't say that to my boss" syndrome. Yet that same boss is probably receptive to constructive ideas. There must be one way of persuading him or her: see **69-77.**

■ Don't feel overawed by 'presence'. Some people somehow fill a room with their personality. Others use the subtle negatives of dismissing you with a glance or seeming uninspired by one of your remarks. The use of silence is particularly important here – see **40, 73.**

■ Don't be threatened or bullied. Some people really do have the ability to do you harm; just as many assume it. When on the receiving end of a threatening innuendo, feign innocence: "Sorry. would you say that again? I didn't quite understand." This can have the effect of making the other side re-think whether they actually possess the clout to turn the threat into reality.

At the same time, remind yourself that it is a sign of weakness to demonstratively wield power. Truly powerful people simply have it. Try and give the power-wielder what he or she secretly wants. For instance, if they are 'Hurry Up' (see **67**), find a way of slowing them down and making them think and talk things over.

■ Use humour. When under threat you are likely to fall prey to an overactive, chattering mind. Remember that you operate better when you gain access to the different skills in both sides of your brain (**32**). It is not corny, or irresponsbile, but potentially productive, to see the funny side of a serious situation.

■ Don't be phased by reputations. Awkward types certainly allow few people to get through to them; regard this as an opportunity. If you can get through, you become one of the few; the benefits could be significant.

■ If faced with a megalomaniac who has something you want, seek an even more powerful person as an ally. Or give up and find another route. If you fail, return to the problem later. Some dictators lead charmed lives; it is ages before they are deposed. So don't wait for their downfall – re-route.

92 *Less conflict*

> **"** *Some have wondered that disputes about opinions should so often end in personalities; but the fact is, that such disputes begin with personalities; for our opinions are a part of ourselves. Besides, after the first contradiction it is ourselves, and not the thing, we maintain.* **"**
>
> – *Edward Fitzgerald*, Polonius 1852

I magine you were watching a tug-of-war contest: two teams trying as hard as they can to pull the opposition into the mud.

During the breaks, each team comes to speak to you, telling you how good they are, and describing the other sides's dirty tricks.

Assuming that neither side ever completely wins, for how long would you watch the contest? You would, of course, eventually get bored.

Think about your own organization. The two tug-of-war teams could be the marketing and sales departments, or sales and production, with the spectators being your customers.

During the breaks in the internal tug-of-war, each team takes the opportunity of pleading their case with the spectators. "Production promised us the prototype by last week." "Who told you that? – Sales will say anthing, you'll have to wait at least a month." Customers find this internal tug-of-war even more boring than the real thing.

Nobody can live in total harmony and one could argue convincingly that they should not have to. In the performing arts, internal argument is sometimes called creative tension and recognized as an essential means of getting the best out of people. However, it does need to be kept at a useful level.

Think about being a spectator at an internal battle: Do you find that usually there is a clear right or wrong, in which case they should sort it out as quickly as possible? Or do you usually find that no one is totally in the right, or that it does not matter much either way? Whichever, you know that a result will never be efficiently achieved until the argument stops.

Every moment that is spent arguing internally is a moment that could have been spent producing an end result.

▶ **Reducing internal conflict**

■ Follow Fitzgerald's advice and concentrate on 'the thing', not the personality; on results, not blame.

■ Keep creative tension to a minimum. Challenge by all means, but do so with the aim of improving the product.

■ Introduce 'quality circles' or 'improvement groups' made up from different disciplines within the organization, with a mix of senior and junior staff. Get them to pick up weaknesses *and* opportunities.

■ When you hear someone publicly criticizing another department, ask "So what are you going to do?"

■ Never be destructively disloyal about your company, or your group, to outsiders. Remember that you too are a member, and that you are, in effect, criticizing yourself.

93 Being aware of other people's time pressures

Are you other people's main time management problem? When you are looking for ways of organizing and motivating yourself, you are in danger of becoming too self-interested; ignoring other people's need to manage their own time. If allowed to develop too far, these blind spots can all too easily stand in the way of opportunity and achievement.

Everyone has a bad working habit that causes colleagues irritation. Use the list below to measure your inconvenience factor:

Telephone:
■ Do you ever fail to telephone back when you say you will? Do you sometimes fail to ask – at the beginning of the call – if it is convenient to talk?
■ Do you rarely make quick calls?
■ For important calls, or calls dealing with complex matters, do you plunge in without first writing a summary of what needs to be said?

Meetings:
■ Do you do all your thinking when you are there, by the seat of your pants?
■ Do you think being a good chairman/woman is desirable, but not essential?
■ Do you sometimes find yourself wishing you could make your point more efficiently?
■ Do you sometimes fail to do what you promised?
■ Do you accept telephone calls in meetings?

Staff:
■ Do you think it unnecessary to say "Excuse me" or "Is it OK to talk now?"

■ Do you interrupt them more than they interrupt you?
■ When they interrupt you, is it to clarify your instructions?
■ When delegating urgent work, do you give people a chance to discuss re-scheduling other important tasks?
■ Do you bother to question people's tendency to be over-ambitious about completion dates?
■ Are most of the jobs you delegate last-minute panics?
■ Do you ever spend time on making your writing more legible?

Visiting colleagues:
■ Do you go and chat to a colleague at least twice a day?
■ Do you think it is inflexible of colleagues to postpone interruptions to more convenient times?
■ Do others have to adapt to your moods? Does the rest of the office always know if you are, for instance, happy, or silently miserable?
■ Do you allow visitors when you already have a visitor?

Generally:
■ Is there a regularly occurring joke about one aspect of your behaviour (like not getting to the point)?

How do you rate?
If you score one 'yes' or more, when are you going to start changing things? All these bad habits are rectifiable. See especially 20, 40, 41, 42, 57, 68, 79 and 80.

If you think you are not guilty on any of these counts, you have a more serious problem: complete lack of self-awareness. Take another look at 18 and 19.

94 *Coping with shock*

S hocks will always be shocking. However, by understanding the process by which shock is absorbed into the human system you can cope with it better. There are six distinct stages in the process, each neatly encapsulated in this telephone monologue. It may have a familiar ring:

> *"(Stunned silence) . . .*
> *I don't believe it . . .*
> *It's all my fault . . .*
> *It wouldn't have happened if he wasn't in such a rush . . .*
> *I was too tired to check it . . .*
> *. . . Oh well, there's nothing we can do about it now."*

Stage 1 – Shock: Usually greeted by silence as the initial impact is felt. The brain needs to assimilate this information, so it buys some time with the next stage.

Stage 2 – Disbelief: "I don't believe it." Some people never get out of this stage, living out a pretence that nothing has happened. This second stage also stalls for time.

Stage 3 – Guilt: "It's all my fault." You take all the blame, regardless of actual responsibility. Some people (see 'Be Perfect' in **45**) find it difficult to move on from this stage.

Stage 4 – Blame: "If he hadn't been in such a hurry . . . " Here is the brain buying still more time to think. Responsibility is pushed out on to other people or events; some find this stage such an effective antidote to the reality of the shock that they get stuck in it completely.

Stage 5 – Rationalization: "I was too tired to check." The logical side of the brain now takes over; it seeks a version for your acting as you did. By accident or design, it often gets the analysis slightly wrong; you may have noticed inaccuracies in other people's rationalizations. However, the brain is moving closer to accepting the experience for what it is.

Stage 6 – Integration: "There's nothing we can do now." You are back to normal. Finally, over a period of minutes – or indeed of years, the situation is accepted. It becomes one more piece of experience on which you can base future judgements; guilt and blame are no longer of prime importance; the analysis is academic: "Oh well, whatever the reason, it's over now."

▶ **Your approach**

If you are aware of the inevitability of the status quo reasserting itself, you will probably handle shock more calmly. There is a temptation, given the knowledge that guilt and blame will eventually be much less important than accepting the new status quo,to ignore these stages, or to try to hurry through them. Better to let them run their course naturally.

Don't try to hurry a victim of shock through any stage just because it seems unpleasant. You may not like to hear a friend loading themselves with guilt, but you should hear them out, then help them, when they are ready to get into the next stage of projecting the blame.

95 *Opportunity*

> **"** *Serendipity: The faculty of making happy and unexpected discoveries by accident.* **"**
>
> – Oxford English Dictionary

T his section is about making those precious accidental discoveries and capitalizing on them. Chance plays a part in everyone's life; pre-planning and assertiveness can make things happen, but chance events are neglected at your peril. What have you done with the opportunities in your life?

 What are opportunities?

Obvious? But how you define them will govern how well you can recognize them. One of the most versatile definitions is that opportunities are time-savers: sudden chances to jump more than one step at a time towards an important goal. The momentum imparts extra energy; opportunities taken are good for morale and self-esteem because they are pleasant to look back on (though dangerous to rest on).

2 Why opportunities are missed

"It might be the wrong one."

"I didn't see it until it was too late."

"I don't come across many where I live."

"It wasn't the right time."

"I thought I'd wait for the next one; but I'm still waiting."

"I could not afford it then."

"It wouldn't be fair on my friends, they don't get opportunities."

"I spend too long thinking about it – when I've decided, it's gone."

"What would people think."

"I wasn't concentrating."

"I don't want to rock the boat."

"You tell me where they are, and I'll take them. They just don't come my way."

"I've got no spare time to do anything about them."

"It may turn out wrong."

"I don't care."

3 ▶ How to make and take opportunities

■ First, know **where you are going.** Otherwise you will not be able to tell a worthwhile opportunity from a waste of time. See **5.**

■ Tell people what you are interested in, **enthuse about your aims.**
Enthusiasm is infectious and the more people you infect, the more there will be to act as agents, or channels for opportunities.

■ **Put yourself about.** Where are your opportunities most likely to occur? There is a famous story about a salesman who stood outside Henry Ford's front gate for three days and nights before a chance encounter enabled him to make his sales pitch: a pitch that would never have happened if he had stayed at home.

■ **Keep your eyes open.** If you really want to succeed, you are less likely to do so on a part-time basis. Your next opportunity is likely to come in some sort of disguise. How will you spot it? Where could it come from – which group of friends? Which company? Which newspaper?

■ **Be flexible on timing.** Opportunities don't come at the most convenient times. Don't miss your chance waiting for everything else to be in place. It may be inconvenient to take on extra assignments now but if it is what you have been waiting for, take it, and sort things out afterwards.

■ **Expect your share of good fortune.** At your most despondent, you see all events as being bad news. If someone then came to you with a good proposal, you would probably reject it on the grounds that it could be much good if he came to you with it. The best antidote to this type of destructive pessimism is to reflect, when feeling optimistic, on what opportunities could come your way. You then have a better chance of recognizing them when they arise, even if you are in a black mood.

■ **Opportunities are usually worth borrowing against.** If you judge the opportunity as a real one, consider borrowing against it. A sound proposition is good collateral; there is nothing like an overdraft for making one realize the idea which caused it.

■ **Don't wait for others.** It is not mean to others to capitalize on your good fortune. If you so wish you can always share the proceeds.

■ **Don't over-analyse.** If in the past you have missed chances by pondering them too long, or researching them too cautiously, then this time try a more cavalier approach. But see next point

■ **Be rational;** don't gamble. Take a calculated risk – there is a difference – see **64.** By knowing where you want to go and by setting your criteria you will be well-equipped to decide. In business, calculated risks are usually wrong no more than 30 per cent of the time. If you never gamble, you will go back to letting life, your job, your narrow horizons control you.

96 *Turning problems into opportunities*

I If you have purposefully read this book you ought, if nothing else, to have a clearer idea than when you started of what you want to do with your life. If you don't, look again at sections **4**, **5** and **6**.

But you still have your problems. Indeed, you will always have your problems, and your mental well-being, now, and in the future, will always be largely governed by how you cope with them.

What would you do if faced by the following situations? They may sound improbable, but, as you will see below, they are not hypothetical problems made up especially for this section.

Situation one

You are a university professor researching into wasps. Some one asks you to run another course, on a totally unrelated subject. You agree, with misgivings, because the new research required will take up a great deal of time you have not got. Then you go to the library and discover that there is virtually no literature on the new subject.

Would you:
– Ask someone else to do it?
– Or turn the problem into an opportunity, and in so doing become a household name?

 The players

The academic was Alfred Kinsey. The course he was asked to run was on marriage, and in the 1940s there really was little research on sexuality.

So, he made a virtue of necessity: he created his own research by asking his students to describe their sex lives. From this original material he was able to publish the Kinsey Reports on the sexual behaviour of the human male, and later the companion reports on female sexual behaviour.

 You and your problems

So how do you treat your problems? Do you let them dictate your life?

What is the single biggest problem currently holding you back? You may find that giving it clear definition ac-

Situation two

You are a 52-year-old milk shake mixer salesman who is always striving for more success than you actually achieve. You have had a long-standing interest in fast-food restaurants as a concept. One day, you arrive at a restaurant which needs eight of the mixers. It is called McDonald's, and its formula is exactly the one you had always reckoned should be exploited in the fast food business.

Would you:
– Say to yourself, 'Back to the drawing board, as usual someone's beaten me to it?'
– Or would you turn the problem into an opportunity and get very rich?

The disillusioned salesman was Ray Kroc. He overcome his disappointment by deciding that if he was to be denied actually starting the fast-food joint, at least he would exploit it. He negotiated the right to franchise the McDonald name worldwide – and made a great deal more than he did selling milk shake mixers.

Situation three

After trying many different methods of making money without much success, you end up selling radio sets in the Canadian outback. They are not going particularly well.

Would you:
– Pack it in and accept that you will never make it?
– Or try a different marketing method which becomes the seed that grows into an international corporation?

Roy (later the first Lord) Thomson turned his problem into an opportunity by setting up a local radio station to encourage use of his sets. This he developed into a small chain of stations, and this was the foundation of the Thomson Organization.

tually helps to create an opportunity-seeking state of mind: it is all too often the woolly, generalized assumption that things are impossible which stops people acting decisively.

A warning: don't, in your new-found enthusiasm, overlook the obvious, and allow opportunities to turn into problems.

In 1848, J.W. Marshall was the first to discover gold in California. But he made no money. Other people bought up the mining rights before he did, and he was left with nothing.

97 *Working as a team*

T hink about the group of people with whom you work. When and if you succeed, will it be due to the team, or individuals? Will you have enjoyed working together? What do you know about each other? Are you dull and fruitless as a group? Does everyone fight to be in charge?

Improving the effectiveness of a team is one of the cheapest ways of improving the performance of an organization. It is often quicker than attending to each individual because good teams can compensate for individual weaknesses.

No team is perfect. Use the checklist below to work out how your team rates. Every member of the team is responsible for improving the performance of the group.

■ **Does your team:**
– Know where it's going, this week and this year? And does it communicate this direction?
– Communicate on a two-way basis? Do members of the team have an opportunity to suggest alternatives or sound the alarm?
– Use emotions well? Are people praised for good work? Is it capable of telling off poor performers?
– Avoid negative use of the emotions? Do people work in a constant mood of fear and depression? If so, is this because of too much telling off or not enough communication? Or does it flatter itself unhealthily when it is successful? How could more critical appraisal be introduced? See **30**.
– Have a clear set of standards? Are people who fail them brought back on to the rails?

■ **Does the whole team:**
– Accept its standards as being not too high or too low?

– Have an effective hierarchy and an effective distribution of jobs? Is it accepted within the team?
– Freely discuss individual strengths and weaknesses without fears or recrimination?
– Publicize news as quickly as possible? If so, no grapevine.
– Know each other better than superficially?
– Plan successfully?
– Distribute the work load fairly?
– Work at full stretch most of the time, avoiding undue stress or boredom?
– Feel in control of its destiny?
– Believe it will be successful?
– Have a way of selecting priorities in emergencies? Is it quick to do so, and does this reflect a perception of important objectives, or the need for an easy life?
– Make the best use of the resources, people, equipment and budget? Is it resourceful at extending these?
– Encourage new ideas? Can it avoid over-criticism, killing them at birth?
– Complain and moan too much?
– Have a way of publicizing successful members to the rest of the team? Are the methods of doing this acceptable to everyone? (Some people are embarrassed to hear 'happy birthday' sung to them, for others sky-writing is too low key.)
– Have an identity?
– Have a way of getting out of scrapes? Is it resourceful? Has it got its Mr. Fix-it?
– Got a method of resolving disagreements fairly and quickly?
– Rightly put the emphasis on results achieved, rather than work done?
– Enjoy itself?
– Have someone to whom you could suggest improvements for the team as a whole? When and how will you take your findings to them?

98 *Mixing business with pleasure*

Should you mix business with pleasure? Of course you should. You should make time for both business and pleasure; but even more important, you should introduce more pleasure into your working life.

Basic steps to that end are covered in earlier sections, especially those which emphasize the importance of not going physically, educationally, artistically or socially bankrupt – see **18, 23, 24, 25,** and **29**.

Here, let us assume you want to take some more specific steps, particularly in terms of enhancing relationships with people outside your organization.

▶ **Restaurant meetings**

This is of course the time-honoured way of combining pleasure with business. Yet I am often amazed at the energy with which executives will strive to achieve expense-account status, only to complain at how boring business entertaining can be.

I believe that the heart of this problem is a selfish lack of interest in the rest of humanity. In the same way as being accepted as a person (**43**) is fundamental to developing one's potential in an organization, so being interested in people for their own sakes is fundamental to getting pleasure out of business-cum-social meetings.

Some people's idea of introducing a personal touch to business relationships is a few statutory enquiries into the other person's home life. Unless such enquires lead somewhere useful, they are better left unsaid.

I never sit over meals with people unless I have a solid motive to study them more closely; to enthuse about an idea in its early stages – where suitably informal surroundings will enhance their receptiveness; or to trade information. Simply wanting to know someone better is not sufficient in itself, although it is very important; the best atmopshere for a business meal is where the motives are mixed between personal interest *and* profit.

Having seen to these priorities, you can then take the necessary practical steps.

■ Match the client to the restaurant. Don't inflict grand surroundings on a guest who would plainly feel uncomfortable. Remember people of high status don't always like to eat in smart places.

■ Think carefully about how many people you want to include. With more than two people, social interactions can become too complex for furthering a relationship.

■ In crowded capital cities where restaurant tables are packed together, you can often hear the people at the table next to you better than your guest. So patronise restaurants who will always give you a table with its share of space. I prefer such places to fashionable or 'power' restaurants who won't guarantee this basic service. Sometimes you can contrive privacy by reserving a table for three or four, but only using it for two.

■ If in doubt about when to start talking business, postpone. Capitalize on the rituals of ordering the meal to keep the conversation general and/or personal. You can heighten a guest's receptiveness by suggesting when you arrange the meeting that there is something to talk about; then keeping them waiting a little longer than might be expected.

99 *A new sense of freedom – with your feet on the ground . . .*

The concept of the 'self actualiser' was first promoted by Maslow, the psychologist, in the 1920s; it has stood the test of time. Essentially he wanted people to be uninhibited enough to allow their talents to bloom. Section **48** describes the idea in detail, and suggests some basic steps towards achieving this state. Here and in the next and final section, are more detailed lists, based on his research, of attributes that add up to self-realization. They describe a type of person uncluttered by negative emotions and hang-ups; someone who finds work a source of opportunity and liberation, rather than a harness. Steadiness – see below – is as much to do with this state of being as the more mercurial, spiritual qualities listed in **100**.

Results-centred, not self-centred	**Objective**
Problem solving	**Takes personal responsibility**
Rational	**Comfortable with the imperfections of life and people**

Free from:
- egotistical pulls
- Short-term self-interest
- need to be comfortable and cosy
- restricting fear of change
- brooding on problems and difficulties

Embodies a close relationship between thought and action

Independent:
- in thought
- unswayed by criticism (positive or negative)
- detached

Action-orientated

Desiring and capable of privacy

Realistic about:
- time
- what is achievable
- limitations
- possibilities
- yourself
- skills
- talents
- disposition
- weakness
- others

Makes up own mind

Does not give way to pressures of:
- the group
- the organization
- the environment
- another's will

Lives in the present (see 50)

100 . . . and your head in the clouds

Creative

A risk-taker

Ability to make sudden changes to lifestyle

Experimental

Pioneering

Empathy
– with wide range of people
– able to have deep relationships
– desires to understand and appreciate others

Builds on failure

Not destructively critical of self or others

Resists the desire to:
– impress
– control
– exert influence or power for its own sake

Unhostile sense of humour

Capable of inspiration

Able to commit attention to others

Positive

Positive

Spontaneous

Able to distinguish good from evil

Natural

Not brooding or controlled by moods

Simplicity of manners

Optimistic

Appreciation of everyday things

Freshness of approach

Motivated
– clearly to see what one wants
– wanting strongly what one sees

Openness

Roger Black (owner of a speedy racehorse named Perfect Timing) was born in 1946 and worked in industry before starting Wellgrove Associates, the management training specialists. Among his clients in Britain and continental Europe are Bass, Sony, BP, Coopers and Lybrand and Thomson Holidays. He was co-writer and presenter of the BBC Radio 4 Series *Good Timing*.

The author gratefully acknowledges the help of John Farndon and Richard Platt in preparing material for this book.

Editorial Director
Andrew Duncan
Art Director
Mel Petersen
Designer
Lynn Hector
Design Assistance
Helen Spencer
Illustrations
Michael McGuinness